MW00782964

CHANGED
IN A FLASH

CHANGED
IN A FLASH

ONE WOMAN'S
NEAR-DEATH EXPERIENCE AND
WHY A SCHOLAR THINKS IT EMPOWERS US ALL

ELIZABETH G. KROHN and JEFFREY J. KRIPAL

North Atlantic Books
Berkeley, California

Copyright © 2018 by Elizabeth G. Krohn and Jeffrey J. Kripal. All rights reserved. No portion of this book, except for brief review, may be reproduced, stored in a retrieval system, or transmitted in any form or by any means—electronic, mechanical, photocopying, recording, or otherwise—without the written permission of the publisher. For information contact North Atlantic Books.

Published by
North Atlantic Books
Berkeley, California

Cover image by John Finney photography/Getty Images
Cover design by Nicole Hayward
Book design by Happenstance Type-O-Rama

Printed in Canada

Changed in a Flash: One Woman's Near-Death Experience and Why a Scholar Thinks It Empowers Us All is sponsored and published by the Society for the Study of Native Arts and Sciences (dba North Atlantic Books), an educational nonprofit based in Berkeley, California, that collaborates with partners to develop cross-cultural perspectives, nurture holistic views of art, science, the humanities, and healing, and seed personal and global transformation by publishing work on the relationship of body, spirit, and nature.

North Atlantic Books' publications are available through most bookstores. For further information, visit our website at www.northatlanticbooks.com or call 800-733-3000.

Library of Congress Cataloging-in-Publication Data

Names: Krohn, Elizabeth G., author.
Title: Changed in a flash : one woman's near-death experience and why a
    scholar thinks it empowers us all / Elizabeth G. Krohn.
Description: Berkeley, California : North Atlantic Books, 2018. | Includes
    bibliographical references.
Identifiers: LCCN 2018015402 (print) | LCCN 2018029106 (ebook) | ISBN
    9781623173012 (e-book) | ISBN 9781623173036 (hardback) | ISBN
    9781623173005 (pbk.)
Subjects: LCSH: Krohn, Elizabeth G. | Near-death
    experiences.—Texas—Houston—Biography. | Death—Religious aspects. |
    Future life.
Classification: LCC BF1045.N4 (ebook) | LCC BF1045.N4 K76 2018 (print) | DDC
    133.901/3092 [B] —dc23
LC record available at https://lccn.loc.gov/2018015402

1 2 3 4 5 6 7 8 9 MARQUIS 22 21 20 19 18

Printed on recycled paper

North Atlantic Books is committed to the protection of our environment.
We partner with FSC-certified printers using soy-based inks and print on recycled
paper whenever possible.

*For the four women—Marianne Greenfield,
Minnie Duval, Francine Greenfield Rosenthal,
and Clara Mae Lewis—whose support and love
helped me to survive, and then to thrive.*

—Elizabeth

---

*For Elizabeth, and for all the other countless
souls out there who have been told that their
otherworldly encounters are nothing more
than hallucinations and their astonishing
gifts simply hopeless wishes.*

—Jeff

A dream is one-sixtieth of prophecy.

—BABYLONIAN TALMUD, BERAKHOT 57B

CONTENTS

INTRODUCTION:
Lightning in a Book

Late in the summer of 1988, Elizabeth Balkin (now Krohn), a wife and mother of two young boys, was struck by lightning in the parking lot of a Houston synagogue.

She did not die.

While the odds of getting struck by lightning (about one in a million in any single year) are significantly better than winning the lottery, surviving a lightning strike is not all that unusual. The survival rate from such an event is somewhere around ninety percent, which means that roughly nine out of ten people who are struck by lightning live to tell the harrowing tale. The energy of such an event boggles the imagination. A lightning bolt can carry as much as *200 million volts* and travel at speeds that can approach nearly one-third the speed of light. Luckily, most of the energy travels over or around the human body in a "flashover effect." This can also take the form of an eerie bubble of light within which time seems to stand still. Oddly, severe burns are not common for a variety of conductivity reasons, but many survivors often suffer significant changes to their biology. Limbs, muscles, nerves, even neurological patterns are often altered forever. And that's just the beginning. Some survivors report that they can now sense storms well before they appear;

others that their computers malfunction, or that batteries drain away in their presence.[1]

Things sometimes get stranger still. Elizabeth's most fundamental understandings of what the world is and how it works were completely transformed. She was one person before the lightning strike. She was another after it. She was changed in a flash.

And in a garden. Elizabeth experienced herself visiting a heavenly landscape, in her case a garden paradise of unspeakable beauty, for two weeks, even though only minutes or seconds passed here. Such a near-death experience (NDE), of course, is not uncommon either. But Elizabeth came back with something else still: a rich body of messages or revelations about the nature and future of the human soul and a whole spectrum of new supersenses, including a troubling ability to dream the details of future disasters. Preposterous? Certainly to our ordinary, everyday experience of the world. Impossible? Well, we will have to wait and see.

I am a full professor at an elite research university. It is *my job* to push against all comfortable boundaries, to question any religious *or* secular assumption about who we are, to imagine the impossible as possible. That's what tenure is for, and I take its privileges and responsibilities very, very seriously. This same professional position also affords me the honor and pleasure of teaching and thinking with some of the finest minds on the planet, from fields as diverse as the study of literature to computer science. I can thus easily understand how and why many of us might be tempted to call the following story "bullshit." But here is the thing: over the last two decades, I have encountered hundreds of individuals like Elizabeth, and I am sure there are millions more. I understand the bullshit charge, as I once held it myself, but I am not so sure anymore. Anomalous superhumans like Elizabeth give me significant pause.

This is a book about one such long pause. It chronicles and then interprets a series of events that could not have possibly happened, but did. I am Elizabeth's friend, cowriter, interpreter, and, at the very end of the book, one of the subjects of her paranormal dreaming. I write about Elizabeth's otherworldly visions and precognitive dreams. She responds by dreaming my life, my family, and my Midwestern hometown. Not exactly your typical book. But this is how it came into focus as we completed the manuscript in the final months of 2017.

HOW THIS BOOK CAME TO BE

The project began in October of 2015, when I was asked to comment on Elizabeth's near-death experience at a public event organized by a young man named Anyang Anyang and entitled "Changed in the Blink of an Eye" at the Institute for Spirituality and Health in the Houston Medical Center. From those initial introductions and conversations, the two of us decided to try to write a book together. We met on a regular basis from early 2016 through the fall of 2017. We also met with family members: Elizabeth's former husband, Barry; her husband, Matt; her three children, Jeremy, Andy, and Mallory; and her parents, Marianne and Larry. With these individuals, I corroborated many of the details of Elizabeth's story, including the event of the original lightning strike at the synagogue, which, of course, was too quick and sudden for anyone to see (although, according to Elizabeth, one person, now deceased, did tell her that he saw the actual strike).

I do not wish to hide anything, including how we wrote this book. I want the reader to know that the book possesses both oral and written dimensions and is "two" all the way through, even when it looks like only one of us is talking or writing. Elizabeth and I recorded our conversations, whose content and direction she generally determined and led but that I also occasionally guided with questions borne from previous conversations with my academic colleagues and other extreme experiencers. Elizabeth then transcribed the recordings, and I worked from them to put together the early base text out of Elizabeth's own words. Elizabeth then took up this base text and completely rewrote it, adding much new material in the process. This is what you get in Part One as "Elizabeth's Story." The next part is different. It is certainly informed by my conversations with Elizabeth, and occasionally I quote these (indeed, each chapter begins with something Elizabeth said to me), but at the end of the day it is a commentary, not a conversation. It is a subjective interpretation, not an objective description. Elizabeth provided feedback and criticism on it at various stages, but these are my views, not hers. This is what you get in Part Two, "How We Are Changing the Afterlife."

The Postscript is in some ways also the conclusion, for me anyway. It recounts an exchange I had with Elizabeth toward the end of the writing process, when she dreamed the thesis that I was trying to express in Part Two. It took her just a few seconds and a few scenes—while she slept no less—to express in image and story what I had just spent a year and a half working through. Typical. Finally, one more thing on how this book came to be, and perhaps why it came to be. The book possesses a particular "local flavor," if I may put it in that Texan of a way. The synagogue in whose parking lot Elizabeth was struck is Congregation Emanu El, which sits directly across Sunset Boulevard from Rice University, where I work and teach. I drive by the synagogue all the time. The parking lot is all of three blocks from where I sit in my office in Rice's Department of Religion. There is something there. I don't know what. But there is something there.

FLASH CARDS

This book is not just a fantastic Texas story. It is also a collection of communications, direct knowings, or revelations about the nature and future of the human soul. These form the beating heart of the book. They can be summarized as a series of seven "flash cards," which go like this:

- We do not die when the body dies. The fundamental core of who we are lives on.

- Each of us has a "double" or angelic guide with whom we eventually merge or unite.

- We reincarnate until we accomplish or learn such a union with our angelic double, after which we then become an angelic guide or double for someone else.

- Time is not what we think it is, nor what we ordinarily experience as such. Information from the future can and does sometimes flow into the present.

- A subtle energetic field surrounds the human body and constitutes in some way or in some part what we have come to call the "soul." The soul is an energetic being.

- The "immediate afterlife," that is, what we see and experience shortly after we physically die, is different for each of us and is conditioned and shaped by our own expectations and needs.

- The "distant afterlife," that is, what many would consider "God" or our final destination, remains a mystery and probably lies beyond any traditional way of imagining such a living presence.

The latter flash of truth is represented in Elizabeth's visions as a Light that glows "beyond the mountains" of the heavenly Garden in which she finds herself and from which she chooses to return to this world instead of journeying into the mountains toward the Light. In other words, Elizabeth's visionary landscape draws a very important distinction between what an individual sees and experiences in a NDE event immediately after death, in her case "in the Garden," and who God ultimately is beyond any and all near-death experiences, in her case "beyond the mountains." This key distinction can be carried in two simple visionary, and very biblical, metaphors: that between the heavenly Garden and the transcendent mountains.

I recognize that many of these messages need to be explained. That's probably an understatement. We will do that in due time, and in two different ways—in Elizabeth's way, and in my way. Again, these are different ways, but they are in deep conversation, and they are friends.

FOUR POSSIBLE RESPONSES

If my previous experience lecturing on Elizabeth's life and others like hers is any measure, different readers will invoke one or two simple strategies within an extremely limited range of responses. Three of these responses are essentially defense mechanisms, designed, I assume, to protect against the vast implications that these stories encode and potentially release upon their readers and listeners. Even these defense mechanisms are useful, however, as long as we are aware of what we are doing. I have encountered only four. They go like this:

1. The Hoax. First, some of us will label Elizabeth's stories as made up, fictitious, or simply fraudulent. This is the bullshit claim with which I began. These labels will usually be silent and polite ones, but I have also heard them uttered out loud after lectures I have given about similar experiencers.[2] This reaction boils down to this: "She is lying. He made it up. It didn't happen." Such a response is often effective because it is comforting. It works to protect the philosophical or religious assumptions of the person making it, which usually can be

6

reduced to some form of religious literalism, scientific materialism, or statistical leveling of the weird truth (more on that in due time, including in the appendix). The fraud charge is, at base, a conservative response. It also works, of course, because there *are* hoaxes and fraudulent cases. But, as the mathematician and logician Kurt Gödel (1906–1978) realized in his own fascination with the paranormal, a fake is often a fake of something real.

2. The Honest Misperception. Second, some of us will accept the honesty of Elizabeth's personal narrative but think that such a story is a complex construction of some kind of cognitive dysfunction, neurological blip, or delusion: some fault of memory, some confusion of dream and reality, some hallucination or pathology, some personal, social, or historical trauma, or, most generously, some statistically predictable coincidence that was inappropriately isolated and emphasized as magical or special. This, too, is at base a conservative response, since it protects and leaves unchallenged the assumptions of the reader. It is no doubt appropriate and correct in some cases and instances, although it should always be kept in mind that psychopathology and experiences of transcendence are by no means mutually exclusive. They go together quite well.

3. The Distraction. Third, when the stratagems of the Hoax and the Honest Misperception fail, some of us will let the stories stand, but we will not allow ourselves to think about them too deeply, much less to follow their implications down the proverbial rabbit hole. We will cognitively wall them off. We will quickly forget about them. We will move on. We will drive home and have a beer. Or watch a sitcom. Or go eat breakfast. Or feed the cat. Or let out the dog. We will, in effect,

distract ourselves and so reset the dials to "normal." This is not an intellectual response. It is a psychological or existential strategy. And it works quite well.

4. The Guiding Sign. Fourth, and finally, when the strategies of the Hoax, the Honest Misperception, and the Distraction all fail, some of us will accept Elizabeth's stories as more or less accurate, if always culturally and psychologically mediated representations of an actual historical event. We will hear them as encouragements to think about the world, and ourselves, anew. Please note that this fourth response does not preclude us from invoking the first three where and when appropriate. There *are* hoaxes. There *are* honest misperceptions. And sometimes we just need a beer or breakfast (perhaps not together, though).

BE CAREFUL

Finally, before we begin, I ask you to be careful with this book, not for the sake of the book, Elizabeth, or myself, but for your own sake. Reading this book, I warn you, will not be an ordinary, banal activity such as, say, reading a cereal box, a newspaper, or a novel. I think of books like this much like the writer Aldous Huxley saw his own library during his first psychedelic revelations on mescaline as reported in his now classic *The Doors of Perception*. According to Huxley, some of the books on his shelves glowed with a special energy or living power. They were alive, and they were beautiful. That is how I think of *Changed in a Flash*. Had this book sat on Huxley's shelf, it would have been one of the glowing ones. I imagine sparks.

In all truth, I think of books like this as glowing "radioactive" catalysts capable of awakening potential superpowers and real secret identities in all of us, but especially in *you*, the reader. You might think that I am exaggerating. I am not.

You might think that I have seen too many superhero movies. I have. Regardless, I am perfectly serious about such convictions, in whatever mythical frame we want to express them. If our press's financial resources were limitless, I would have asked them to produce a book with a tiny battery embedded in its spine that would gently but literally shock each reader who picks up the book.

Okay, maybe that is not such a good idea. Still, this is how I think of this book: as an electrical living thing capable of zapping and rewiring anyone who ventures too close to its truths. If we can speak of "lightning in a bottle," perhaps we can also speak of "lightning in a book." That anyway is how I imagine the true nature of this book—as living lightning zigzagging through the words on the page and into the eyes, brain, and soul of the reader.

If I were you, then, I would pick it up with care. You will see. Or, better, you will be shocked. I was.

Jeff

December 31, 2017
Houston, Texas

PART ONE

Elizabeth's Story

1

CHANGED IN A FLASH

Not to transmit an experience is to betray it.

—ELIE WIESEL

The most dramatic thing that ever happened to me is something I did not talk about for almost thirty years. Tell me, who would have believed a woman talking about how she died, left her body, went somewhere else, met and talked to God, and then came back to discover that she now had precognitive abilities? True, a few medical professionals and scholars had begun to study the "near-death experience," as Raymond Moody coined the term in 1975, just thirteen years before my own. But it was still a new topic in the late 1980s. The subject was treated more as a mental aberration than an important phenomenon in its own right. It would take another three decades of study on the part of doctors, scholars, and scientists before I felt comfortable enough to say, "Hey, that happened to me. And it is real." I am ready to speak now. What follows is my story.

◆ ◆ ◆

Jean Albert Duval, my maternal grandfather, died on September 5, 1987. His death was very hard for me. Then, almost a year later, in July of 1988, my maternal grandmother, Minnie Duval, passed away. My grandparents had always been very stabilizing forces in my life. I fell to pieces…just fell apart. I did not grieve normally. It was like grieving on steroids—a kind of hypergrieving. It was beyond bad. It was horrific. I was twenty-eight years old.

I was not present when Grandpa died. I was with my husband and children visiting my in-laws in Memphis at the time. However, I was in the room of the nursing home with Grandma when she died. Actually, there were three of us in the room with her: my dad, my aunt, and myself. Mom had stepped out to look for her brother. Dad was standing on one side of the bed. My aunt and I were on the other. When my grandmother took her last breath, all three of us turned at the same moment to look up to the same corner of the room, the one above the left foot of her bed. We all felt embarrassed by this, I think. We looked at each other as if to say, "What are you looking at up there?"

I think we were all uncomfortable with the idea that we were somehow not paying proper respect to Grandma lying there in the bed. But she wasn't there. I knew, and I think Dad and my aunt knew, that Grandma's essence had left her body and was now somehow suspended in the upper back corner of the room. There was a residual energy that had not yet left. When Mom's brother arrived, we left him to his grief. A short time later, he opened the door and came out. He told us that when he had entered the room, Grandma was still there. He left when he could no longer sense her presence in the room.

I had never previously experienced the death of anyone like this before, much less the death of a woman I had adored since childhood. The clear sense of Grandma's presence in the room after she died gave me my first hint that there may be other realms between or beyond what we think of as "life" and "death."

MOURNING AND SHOPPING

When Grandma died, the first anniversary of Grandpa's death was just around the corner, in early September. I missed them both terribly and decided to make myself feel better with some "retail therapy." Neiman Marcus is an upscale department store anchoring one end of one of the most impressive shopping centers in Houston. I studiously avoided the place. It was too extravagant for our growing family's budget. But on this occasion I was drawn to the store to buy myself something especially fine to wear to synagogue for the service in which my grandfather's name was going to be read on the first anniversary of his death.

What I found in my shopping foray was a beautiful black-and-white suit and a stunning pair of black-and-white pumps. I was thrilled at the prospect of wearing such a gorgeous outfit. I was also petrified. There was no way to kick sand over the credit card charge that would hit our monthly bill, and no way to keep such uncharacteristically elegant clothes from my husband, Barry. Unless I hid them, which is what I did as soon as I got home.

The reading of the name of the deceased on the anniversary of their death is a significant event in Judaism. The anniversary is called a *yahrtzeit* (something like "annual memorial") and is held on the Sabbath nearest the date of the death. The name of the deceased is read during the service, and a prayer called the Mourner's Kaddish is recited by those in attendance. The Mourner's Kaddish, or simply Kaddish, is a short prayer that is memorable for its rhythmic cadence and the special sense one gets, or that I get anyway, that the words are so old that dust falls from them as they are spoken. Reciting Kaddish is always a sad task, one that I try to avoid. I dreaded it especially on this day, September 2, 1988.

My husband, Barry, was out of town on business, so I took our two little boys, Jeremy and Andy, to services. Jeremy was four, Andy two.

With Barry out of town and given the importance of the event, it was the perfect occasion for me to wear my gorgeous new clothes. I wanted the boys to look equally fashionable. I dressed them in the cutest summer suits, madras plaid jackets, and navy blue ties. With their dark hair, blue eyes, and dimples, they were stunningly handsome.

That Friday afternoon we were running late for Shabbat services. Still, as we were leaving the house I decided that I wanted a photograph of the three of us. At the time, I was a little upset with myself for stopping to take a picture, since we were already going to be late. However, something was compelling me to take the photo. I had a brand new camera with a timer on it. So I quickly set it up on the tripod, gathered both boys in my arms, and smiled as the camera captured us in the last photo taken of the "old Elizabeth"—me, in my beautiful black-and-white ensemble, the last snapshot of the woman whose life was about to change forever.

Figure 1.1: Elizabeth with Andy (left) and Jeremy (right), about thirty minutes before she was struck by lightning. September 2, 1988.

THE STRIKE

I got the boys in their car seats and backed the car out of the driveway into the waning sun of a late summer afternoon. As I turned into the synagogue parking lot fifteen minutes later, a single large thunderhead blocked out the bright sun. It began to rain. Then thunder boomed. Suddenly, I was in the midst of a furious storm with the rain pouring down in sheets. It had come out of nowhere on what had earlier been a sunny, beautiful day. I certainly did not want to get out of the car in that storm. I also didn't want to sit in the car with the boys, though, because services had already begun, and I didn't want to risk missing the reading of my grandfather's name.

We were parked a few hundred feet or so from the synagogue door. I told Jeremy that I would open his car door and let him run to the awning that covered the entrance to the synagogue. I told him to wait when he got there. Jeremy took off. Once I saw that he was safely under the awning, I climbed over the seat into the back, got Andy out of his car seat, and prepared to open the car door. The storm had worsened. I always kept an umbrella in the car. I grabbed it with my left hand and opened the car door into a rainy squall. I knew that if I tried to carry Andy and manage the umbrella in the wind, we both were going to get soaked. So I set Andy down, took his tiny left hand in my right hand, and grabbed for a more secure grip on the umbrella with my left hand higher up on the metal shaft. I pulled the umbrella down very close to my head.

Andy and I had taken just a few steps when the air cooled perceptively and my skin and scalp prickled with a sudden chill. Or so I thought. Suddenly, I felt a crackling, like static electricity. There was just enough time for me to think, "Oh. This is really bad. This is stupid. I shouldn't be holding an umbrella." It dawned on me just how foolish it was to be crossing a parking lot in a storm holding a collapsible metallic lightning rod in my hand. I even actually thought, "Oh, this is really, really stupid because look at that. My wedding ring is touching the metal shaft of the umbrella." All of these thoughts rushed through my mind as I consciously thought, "Let go of the umbrella." But I couldn't let it go. My hand was frozen in place, tightly gripping the shaft of the umbrella.

It was as if I had somehow beckoned or conjured up precisely what I feared. A small tine of lightning branched off from a larger fork and struck the tip of my umbrella. I know this because I was later told by a man who had witnessed the whole thing that he had seen a bolt of lightning with tiny little fingers coming off a larger bolt, which is what struck my umbrella first. That tiny finger of electricity did not knock me out. It only served to paralyze my arm and hand around the shaft so that I could not let go of the umbrella.

Then the big one hit. The power was unbelievable. The blinding light, deafening explosion, and crackling energy all hit me at once, changing, charging, and charring me.

It is difficult to explain what it was like. In terms of the physics, I know now that thunder happens when the channel made in the air by lightning collapses. Andy and I were in that channel as it rushed back together. The deafening noise that resulted literally split our eardrums. But, for reasons I did not understand at the time, I felt no pain at all. Andy sure did, though. He was screaming with his hands to his ears as Jeremy, also screaming, ran toward him from beneath the awning. Jeremy grabbed Andy's hand and pulled him toward safety. Both boys continued to wail: Andy from the pain of his burst eardrums; Jeremy because he had just witnessed his mother killed by a bolt of lightning.

As far as I understood the situation, I was heading toward the building with my screaming boys. I followed them into the synagogue lobby, where we saw someone that we knew walking back toward services from the restroom. The man immediately came over to Jeremy and Andy and asked them what was wrong. They knew better than to be disruptive during services, of course, yet they couldn't seem to stop wailing.

As the man was trying to calm them down and figure out what had happened, I stood there wondering why no one was paying any attention to me. I also wondered where my umbrella was. I knew I'd had it in my hand, but it was gone now. I looked back out the narrow window in the synagogue door and saw the smoking skeleton of my umbrella lying on the parking lot in the rain. My gaze shifted to the right. About twenty feet away from the umbrella, I saw a crumpled figure lying on the pavement. I saw *me*.

Believe it or not, my first thought was: "Oh God, not the shoes! *Damn.*" I saw that the soles of my new pumps were burned and blown clean off. They had exploded as the only thing between me-as-lightning-rod and the wet ground. I could see my charred feet protruding from their remains. So I looked down at my feet where I believed I was standing in the lobby. I saw that my perfectly intact pumps were still on my feet *but were not touching the ground.* I was hovering a few inches above the carpeted floor. That was confusing, to say the least. It didn't help clear things up that I was also lying in a heap in a grease puddle outside.

As this was all transpiring in my (... in my *what?* in my head out there on the pavement?), the man that had approached my boys went into services and, from the back of the room, asked if there was a doctor that could help. Now this is a very large Jewish synagogue near a major medical center. About forty physicians stood up and rushed toward the back.

I saw that my children were in good hands, so I floated back outside to where my body lay. I was looking down at myself. I know it is difficult to imagine, but I was really pissed off about the new shoes and outfit. I was thinking, "*Get up.* You're lying in the rain in a grease puddle. You are never going to get the stains out of the suit." Then, like a bolt from above, it hit me hard: "Oh, wait a minute. I'm not getting up *because I'm dead.*"

BLACK AND WHITE

As I hovered there over my body, I suddenly got it. I went from "Shit, my shoes are ruined" to "I was *so* wrong about so much." Thoughts came rushing in all at once. I thought about those people who believed in an afterlife and who I had secretly ridiculed for years. They had been right all along. I was looking at my body and thinking something like: "What a waste. You were so wrong. How could you have been so wrong? You lived for twenty-eight years and learned so little."

About what was I mistaken? So much. To begin with, my black-and-white thinking was wrong. I had always been very rigid in my beliefs. Everything to me had been right or wrong, alive or dead, black or white. There was no wiggle room at all. I suddenly realized *nothing* is black and white. And there I was, lying in the rain, and honestly, I was in a grease puddle that made *everything look gray*. All of the black and white that defined my life up to that point was gone.

My new view of my old self was harsh. I saw myself lying there in a kind of blur that was rapidly becoming infused with gray. The splendid white of my new suit was already a dingy, greasy gray. What I comprehended that disturbed me so was that the black-and-white, sharply defined borders that neatly defined my previous life were also blurring, graying now. Suddenly, the sharp divisions that had ruled my routines no longer mattered. This was not something I reasoned myself toward or even "thought" about. It was an understanding that came to me instantly, suddenly, shockingly. It was more like an awakening than a thinking. I looked at my body on the ground and knew that whatever had just happened to me had given me an insight that the woman lying there could never have grasped on her own, even seconds earlier.

Then something else happened, something deeply connected to my childhood. I had been sexually abused as a child for six years by a teenage boy who babysat for us. He is now a registered sex offender.

My final thought as I left for the afterlife was this: "You know how to do this. Remember?" I was thinking of how I learned to leave my body during the abuse by the babysitter, and then return when it was over. I understand that psychiatrists may call my out-of-body experiences as an abused child "dissociations." I think of them as repeated rehearsals that enabled me to survive a lightning strike years later. Those two defining life events—one horrible (the childhood sexual abuse), the other beautiful (my visit to heaven and conversation with God)—were linked by the near-death experience itself, and and by what was what was now rushing through my mind.

2

THE GLOW AND THE GARDEN

Sometimes when you go looking for what you want,
you run right into what you need.

—WALLY LAMB, *The Hour I First Believed*

As I was processing all of this, really in just a fraction of a second, a warm, inviting, golden glow appeared to my upper right. I sensed it as much as I saw it. It was not a fixed light but more of a moving beacon that seemed to want me to follow it. That is, there was no defined form to the glow. It was not round like the sun. It was more like the glow around the sun. In any case, I understood that I was dead and that my children were safe with my family and the community at the synagogue, so I gave in to the temptation and followed the beckoning glow.

Things suddenly got, well, *stranger* than they already were. For example, I immediately understood that time is not linear. Things were happening in my field of vision and new capacities were awakening within me, but they were all taking place at the same time, all at once. Moreover, my movement was not encumbered by my physical body. Whatever I had become floated or flew toward the warm glow. As I followed the glow, it led me to what I will call "the Garden," although it was unlike any garden here on earth. Many things about my visit to the Garden I now struggle to describe. They are simply not imaginable or thinkable. We just cannot perceive the Garden "where" and "when" we are now. And so the words to describe them do not yet exist here. Maybe they never will. Perhaps they are not supposed to exist here.

But I will try to describe what I saw using our existing language and vocabulary. The glow led me to a beautiful bench made of what appeared to be hand-carved wooden scrollwork, which had been sanded and polished until the wood was glossy. The graceful curves and swirls of the deeply carved wood felt like satin to my touch. It was so incredibly beautiful and elaborately ornate that it looked like an antique throne built for two. The unique beauty of this bench was only surpassed by the otherworldly comfort I felt when a familiar voice welcomed me and told me to sit on the bench. The voice was that of my beloved grandfather whose death a year earlier, of course, I had been at services to commemorate when I was struck by lightning.

I took a seat on the ornately scrolled bench and found that it immediately conformed to whatever my individual body had become as soon as I sat down. The morphing bench was surrounded by an abundance of plants, the likes of which I had never seen before. The plants blossomed into magnificent flowers that seemed to explode with colors from another color and light spectrum not accessible here. My grandfather's soft, familiar voice, complete with the French accent that made it so distinct in this life, immediately put me at ease. The voice said that audible speech would disrupt my absorption of my surroundings, so he was going to speak what I had come there to know in my head, silently, telepathically. I have come to believe that this was actually not my grandfather, by the way. I think it was God using my grandfather's voice to put me at ease.

The soothing voice was a calming vocal presence that I perceived yet did not hear. He knew things about our family that only my grandfather, and perhaps God, would know. This presence imparted information to me that implied a vast grasp and knowledge of where I was and what choices I would need to make if I chose to "go back." He relayed the clear impression that the choice to remain in the Garden or to reoccupy my burned and soaked body was mine to make. I understood that I could take all the time I needed in making the decision to stay or return, and that I would be given information that would help me make that most difficult choice.

I was dead, but I was more alive than when I had been that twenty-eight-year-old woman with the child and the umbrella in the synagogue parking lot a few seconds earlier. I was surrounded by and suffused with an unutterable feeling of unconditional love. The love was all-encompassing and embraced me in every way: in the palpable scents that hung in the air around me like ornaments; in the soothing sound of a gently babbling brook nearby; in the cadence of the gorgeous otherworldly music surrounding me; in the visual floral feast before me; and in the deeply comforting knowledge that I was safe, protected, and unconditionally loved by God himself.

The glow that I had initially followed into the Garden had moved away from me. It was still to my upper right, but now it was behind a range of mountains whose outlines in the distance were backlit with the shimmering light of the warm glow from behind them. I resisted the impulse to follow the beckoning glow to the mountains, since the peace, comfort, beauty, and unspeakable love that surrounded me where I was sitting were all that I could ever want. The sound of the brook nearby, the music in the air, the sweet scents of the blossoms and grass, and the vivid colors of the sky, mountains, and flowers, lulled me to depths that I had never known my soul to possess.

Regardless of whether my companion on the ornate bench was my grandfather or some other being higher up the ladder, I knew that I was not alone in the Garden. I did not turn to look at my companion because

I somehow knew that it would be overwhelming for me no matter what (or whom) I saw. I did not want to disrupt the visual and emotional perfection in which I found myself by seeing something I could not emotionally absorb. I knew that the abundance of love that this presence communicated to me was an immersion in spirit, the memory of which would never leave me. Still today I can draw on that memory of unspeakable love whenever I need to do so. I could have happily, willingly, and gratefully remained there for eternity. It was a gift, tailored to me, from a higher being that loved me unconditionally.

The landscape was clearly meant to comfort and assure me. The sound of flowing water, be it a brook, stream, waterfall, or ocean waves, is something I have always found to be gentle and soothing. A view of any scenery has always been enhanced for me if there is a body of water there. I think that is why it was so prominent among the other sweet sounds and music that permeated the Garden. The presence of all that I found to be warming, loving, and inviting taught me that, in this place, all who arrive encounter and perceive whatever is most comforting and reassuring to them. My source of comfort was the unmatched beauty of my surroundings and the all-embracing feeling of unconditional perpetual love, all captured in the Garden. This was *my* heaven.

Jeff has encouraged me to say more at this point. So let me put it this way. Let me say that I understood that all who come to this wondrous place are soothed and welcomed by whatever they find most comforting and pleasurable in life. Therefore, I was not surprised to find that *my* particular heaven took the form of a lush, perfectly manicured garden. Someone I saw in the distance may have expected his or her heaven to be a snow-blanketed forest. I instinctively recognized that while I found myself in a beautiful garden, someone else there might encounter a snowy forest, a boundless meadow, or a serene beach. Yet we were all in exactly the same place. We were in heaven. I also understood that in heaven one's own appearance projects the best of whatever one believed oneself to be in this life. Each of these kindnesses, moreover, added to my ease during my visit to the Garden.

I feel so inadequate to convey the totality of the place where I was. As I tried to explain earlier, time in the Garden is perpetual. It is layered with events and sensations that all occur at once. This changes pretty much everything. For example, all the lines that I had drawn in my previous life to separate past, present, and future had vanished. As I attempt to write what I experienced, I am left only with those explanations that I once received from those whose experiences I mocked. One of the many ironies in this redirection of my life is that I now hold to be true what they did—most fundamentally, that there are connections to something much greater than ourselves. I also now understand that it is possible to return from another realm or dimension and be completely unable to help those who have not beheld it to understand that it exists at all. Something can be perfectly true and completely unbelievable.

The knowledge that was being transmitted to me as I sat on the ornate bench in the presence of the loving being who spoke in the voice of my beloved grandfather was also being shared with the other humans there, humans whose forms I perceived in the distance. Everyone was in pairs. No one was alone. They were dressed in what I knew as street clothes. And they were all beautiful, youthful, healthy, and perfect. I wondered, "If they are perfect, am I?"

I looked at my left hand, curious to know how the burn from the lightning strike had affected it. Remarkably, my hand looked as if it belonged to a younger woman. There were no chipped nails or wrinkles, and certainly no burn from the lightning. There was also no wedding ring. All I saw was the taut, smooth, pristine skin of myself at eighteen or so. The skin on my hand was *perfect*.

Although I saw people in the distance, no one approached me. Nor did I approach any of them. Why were they all paired up with someone? Did I appear to them to be alone? These questions were immediately answered by my companion, who told me that I was also part of a pair, and that he was the other half.

This raised more questions for me. Could the other people there see two of us? We must have appeared to the distant human forms as they did to me—as a pair, and as beautiful as I ever was at my best. Did this partner of mine look like my grandfather at age ninety when he died, or did he look eighteen like everyone else there? Or did he have an entirely different appearance? I don't know because I never turned to look at him. I think I was not supposed to see him because I would have been overwhelmed at the sight of my beloved grandfather.

Or by the beauty of God himself.

THE TWO-WEEK CONVERSATION

My guide in the Garden gave me knowledge and entertained my questions for the entire two-week period I was there. My questions were answered instantly. As quickly as I could conceive the questions, I received the answers. I understood the passage of time in the Garden realm by observing the movement of the three celestial bodies that orbited and revolved above us. These moon bodies or planets were vividly bright orbs that looked, as best I can describe them, to be what we would call violet, although violet here on earth comes nowhere close to the intensity of violet in the Garden. This ability to read and understand the movement of the orbs as a calendar of sorts was one that I found I already possessed. By instinctively "reading" this "calendar," I came to know that my visit to the Garden lasted two weeks. I instinctually knew how time worked and passed in the Garden realm, just as I know how it works where we presently reside.

I know that this appears to contradict what I explained earlier about the simultaneity of time in the Garden. Why there was a way to ascertain the apparent passage of time in eternity, where everything happens at the same time, became clear as my guide imparted knowledge to me. I am not sure I can explain it, but let me try. As I wrote previously, everything appeared to be happening all at once. But once I began to converse with my companion and receive information from him, time seemed to become linear again for the duration of my visit (or so is my memory *here*). I have come to understand that this happened not because time actually became linear for two weeks, but because I would have no other way of "decoding" the information I received in the Garden here in this world. The only way I can understand *here* what was told to me *there* is to remember it in linear terms. I know this is confusing. I honestly do not know if the near-death experience itself was linear, or whether I just need to remember it in those terms in order to decipher it. My gut feeling is that (a) time there was not linear, but (b) linear time is my only frame of reference here.

The presence told me that I was welcome to stay there or return to my earthly body. The choice was mine. His job was to help me make the decision by answering questions I had about my life, my family, and the future. He also explained that, if I decided to stay, he would escort me from the Garden along a path and over the mountains to where the glowing beacon still patiently awaited my arrival.

It was not an easy choice. Returning to earth seemed to involve the risk of losing the fortifying sense of love without bounds or time that I knew there. I did not know then that this gift of incomparable love I felt would be with me forever on some level, regardless of whether I decided to stay there or return to my body.

Not all of what I was told there was ethereal in nature. For example, I was told that George H. W. Bush would shortly be our next president, and that the Cincinnati Bengals would play in the 1989 Super Bowl. These things might seem trivial or even silly to some (American elections and football games in heaven?), but I do not think that the specific events themselves were the point of the information. That is, I do not think that heaven is about politics or sports unless the deceased is a former politician or athlete. I think this information was given in order to help me grasp the nonlinear nature of time. Having the knowledge of *future* earthly events taught me that those events had already happened in the *past* yet still were going to happen again ... in the *future*. In short, I was realizing the relativity of time, relative, that is, to where one is in time.

This is going to take some explaining, and I am not sure I can. But let me try. It seemed to me that eternity itself was keeping an accounting of time. I understood that since time doesn't really exist as we think it does here on earth, someone or something in eternity is keeping track of every event that has happened, is happening, and will happen. I comprehended this concept of simultaneous time while I was in the Garden much more clearly than I do here. This is why, I think, it was so important that I be given information about future events: so that if I decided to return to my earthly body I would have a "trigger" to remind me of the simultaneous nature of time.

And in fact, this trigger worked beautifully. When George H. W. Bush was elected eight weeks after my trip to the Garden, suddenly my lessons on the simultaneous nature of time came rushing back to me. Suddenly, I remembered. Prior to the election, my lessons about the nature of time were buried so deep that I had yet to draw them forth since my return. The presidential election and then, a few months later, the Super Bowl served to remind me how real the Garden was and how the true nature of time works. Even though I do not understand the concept of simultaneous time here as well as I did there, I know that it is true, and I never question it.

My companion told me two things that clinched my decision to leave the Garden and return to my still unfinished life. Both involved my children. First, he told me that if I returned to my life, I would have a third child, a daughter. He explained that she had already selected Barry and me as her parents. As he told me this, I understood that reincarnation is a fact. This was a topic to which I had previously not given much, if any, thought. Had I thought about it, I would have laughed it off as impossible. But suddenly I knew it to be a very real process. Nevertheless, he told me not to let this future third child color my decision too much, because if I decided to stay in eternity, my future daughter would simply select other parents. In other words, she would return regardless of my decision.

The second thing he told me that helped me decide to return was that my marriage to Barry would not withstand the changes in me that this whole experience had wrought. If I chose to return, I was told that Barry and I would be facing a divorce in the future. This was a clincher for me, as I knew that I wanted to be the parent to raise our children. But in order to do this I first had to be there, of course, which meant coming back. Divorce or no divorce, I felt very strongly that I needed to be the one to raise them, which made the desire to return even stronger.

The missing wedding ring on my smooth hand when I looked at it in the Garden might have been a harbinger of all of this. Still, I had a hard time believing we would get divorced. Barry and I were perfectly happy with each other and our growing family. What I did not yet realize was that the Elizabeth who returned from the Garden was not the same Elizabeth who had been struck by lightning in the synagogue parking lot. The new Elizabeth would see life in varying shades of gray. Nothing would be black and white ever again. I was simply not the rigid, opinionated, well-defined person Barry had married.

So I opted for the return ticket. It was apparent that my time as a walking, talking, stained, burned, and insecure human being was not yet over. Even if there was a slight chance of divorce, I knew that I wanted to be the parent to raise Jeremy, Andy, and, if my guide was correct, our future daughter. I had a burning curiosity to meet this daughter whom I already loved.

My partner in the Garden cautioned me that going back would be physically very painful. The burns on my feet and body and my burst eardrums were injuries that I had not yet felt because I had not been in my body to suffer them. By reclaiming my physical self, I was also agreeing to accept whatever physical pain was there to bear. I understood from my guide that I would have to spend about three months off my burned feet. My companion reiterated that I needed to remember the overwhelming feeling of unconditional love because I would possibly not directly experience it again until I returned to the Garden at the point when I leave this particular life and body for good.

He also told me about another kind of pain I would feel as I returned to my body. He said he would have to "help" me back into my body by hugging me tightly, so tightly it would feel as if my bones were being crushed. He explained that this was necessary because my expanded soul was much larger than my body, and it needed to be squeezed back into my physical frame. My understanding of the unconditional love, and everything else I had been taught in the Garden, was now part of who I was. This knowledge and understanding had expanded the size of my soul, which was now much larger than it had been when it departed my body. As promised, the hugging was bone-crushingly painful and suffocating as he lovingly squeezed me back into my burned, wet, gray body.

I "woke up" on the wet asphalt of the synagogue parking lot.

BACK

I gasped for air. It filled my lungs and revived every cell in my body, except for my immobile left arm and hand. These were frozen, paralyzed in the same posture and grip I was in when the lightning struck. I don't think my body had moved at all from the position it was in when I was struck and fell in a heap on the pavement. I really cannot say if I was breathing at all during the couple of minutes here that I was gone. What I can say is that my left arm was still frozen in place, my beautiful new suit was now a permanently greasy gray, and the soles of my once gorgeous new pumps, still on my feet, were no more. They had taken the force of the electrical current as it grounded out through me and then through them.

My eyes opened, and I could see people rushing toward me from the synagogue. An initial sense of confusion overcame me as it dawned on me that, while I had been somewhere else for what I experienced as two weeks, here in the parking lot it was likely not more than a couple of minutes that had passed. I could not understand how it was possible to have received so much information and be so completely transformed in such a short time. It was all so disorienting.

Serendipitously, one of the many physicians at services that evening was a doctor who had extensive experience treating victims of lightning strikes and electrocution. He was a white-water rafter and had helped several people who had been struck by lightning while rafting, which, apparently, is not an uncommon experience.

I eventually learned that the relatively modest injuries I sustained from my lightning encounter were probably due to how I was struck and the nature of lightning itself. Lightning transmits its incredible energy ever downward as it seeks the earth and grounds out. From the tip of my umbrella, the charge apparently flowed through the metal frame to the place on the metal shaft above the wooden handle where my wedding ring had been in contact with it. Had the lightning hit higher on my body, say, on my head, my experience would likely have been very different. My "near-death experience" probably would have been a "death experience."

When I awoke, it was still raining, but not as hard. I remember being helped into the synagogue and placed on the couch in the rabbi's study. I was in and out of consciousness, and really, really tired. The doctor was there. I recall him telling me to open my eyes. But I was so tired. I was able to open them, but I could keep them open for only a couple of minutes at a time. The doctor examined me and concluded that I had a mild lightning injury, an MLI. No hospitalization was necessary at that point. He listened to my heart with his stethoscope and said it sounded fine. He explained that I had keraunoparalysis (lightning paralysis), and that it would be temporary. The paralysis lasted for about six hours but did eventually subside. He also encouraged me to have the burns on my feet and left hand looked after and told me I'd have to keep off my feet, which meant bed rest, until they healed.

Looking back on it all now, I confess that it feels a bit outrageous that the doctor did not feel that I needed to be checked in to a hospital. He did tell me that, if I were to go in, they would simply call him in as the resident lightning specialist, and that he would do exactly what he just did and tell me the same exact things. So there was some practical sense there, I suppose.

Hospital or no hospital, I was back now.

But I was no longer me.

3

THE PORTFOLIO OF STRANGE THINGS

He's got to have the ability, and it seems to be fairly rare, to see
things as they are and at the same time as they might have been.

—JACK FINNEY, *TIME AND AGAIN*

The experience of being struck by lightning and the immediate effects that it had on me both in the Garden and afterward—the differences in perceiving color and sound, the new knowledge, and the new understanding of time—were just precursors of the ways in which I was about to change. Something in me had "opened." I also now *thought* differently. I was much more comfortable now with ambiguity and complexity, less infatuated with black-and-white thinking or judging. I even literally *saw* differently. It began with the colors.

THE COLORS OF OZ

One of the first things that struck me within the near-death experience itself was the shift from black and white to an otherworldly vision of brilliant, vibrant, living colors. This was not just a visual change. It was also a symbolic one. The Garden was suffused with astonishing light and color. It was all *alive*. What a contrast to the grays and grease of the parking lot!

It was *so* clear to me then that the definite separations, the clear either/or thinking that had defined so much of my life, are simply not the way things really are. For twenty-eight years I had not been living in the actual world. I had been living in an illusory world of my own judgments and learned responses. I had been wrong, and I felt no shame in admitting that to myself throughout the near-death experience. It was a bit like Dorothy finding herself in Technicolor Oz. "Toto, I've a feeling we're not in Kansas anymore."

Or Texas.

"JUST KNOWING"

And the living colors were just the beginning. The new convictions and capacities I had acquired in the Garden began to show themselves in other ways, ways that surprised and frankly shocked me. Indeed, these convictions and capacities were so strange at first that I honestly believed I was losing my mind.

Here is an example. Three months after my visit to the Garden, the certain knowledge of the death of a woman I knew of but did not personally know showed itself to me in a dream. I simply knew that this soul had transitioned out of this world and into the next. I awoke with a single question for which I had no answer. I had no real connection to this person, so why me? "Why tell me?" I asked the universe. The answer came quickly. The point of knowing was not the content of the knowledge. The point of knowing was to show me *that I could know*. But there was more. The point of knowing was also to show me that I could know such things *before they happened*. Because I was still something of a skeptic, the universe set out to force me to believe in my own new abilities.

At times I would see (and still see) words, texts, pictures, even movies that convey with instant conviction things that I would have no way of knowing or no reason for even guessing. When this first began, I found it reassuring that at least there were no audible voices telling me these things. As long as I wasn't hearing voices, I told myself, I must not be going completely nuts.

It has taken me years, decades really, to trust the different forms of how I receive information about different events. I have come to understand that the way in which I know of events in advance has something to do with slipping through different dimensions of time and space. More on that later. But back when all of this was new to me, knowing about the death of someone I did not personally know was simply perplexing. I had no idea how I would ever be able to prove this knowledge to anyone, including myself. So I told no one. I didn't want people to think I was crazy. At the time I thought I had reason to question my own sanity.

The morning after the dream of the woman's passing, I had to find out if it was true. I felt compelled to go see an acquaintance at the pharmacy where he worked as a pharmacist, since I knew that the person whose death I had sensed was someone this pharmacist knew. I drove over to the pharmacy and hesitated before I went in. Somehow, I wanted my precognition to be accurate. I wanted to prove to myself that I actually had this ability. Yet I also wanted it to be a fluke. I was torn. I wanted some way to justify going back to my much simpler black-and-white existence. I wanted to pretend that nothing had really happened and I was the same person I had always been. That was not going to work.

I walked up to the pharmacy counter where this acquaintance was filling a prescription. He looked up and, after a few brief pleasantries, told me that a longtime customer of his had died early that morning. He has always cared about his customers, and I heard the emotion quiver in his voice as he spoke. I was deeply shaken, too, if for different reasons. I expressed my sympathies and rushed back to my car. Somehow I had been shown knowledge of this woman's passing that turned out to be true, despite the fact that I had never even met her. I was not just confused. I was frightened.

The dream of the woman's passing was just the beginning. My feet were now healed, and I was able to get around. But my charred feet had kept me in bed for long spells. I had slept a lot, and my sleep had been filled with dreams and nightmares, some of which I remembered when I awoke. This already was a bit strange because up until this point in my life, I had never once been able to recall a dream, even if I had just awakened from it. I remembered nothing. Now I did.

At this early stage in my new life, it had not yet occurred to me to document the timing of my dreams and the incidents they appeared to display or predict. Occasionally, I would tell Barry or my mom when I had these dreams. It made Barry uncomfortable to hear them, so I didn't tell him about all of them. My mom, on the other hand, was interested and seemed to enjoy our discussions about my precognitions. It was after my first plane crash nightmare that I realized I needed to document my precognitions. And yet I still didn't know how to do that.

The first plane crash nightmare I had was on July 16, 1996, about eight years after my near-death experience. It really rocked me badly. In the nightmare I could see the letters "WA" on the wreckage and thought it was a World Airways flight. I knew there were 230 people on board, and that none of them had survived. I knew that the plane crashed in water, and I knew it was flight 800. I called my mom and told her about my nightmare on the morning of July 17, 1996. The next morning, July 18, 1996, Mom called me to tell me to turn on the news, quickly.

And there it was: TWA Flight 800 had crashed in the Atlantic Ocean with 230 people on board. No survivors. This particular nightmare really upset me because of its accuracy. TWA was an acronym for Trans World Airlines, an airline that was in business until 2001. I just had not seen the "T" in my nightmare. Other than that detail, my nightmare had been spot on. Distraught, I shared the information with Barry, even though I knew it would be more than he could handle. He moved out of the house within ten days. Our divorce was final a year later. This specific nightmare did not cause the demise of our marriage, but it sure didn't help. For the record, Barry and I had our daughter, Mallory, in 1990, two years after my near-death experience. We divorced in 1997, almost nine years after my trip to the Garden.

I had not asked for any of this, but I recognized that I needed two things. First, I needed an answer to the lingering question of why this was happening to me. And I needed a way to document the accuracy or inaccuracy of my dreams. Mostly this was for my own sake, so I could convince myself that I was not crazy. It was not until 2008 that it dawned on me that I could email brief recounts of the dreams to myself right after they occurred so that they were date-stamped and time-stamped. I never imagined that anyone other than me would see these emails, which I wrote for my own self-confidence and reassurance.

Please remember that I was a mom to two young boys when all this started. I did not approach any of this as some kind of scientific experiment or academic case study. I had no time for this. Actually, what I felt most was anger. I had no desire or wish to become some radio receiver to the cosmos. I didn't want the moral burden of these premonitions, visions, and nightmares. But try as I could to ignore them, they continued to plague me. And every one of them was made of the same damned stuff—that undeniable knowledge that these horrific tragedies were perfectly true. I had no idea how I could make anything positive come of them. I was frustrated, and I was angry.

These visions have never stopped occurring. Nearly thirty years after the lightning strike, incidents of clear knowledge continue to come to me, occasionally even when I am wide awake. Here is a simple example. One day in February of 2003, my second husband, Matt, and I were driving to meet some friends for dinner. I turned to him, grabbed his arm, and said, "Earthquake, an area in western China." That was early on a Sunday evening in Houston. Sometime in the early morning hours on Monday the earthquake hit in China. It happened too late for the Monday papers in the United States and was in too distant a rural area to attract media attention—at least as far as we knew. But in the Tuesday paper there was a brief article on the international page about a severe earthquake that had taken place in western China at approximately the same time that I had grabbed Matt's arm and told him it was happening.

People often ask Matt if he believes my stories. His first instinct is always to doubt. However, he has been with me many times and witnessed these things firsthand. It is simply a matter of honest observation for him. He says that he cannot *not* believe them. He lives with them, after all, and although he cannot understand much of what I may relate (who can?) and has no means to explain any of it, he knows that these precognitions happen. He might as well deny that the sun comes up in the morning. These things are simply a part of our world.

PHONE CALL FROM THE DEAD

As I have already made clear, many exceptional things have happened to me since my near-death experience. One of the earliest and strangest took place in the spring of 1990, a year and a half after the lightning strike. I had recently found out I was pregnant with my third child. Barry and I were sound asleep in bed. It was about 3:30 A.M. when the phone on my side of the bed rang. This was back when people only had landlines plugged in to the wall. I think we are all conditioned to expect the worst when the phone rings in the wee hours. It is usually news that is urgent, important, and not good. No one calls at 3:30 A.M. to give you good news.

I love my sleep. At the beginning of my third pregnancy, after chasing two active boys around every day, I relished it. So I did not really wake up when the phone rang on my side of the bed. It was Barry's shaking me and telling me to get the phone that finally roused me. I hesitated to answer because I feared it would be bad news. That is not exactly how it played out, though. My hesitant "Hello?" into the phone was answered with the soft, French-accented voice of my dead grandfather. This time I knew it really was him. "Hello, darling," he said.

"Darling" is what he always called me. Stunned, I asked why he was calling me. Barry, who was now wide awake, kept asking who it was. I shushed him. He did not need to talk to my grandfather, and I didn't want to waste precious airtime with him. I asked my grandfather where he was. The conversation went something like this:

"You know where I am. You've been here and seen it."

"But why are you calling me?" I asked.

"I need you to tell your mother something for me."

"Then why are you calling me? Why not just call her? I can give you her number if you need it."

"I have tried to contact her, but she can't hear me. But since you were struck by the lightning, you can hear me. Contacting the living takes a terrific amount of energy, and I don't have long to talk. There is something that I want you to tell her for me."

"Of course I'll tell her."

He then relayed what was, to me, a mundane bit of family information that he felt my mom needed to know.

By now, Barry and I were both sitting straight up in bed, wide awake. Barry was still pestering me to tell him who was on the phone. I was still ignoring him. I needed to know something from Grandpa, so I asked, "Did Grandma find you?"

At that, Barry got angry and said, "Who the hell are you talking to?" I ignored him.

Grandpa answered: "Yes. She is fine. We are together. All is well. She is whole again."

Grandma had dementia when she died. The woman she was had gotten lost. At the end, her life was a ride on a bridge that crumbled as she crossed. I was so happy hearing this news.

"I have to tell you something," I said to Grandpa.

"I already know. You're pregnant. And it's a girl, just as you were told it would be."

His voice became weaker, fainter.

"I can't hear you well," I said.

"I have to go. This is taking a terrific amount of energy. I can't do this often, but I will call you again. Please remember to call your mother and tell her what I said."

"I will, but please don't hang up," I pleaded.

"I will talk to you again. I just can't do it right now. You need to remember, remember when you were here, the feeling of unconditional love. Never forget that."

These were the words, of course, that I had also been told when I was in the Garden and had made the decision to return to my body. I begged him not to go.

"Remember the unconditional love. You will have this feeling again as soon as we hang up."

And with that, the connection faded away.

Our bedroom immediately filled with an odorless smoke. It was just vapor, as if we were in a dense cloud. In any normal circumstance, of course, if our bedroom filled up with smoke, both of us would be running to get the boys and get out of the house. The situation was anything but normal, though. Inexplicably, while we were both sitting in this thick mist, or whatever it was, neither of us acted or reacted in fear. And neither of us spoke.

Then things got stranger still. At the far end of the long hallway that extended from our bedroom to the children's rooms, I saw a bright red light shining through the fog. Like a laser pointer, it pierced through the mist. When I saw that light, I was immediately overcome with the same palpable sense of unconditional love I had experienced in the Garden and had been told moments before to never forget. This must be what he meant when he said, "You will have this feeling again as soon as we hang up." Somehow, the light carried the love. Suddenly, the light vanished and the fog dissipated completely in an instant. It was all just *gone*, as if nothing had happened.

Barry turned to me and now calmly asked who had called.

"My grandfather," I replied.

"Which one?" he asked.

I told him. I then asked him, "Did you just see anything?"

He replied, "What smoke? I'm going to sleep."

Clearly, he had seen what I had seen but would not talk about it.

After that exchange in 1990, Barry and I never talked about that night again for almost twenty-one years, until 2011, to be precise. By then, we had divorced, had both remarried, and had traveled independently to Jerusalem to attend the rabbinical ordination of our son Andy. By this time, I had taken to telling my adult children about some of the extraordinary things that routinely happen to me. I don't know if it is because he was holding my hand when I was struck, but Andy in particular has always taken a very special interest in my experiences. Jeremy and Mallory have as well, but I often wonder if Andy's proximity to me at the time of the strike somehow affected him spiritually. I mean, he grew up to become an Orthodox rabbi.

On the night of his rabbinic ordination, at a dinner celebration in his honor, Andy casually asked Barry if he remembered the night when I was pregnant with Mallory and the phone had rung. My ears perked up and tuned in to their conversation across the dinner table.

"You mean the call from her grandfather? Yes, I remember."

Of all the cynics and doubters of my experiences whom I had encountered through the years, none had matched Barry. This was especially true during our bitterly contested, quite ugly divorce. As Andy asked him about the call, I listened, stunned, as Barry recounted it just as it had happened. He remembered the details as if it had happened just the day before. Barry can admit to the events themselves, but, like so many others, he hesitates to jump to any conclusion about whether or not I was really talking to my deceased grandfather. But the fact that Barry admits to having heard the phone ring, hearing my half of the conversation, and seeing the smoke and its instantaneous disappearance is enough for me. I cannot make those who either refuse to believe or lack the capacity to believe what I experienced believe me. Nor do I want to try.

I called my mom the day after the phone call in 1990 and told her the information that her father had wanted to convey. She asked me how I knew that. I recounted my experience of the night before. Our short conversation ended with Mom in tears. "I know he has tried to talk to me. I try so hard to hear him, and I just can't."

I find it puzzling how different we all are. On one side is Barry, who actually witnessed this communion across the two worlds yet cannot bring himself to fully believe what I suspect he knows to be true. On the other is my mom, who fully believes in these exchanges between the two realms but cannot bring the experience about, no matter how much she may want to do so. I should add here that, as time has marched on and life has dealt Barry some pretty swift blows, he has become more of a believer and much less cynical in recent years.

IN THE GENE POOL

It is not that Mom lacks any spiritual experiences. Quite the contrary. As I alluded to earlier, Mom is a spiritual person. When I was a child, she never told me things like "death is the end of a person's existence" or "when people die, they are gone forever and you won't see them any- more." Because of her spiritual nature, it does not surprise me that she has stories to tell about strange things that have happened to her. What has really stunned me is my dad.

Dad has always appeared to be pretty conservative in his ideas on matters of the spirit. Growing up, I always got the feeling that his take on death was that it is final. So I was quite shocked when Jeff was interviewing him for this book, and he told us the following story about "Pop" (my beloved maternal grandfather) with tears in his eyes:

In 1971, when I was moving into a new suite of dental offices, Pop gave me a tiny little potted plant for the new office. It was a Dracaena compacta and was about three inches tall. This is a very slow-growing plant. I always took great care to water it and take special care of it. In 1977, it moved with me to my new office, and then in 1984 it moved to the balcony at our home when I retired from dentistry. It was about the healthiest plant I have ever seen. By 1987, it stood eighteen inches tall and was lushly vibrant. I remember watering it on September 4, 1987, and thinking to myself how remarkably healthy it was for a houseplant that was sixteen years old. The next day, September 5, 1987, Pop passed away. I had always watered all of the plants on the balcony every other day, so I went out there on September 6 to water them. I was shocked to see that the sixteen-year-old Dracaena that had been amazingly healthy two days earlier was dead. It was as if when Pop died, the life energy he had always supplied was gone, and the perfectly healthy, vibrant, lush plant literally wilted over and died.

Dad had never told me that story. I began to wonder to myself if something genetic was going on, something within our family line that made us all experience these strange things. Then Dad went on:

There is another story, if you want to hear it. When Ronnie [my dad's younger brother] died, and we were at his funeral, do you remember what happened, Elizabeth? As the rabbi was eulogizing him and everyone was around the gravesite, a big black grackle bird flew into the tree right above the rabbi. It was cawing and cawing so loudly the rabbi had to stop talking. This bird actually interfered with the funeral service. I know that was my brother commenting on his own funeral.

These two stories would not have surprised me at all coming from my mother, but my *father?* Really? I did not remember the grackle at my uncle's funeral, but my dad sure did.

Mom and Dad both grew up in Houston in the 1950s. It was a simpler time, a time of social conformity when everyone wanted to fit in and be like everyone else. Adolescents were prevented by peer pressure from talking openly about the supernatural. Nobody wanted to be anything other than like everyone else.

In her mid-teens, Mom was a participant in a storytelling competition. She was drawn to a particular story she had read about a man who was sentenced to prison and died while incarcerated. The prison setting of the story was unsettling enough for her audience of teenage girls, but what really took them by surprise was that the death of the prisoner was not the end of the story. The man becomes a spirit and is able to see what is taking place in the prison even as his dead body remains in his cell.

Mom remembers two things about her storytelling experience. First, she recalls winning second place in the competition. Second, she remembers the looks on the faces of the young girls to whom she had told the story. They were shocked by her selection of such an unconventional topic. I think this early dalliance with the realm of the supernatural kindled an interest in my mother that has grown through the years.

But it was on a cruise to Alaska that Mom became really convinced that there is a pervasive unnamed force in the universe that operates in strange and wondrous ways. She and Dad had convinced a couple who were friends of theirs to go with them on this cruise. These friends had a son who had been recently murdered. This was to be their first trip away from Houston since their son's tragic death. Mom and Dad were under great stress as well at the time of this trip. This made the cruise particularly welcome but also fraught with remnants of life that could hardly be banished by simply leaving home.

Among the many changes one notices when boarding a plane in Houston and landing in Alaska is the nature of the light in the northern sky. Long summer days in Texas are remarkable for the intensity and duration of the sunlight. But for the heat waves shimmering up from the steaming concrete in Houston, the vista that the bright sunlight opens up expands without interruption for miles once you leave the big city. On the water in Alaska, however, the opacity of the sunlight blurs rather than sharpens the sky. Night is a shadow of itself that far north in summertime, and the fuller morning sun following the feeble night is rejuvenating.

It was on such a morning during a stroll around the deck on the ship, arm in arm with Dad, that it happened. To put it simply, Mom was surrounded by a beam of light that shone down on her from above. No one else saw it, not even Dad. To this day, Mom is convinced that the light that surrounded her was sent by God. A wave of serenity washed over her, and vivid images of a rich, deep fabric calmed the concerns she had felt only moments before. The experience of the peace that this moment brought her told her that everything is surmountable and that no strife, whether from within or without, cannot be calmed. It has stayed with her ever since.

It was years before Mom took the leap and talked about this experience. She tossed out a couple of hints to close friends, but their reactions were disbelieving, even disparaging. So she kept it back. She also feared that if she were to divulge the secret of this special moment, she might somehow diminish its potency.

There have been other experiences, too. Mom is also a staunch believer in reincarnation. She has had several vivid experiences in her adult life that have served to convince her of two things: first, that she has had many previous lives; and second, that she has cycled back through incarnations with souls with whom she has lived in other lives.

I mention all of this for a reason. After all, with a family line like this, perhaps it made it easier for me to become who I am in an unaccepting world. Maybe I was destined, fated to become who I am.

THE WOMAN (NOT) UPSTAIRS

We do have words for some of this, of course. Jeff would call them "strange words," by which he means that they occupy ambiguous or uncertain places in our language and culture: We use them, but we don't quite believe in them, and we often make fun of them. These words are disreputable, never quite respected, and yet they do not go away either. I think Jeff would say that they do not go away because they name something that is real, something that is a part of our world and probably our own nature.

My knowledge of events before they happen, for example, is called precognition. My observance of ghostly phenomena that take place at the point in space and time that we call the present is sometimes called an apparition. I know both kinds of experiences well.

There is a spirit who lives in my house. I can sense her. I can also sometimes see her. She hovers on the second floor of our home, moving from room to room. She does not interact with us, nor does she make herself known in any way but for her floating spectral presence. Our dog McKinley used to sense this presence and bark as she looked up toward our second floor. Several times I heard her bark when I was in another room. I'd come into the den that opens up to the second floor to find McKinley barking at the figure that I could sense and see as well.

I kept the sight of the floating woman to myself until Andy was in high school and came downstairs one morning to ask if I had been upstairs. He thought he had seen, or sensed, someone in his bedroom. And then he thought he may have sensed a woman standing behind him as he was looking in the bathroom mirror. When I asked him to describe what he had seen, he hemmed and hawed and then said only half jokingly, "I may have imagined the whole thing. Maybe it was a ghost."

He said that the apparition was not terribly frightening to him. He sensed no ill will from it. He told me it was a young woman and proceeded to describe her clothing, *exactly* as I had seen it. Andy was somewhat amused that, in addition to his mom, only he and our dog McKinley had seen the woman. If he ever saw her again, he never spoke about it.

Eventually, I decided to tell Matt about our additional resident. He had never seen her but was very amused whenever the dog or I saw her. McKinley passed away in 2015, but she used to sit at my feet when Matt and I would watch television at night. Occasionally, something would catch my eye, and McKinley and I would look upstairs at the open balcony at the same moment. McKinley would whimper or bark. She clearly saw the apparition, just as I did. McKinley would not look away until the woman had floated out of our view. We have a new puppy now, Charlie. I am curious as to whether Charlie will see or sense the woman the next time she shows herself.

To my knowledge the only other person who has seen our boarder was a friend of Mallory's. When Mallory was fourteen or fifteen, she had a group of five or six friends over to our house one Saturday night to watch a movie. They were all crammed together on our sofa watching the movie when suddenly one of the teenage boys yelled, "What is that???" He was looking upstairs at the balcony and pointing and screaming. None of the other kids saw anything. He was truly terrified, though, as evidenced by the fact that he wet his pants and went running and shrieking from our house. Although he and Mallory remained friends, he would never set foot in our home again. It was after that episode that I decided to fill Mallory and Jeremy in on the fact that someone, or something, was living upstairs with them. They were fine with it. To my knowledge, they have never seen her.

My sense of the woman who (doesn't) live upstairs is that she is seeking something. She reminds me of myself just after I was struck by lightning, when I was "hovering" until Jeremy and Andy were safely inside the synagogue. My "hovering," I believe, ceased when I knew that they were safe and in the hands of people who loved them and I understood that I was dead. Knowing that, I could get on with being dead, and that's when I went to the Garden. Because of the way she behaves, I sense that the woman who is (not) upstairs is caught somewhere between realms. Her marginal status is what may explain her movement from place to place. I think it is also why she does not appear to be conscious or to direct her movements with any purpose. She does not appear to see us, nor does she attempt to interact with our household in any way.

I think it is significant that the woman never comes downstairs. We built this house in 2003. It is built higher off the ground than the house that previously sat in the same spot. We had to build it higher to be up out of the flood zone. We also lived in the house that occupied the same spot previously and never sensed or saw any apparitions. Perhaps the woman (not) upstairs is a leftover remnant of energy, a scrap of charged matter, the residue of some memory encoded into the space where the upper part of our house now sits. I don't know.

4

THE HAUNTED NECKLACE AND
THE RAINBOW WORLD

*The object becomes aesthetically significant when it
becomes metaphysically significant.*

—JOSEPH CAMPBELL

The precognitive dreams, the phone call from the dead, and the woman (not) upstairs—these things do not exhaust the portfolio of strange occurrences that is now my life. Sometimes, for example, I feel that inanimate objects have a unique "vibe" to them. It is not an aura that I can see exactly. It is more that I can sense certain energies around or within the object. Even though I understand that they are not living beings, I cannot deny that I sense at times that a nonliving object possesses a certain living energy. Such was the case with my necklace.

THE HAUNTED NECKLACE

In 2005, I had planned to meet a friend for lunch in Rice Village, a shopping district in Houston near Rice University. I was running early, and she typically runs late, so I knew I had some time to shop before lunch. I walked into a women's boutique, just planning to browse for a few minutes. This was not a store where I often bought clothing, and in fact I do not really care for their clothing. But something drew me in there that day. I quickly lost interest in browsing the clothing and made my way over to the accessories.

This particular boutique carries a fairly wide selection of costume jewelry under its own label. Even though it is costume jewelry, it is rather expensive and very well made. Each piece of this store's clothing, accessories, or jewelry has the name of the boutique somewhere on the item. In the case of their jewelry, the store name is stamped onto a tiny oval metal tag that hangs from the clasp.

Almost immediately, my eye was drawn to a gorgeous necklace unlike any of the store's other jewelry. Most of the store's necklaces are heavy metallic pieces, silver, gold, or bronze in color, but this one was different. On a bronze-link chain, about eighteen inches long, hung the most eye-catching, multicolored stone I'd ever seen. The stone itself was oval in shape, about three inches tall and two inches wide. Something about the colors in the stone—vibrant gemstone hues that changed color, depending on the angle from which one was viewing it—reminded me of the Garden. Sapphire blue, ruby red, emerald green, amethyst purple, vibrant rose-quartz pink, and velvety tourmaline yellow all worked together to make the object almost come alive. I reached out and picked it up.

As soon as I touched it, I knew it would be mine. Holding the necklace, I suddenly felt as if I were a little girl again, sitting in my grandmother's musty attic going through the trunk of old dresses she had brought with her from Europe when she immigrated to the United States as a young teen. I was transported to another place and time. Oddly, though, this particular necklace had no price tag on it. Every single accessory had a price tag, except for this one necklace. I also noted that it did not have the signature metal tag hanging from the clasp.

I carried it to the register and set it down in front of the woman tending the counter, whose nametag indicated that she was the store manager. She was quite perplexed that there was no price on the necklace. "Oh! This is beautiful. I've never seen it before. Where did you find it?" I pointed out to her where I had found the necklace, among all the other jewelry that looked nothing like it. She pulled out a gigantic binder of computer printout paper that was supposedly a complete inventory price list of every item the store carried. But, just as I suspected, no necklace matching the description of the one lying before us on the counter was listed.

After spending a solid fifteen minutes looking through the inventory binder, she walked over to the accessories area of the store, where she held and looked at some of the other necklaces, trying to gauge the price of the one I wanted. She returned to the register and again looked through the inventory binder, still to no avail. Finally she told me she just could not sell it to me. She didn't think it was from their store, and she had no idea how to price it. I was clearly upset by this. I told her I just had to have it, at any price. She suggested that I go to lunch and come back after I ate. She would keep looking for the price and see what she could do.

I knew, though, that if I left the store without the necklace, I would never get it. So I insisted that she name a price and let me buy it. Finally, I wore her down, and she agreed. We arrived at a price that was in line with the other necklaces. I walked out $140 lighter, but with a necklace I really loved and couldn't wait to wear.

The first time I wore the necklace was to work. Due to the vivid and varied colors of the stone, I could only wear it with a few solid-color outfits. At the time, I was working for a homebuilder selling custom homes. I had a beautiful office and an assistant who had a good eye for nice things. "That necklace is gorgeous," she gushed. "Where did you get it?"

I told her where I bought it, and we chatted for a few minutes until I headed back to my office to start the day. A couple of hours later she came back to my office visibly upset. She told me that a young person to whom she was very close had just unexpectedly died (her sister, I believe), and she needed to leave. I felt terrible for her. She was out for several days.

The second time I wore the necklace another person's death, quite unexpected, was announced to someone I was with. Again, it wasn't someone I personally knew, but the news certainly affected me. It did occur to me that the same thing had happened the first time I had worn the necklace, but I did not think too much of it. It was just an odd coincidence, I reassured myself.

Until, that is, it happened again two weeks later the third time I wore the necklace. I was talking to a prospective buyer about building a new home when he got a phone call. He needed to leave immediately, as someone had died, again unexpectedly. I immediately took the necklace off and knew that I would never wear it again.

But here was the odd thing (or another odd thing). As I held it in my hand, I realized that, just like the first time I touched it in the store, every time I touched this necklace I was immediately transported back to my grandmother's musty attic and her trunk of old clothes. This was not a fearful thing. It was in fact a wonderful memory for me. As a child, I used to love going up into Grandma's attic with her. There were so many treasures up there. She and I enjoyed going up there, especially if it was raining. It felt very cozy when we could hear the rain on the roof above us while we talked and I played in the attic. I would dress up in her old clothes, and she would regale me with stories.

Happy memories or no, this necklace was clearly cursed, or haunted, or something. I decided I had to rid myself of it. The coincidental deaths or the juju that emanated from it were just too much. But how exactly was I to dispose of it? I could hardly give it to someone: its evil vibrations would simply attach themselves to the recipient. This is why I also felt that I could not simply return it to the store or, for that matter, place it somewhere that it could wind up around the neck of an unsuspecting woman. I realized that the last woman who had it had most likely left it in the store intentionally to get rid of it. I also knew that there would be some very bad karma if I threw it away.

So I took the cursed thing home and put it in a small, airtight plastic container that I then sealed with duct tape. "Sealed" is probably an understatement here. I wound the tape over and over around the plastic container so that it would be very difficult to ever open it again. But that was not enough. I did not want to keep it in the house, but I also did not want to curse anyone else's property with it. So I carried it outside to the farthest back corner of our backyard and placed it on the ground behind some shrubs against the fence. Eventually, though, I concluded that was not enough. I began to worry that someone, the yardman perhaps, might find it. The dark feeling the necklace gave me motivated me to do a better job hiding it. So a month after I set it out against the back fence, I decided to bury it. When I went out to the backyard with a shovel, however, the container was no longer there. It was nowhere to be found. I felt really bad about this, but what could I do? I hoped that an animal rather than a person had found it.

About a week later, I opened the front door one morning to get the newspaper. There was the little plastic container, still tightly sealed with duct tape, sitting on my doormat. I absolutely freaked out. Crying and shaking, I immediately got the shovel, dug a hole in the back corner of the yard, dropped the plastic container in the ground, covered it with dirt, and firmly tamped it down. Finally, I thought, I could breathe easy. That sucker was *buried*. I preferred not to think about how it had gotten to my front doormat.

Three years passed, and my daughter Mallory was about to get a new car. We were going to give her old car to her brother Andy. Jeremy, Mallory, and I spent about an hour cleaning out the car. As is typical with a teenager's car, bits of trash and various abandoned objects had accumulated over the years in the trunk, under the seats, in the console, and in the glove box. We got it all cleaned out. I decided to make one final pass through the car. I checked the trunk, the glove box, the console, and under the back seats. Then I stuck my head down on the front floor under the steering wheel to check that nothing was left under the driver's seat. A glint of something caught my eye. I reached under and pulled out *the necklace*. It was not in the plastic container, but it was covered in moist, freshly dug dirt! I dropped it like a hot potato and started screaming at Mallory, "Where did you get this?!?! What are you doing with it?!?!" Clearly, it had been dug up, *recently*. Mallory had no idea what it was or how it had gotten in her car.

I was really upset. I took the necklace home and just left it outside, loose on the ground in a corner of the front porch. The next day it was gone, and I haven't seen it since. It could have been picked up by the mailman, the yardman, or even an animal. I have no idea. It has been more than nine years now. God help me if I ever see it again. I don't know that I could take it.

What does the haunted necklace have to do with the lightning strike and near-death experience? I'm not sure. Two things occur to me, though. First, before the lightning strike of 1988 I don't know if I would have realized the connection between my wearing the necklace and people dying. Maybe. Maybe not. Perhaps more substantially, I am fairly certain that I would not have been capable of experiencing the wonderful flashbacks of time spent with my grandmother whenever I touched the necklace. But what do these happy memories have to do with these sad deaths? Again, I simply don't know.

One positive thing did come out of this otherwise quite dark series of events. My experience with the necklace inspired me to read about objects that are believed to be imbued with some kind of supernatural power. Through my research I came upon the name of Bruce Greyson, MD, who was at that time a professor of psychiatry and neurobehavioral sciences at the University of Virginia, and who has focused his distinguished career on the very topic of near-death experiences. Though he was not able to advance my understanding of the strange events associated with the necklace, he was all ears about the lightning strike and the changes in me that resulted from my near-death experience. We have carried on a series of very constructive conversations ever since.

SEEING ENERGY FIELDS

I do not understand the connection between all of the phenomena I have experienced since September 2, 1988. They appear to be related, but how? Clearly, the near-death experience has changed my life, and the paranormal currents that emanate or radiate from this original explosion continue to change me almost daily. It is as if the voltage I received when that tiny finger of electricity touched me charged me with an energy that pulses through everything. It is as if the energy of that lightning was somehow alive and has somehow made me more alive, more sensitive to my surroundings. I can *see* this energy now. I can also *feel* it. This is not a question of faith or belief. It is all about sensing new dimensions of the world. To see and palpably feel the energy is proof to me that my experiences are real. Perhaps the most obvious example of this is my ability to see and sense "auras."

Put most simply, an aura is a field of light generated by an energy-producing entity. That entity can be anything from the sun, whose aura gives life and light to our world, to a light bulb, whose filament brightens when fed electricity. But here is the thing. I also see auras as the vibrancy emanating from living things—plants, animals, and humans. Unlike the auras from a light source like the sun or a light bulb, auras of living beings, in my own experience at least, are delicate, evasive, and always changing.

In order to see these auras I have to unfocus my eyes. A white background aids me in detecting them, although that is not always necessary. For this reason, I have to ascribe some external visual stimulus, some objectivity, to them. Otherwise, what difference would the change in background make to an image of a person surrounded by light and color, if this is all only in my mind? No, I really see these energy fields. They are there. But they are not exactly simple electromagnetic phenomena, like the light of a light bulb. I also believe, for example, that a blind person is capable of *feeling* auras instead of seeing them visually. If I close my eyes and put my hand into someone's energy field, the color and texture of the aura are something I can usually, but not always, sense. They are not just "light" or "energy" then. They are also something more.

A good way to practice seeing auras is to look at the old *Magic Eye* books. Those picture books have fuzzy patterns that, if you stare at them long enough, will focus into clear, three-dimensional pictures. The trick is to unfocus your eyes and look *through* the patterns. Once you get the hang of that, the three-dimensional images almost jump off the page at you. Auras work the same way for me. I can look at a person, a tree, or a dog, for example, and unfocus my eyes to look through the living being. When I do that, the outline of an aura just pops out at me.

The auras are different colors and textures, depending on the health and emotional state of the being. Accordingly, the colors and textures of the auras around people are continually in flux. One day I may see a steady, solid, blue aura around someone, and the next day I might see the same person surrounded by a wavy green aura. Sometimes the auras shimmer and sparkle. I have never studied what the different colors and textures mean, but I definitely see them. The only one I know the probable meaning of with any degree of certainty is a black aura, which I have only seen once, and which evoked a feeling of dread. My sense is that a black aura bodes ill for the person generating it. I do not know if what causes it is physical (say, an illness) or what such an aura might signal or represent: a comment on the mental status of the person (i.e., depression), an indicator of the remaining duration of this person's life, or perhaps a corrupt moral character.

The one and only time I recall seeing a black aura was in 1992, and it was around someone I knew. In fact, it was someone to whom I was related (but whose identity I will not reveal for the sake of the family's privacy). I was driving and had stopped in the left lane at a red light. I looked over to my right. In the car stopped next to me was a close relative of mine. He looked at me but didn't smile or acknowledge me at all. I said out loud to Mallory (who was only a little over a year old at the time) strapped in her car seat behind me, "Look at that! 'Joe Smith' has a black aura! I've never seen one of those before!" I had no idea what that indicated but thought it was strange that he didn't respond to my smile and wave.

Four hours later he had a massive heart attack and died. This was a young man, and it was as devastating as it was surprising. No one in the family suspected that he may have been sick. And given how young he was, a heart attack was totally unexpected. Except that his aura was projecting something negative that I saw clearly. Had I understood then what a black aura might indicate, perhaps I could have intervened and gotten him to a doctor. But this was very early in my post-NDE life, and I had no idea what auras meant or how to interpret them. All I knew was that I could see them, whereas prior to 1988 I could not.

The ability to see auras is something I acquired from my lightning strike and subsequent near-death experience. But this capacity is quite different from the precognitive dreams in the sense that it is much trickier to demonstrate. It is as if I were suddenly gifted with a visual system that can perceive along a wider spectrum of visible light. Most people can't see the particular frequencies of this light spectrum, so they don't believe me when I tell them that they are there. But they are there.

As I explained earlier, as the changes in both my perception and the ways in which I perceive have changed, I began several years ago to document those things that I think are to take place in the next (future) manifestation of this eternal present (more on that latter idea later). Put more simply, I began to intuit or see future events in my dreams (nightmares, actually) and, eventually, in my waking life. But this ability can be observed empirically—and it is extremely convincing to anyone who witnesses it up close, like Matt. This is because these historical events have a proof point in them, that is, an objective reality that others can see for themselves and acknowledge as part of our world. What happens is that a vision that has come to me previously in a nightmare will subsequently appear on television, on the internet, or in an article in the newspaper. That's the proof point. I know what these visions mean to me when they occur, but reading about them or seeing them on a screen is proof that I did in fact precognize them, and that I am not crazy.

With auras, though, there are no proof points. I can't produce a photo from the media or a news report proving that "Joe Smith" had a black aura and then died of a heart attack a few hours later. You either believe me, or you don't. And I understand why you may not believe me—because you don't see auras. But is this really a valid reason to tell me that I am not seeing what I'm clearly seeing? I see auras, but I have no idea what they mean, which implies, of course, that I think they mean something. I do think that auras carry information, that they can speak to us, as it were. I don't have any idea if other people that see auras would see the same colors and textures that I see around living beings at any given time. Jeff's opinion is that they probably wouldn't. What I do know is that when I returned from my near-death experience I found that I had this new ability to see, sense, and interact with energy. Whatever these auras are, my own capacity to see them has something to do with the lightning strike and near-death experience. Of that I am certain.

MONDAY IS RED

Another odd result of my near-death experience is that I now have what neuroscientists call synesthesia. Actually, I don't know if the synesthesia is a result of the near-death experience itself or is a function of being electrocuted. Either way, I never had it before September 2, 1988, and it wasn't until decades after my trip to the Garden that I first heard the word, much less understood what it meant.

Jeff tells me that the word combines the Greek prefix *syn-*, which means "together" or "with," and *(a)esthesia*, which indicates the capacity for sensation or feeling, hence our English word "aesthetic." The word, then, signals a sensation or feeling that combines or puts together sensory modes that are not ordinarily linked. Synesthesia is essentially a neurological phenomenon in which the senses crisscross or fuse so that an individual might "hear" colors, "see" music, "taste" shapes, and so on. It sounds unbelievable, but it is actually much more common than people might think.

Let me pause here to make another observation. I often go back to my two weeks in the Garden to find an explanation for some of the strange aptitudes I have developed since I was struck by lightning. I don't know if this return to the Garden and the understanding it generates are plausible explanations or comprehensible to anyone else, but they seem to work for me. This process is closer to groping than it is to a logical search. It's more like working with a puzzle. I have something odd occur to me, or all of a sudden I recognize a new sense to my being. I go back to the Garden in my mind, searching through my memories of my time there until I find how this new anomaly might fit with what I experienced when I was there. I try to make it less strange, to fit it in somewhere. In essence, the Garden is my way of arranging and coordinating the portfolio of strange things that always seem to be happening in and around me. The Garden is my way of making sense of what does not seem to make sense.

I believe that the influx of information and new teachings that were instantly "downloaded" into my consciousness when I was in the Garden occurred at the same time that I was being mesmerized by the sights, sounds, and colors of my surroundings. I was being subjected to all of these things at once. I believe that the stimulus of everything that I was experiencing and learning became conflated or—and this is harder to understand—somehow the sensory beauty and the information were the same thing. *Somehow what I was sensing was also what I was learning.* There was information or knowledge in the colors and sounds. There were teachings in the images. Jeff calls this the "symbolic function" of the Garden, but I will let him explain that. What I can say for certain is that I was overwhelmed by the stimuli to my senses.

I think the Garden experience flowed out of the near-death experience and into my daily life, partly through all of the weird stories I am telling you, but also through a new set of abilities to sense things through multiple and unexpected senses: in short, through synesthesia.

Shortly after my sojourn there, I was lying in bed with burned and bandaged feet. Perhaps this made me more attuned to the nuances of my perceptions. In any case, I began to realize that, whenever I heard a day of the week mentioned, I immediately and distinctly associated that day with a color. If Jeremy mentioned that he wanted a friend to come over on Tuesday, I would see blue. If Barry said he wanted to take the boys to the zoo on Saturday, I would see orange. The specific colors associated with the days never varied. Monday was and still is always red, Tuesday is blue, Wednesday is yellow, Thursday is green, Friday is yellow, Saturday is orange, and Sunday is brown.

This is not to say that, because I know Monday as a red day, all people with synesthesia see Monday as red. All I am saying is that the colors *I* associate with the days never vary for *me*. They probably will vary from person to person, but not within a specific person. The same is true for the months of the year. For example, August is orange. Odd. Maybe it was the time I spent in the Garden immersed in meaning, knowledge, and sensual stimuli all at once that did this to me. Maybe it was the lightning strike that rearranged some synapses or "rewired" my brain. I do not know, and it really doesn't matter to me. This is my experience and world now.

It was not long after I acknowledged to myself my newfound way of seeing the calendar as colorful that I realized I was doing the same thing with numbers. The digits from zero to nine all evoked a sensation of color within me. Zero was and still is white, one is orange, two is blue, three is yellow, four is blue, five is red, six is purple, seven is yellow, eight is green, and nine is orange.

At different times in my life, particularly in childhood, I have suffered from obsessive-compulsive disorder (OCD). Synesthesia is an OCD sufferer's nightmare. This is how it works with synesthesia. The confluence of colors matters a great deal. I don't know whether to thank my OCD or my synesthesia when, in a moment of serendipity, August 9 falls on a Saturday and I am eating an orange, or to curse them if my birthday, which is a yellow date in a yellow month, falls on a Monday, which is red. Some people consider it a good day if their hair looks good and cooperates that day. For them, a good hair day makes for a good day. I consider it a good day if the eighth of May falls on a Thursday and I am eating broccoli—all green. I'm not completely over the sense that synesthesia is weird, especially with stuff like this. In the words of one of my heroes, Kermit the Frog, "It's not easy being green."

Occasionally, the outfit I choose to wear for the day has to do with the color of the clothing and the day of the week. What I choose to eat occasionally is an intentional choice based on the time of day and the color of the food. If I am hungry for a snack at 3:00 P.M., especially on a Wednesday, I likely will reach for a banana rather than an orange. I like oranges much better than bananas, but odds are I would save the orange for Saturday at 1:00 P.M. I am not nearly as rigid as that sounds, but given the choice, the colors of the numbers and days do enter my mind. And sometimes they do color (pun intended) my choices of what I eat and when I eat it, and, of course, what outfit I may wear on any given day. If my OCD were very severe, which thankfully it is not at this point in my life, it is easy to see how synesthesia could wreak havoc. Having said all that, though, the OCD does wax and wane according to the level of stress I am experiencing, so at times the synesthesia does figure more prominently in my decision-making processes than at others.

Synesthesia is apparently fairly common. There are more than twenty different types of synesthesia; I have a version called Grapheme-color synesthesia, the most common variety of the condition. A person who experiences Grapheme-color synesthesia will involuntarily associate letters, numbers, or even words with specific colors.

BORN THAT WAY?

One interesting theory about synesthesia is that it may be genetic in some cases. My parents don't have it, nor do my sisters. However, my daughter, Mallory, has it to a mild degree, as do my aunt and my oldest son, Jeremy. The fact that I didn't have it until after I was struck by lightning leads me to believe that in my case it was either not genetic, or that the necessary genes were there but were dormant until the lightning strike activated them. The lightning strike might also explain the fact that Mallory experiences synesthesia as well. After all, I conceived her following my contact with lightning, which may have activated that particular gene expression. Again, I don't know. I am certainly no geneticist. I do wish someone would study these things, though.

As I already mentioned, my son Jeremy, who was conceived and born before the lightning strike, also has synesthesia, and to about the same degree as I have. It is really difficult to try to differentiate the synesthesia from OCD. One manifestation for Jeremy is the ability to count the letters in a sentence almost instantaneously. By the time the sentence is spoken by someone challenging Jeremy, he can easily report the number of letters in the sentence. By way of example, I can say: "Jeremy, have you seen the car keys I left on the table?" He would instantly say, "forty-two," just as the word "table" came out of my mouth. I have never known him to be wrong. He even had a brief brush with fame via David Letterman's "Stupid Human Tricks," thanks to this ability. How odd that someone named Letterman would be interested in interviewing someone who is literally a "letter man"! Jeremy didn't make it onto the show because the producers felt that there was no way to prove to viewers that it wasn't a setup where he had been given the sentences earlier. He came very close. But all he got was a T-shirt.

I think Jeff would jump in here and say something like, "Isn't it ironic how, in this case, because something can be faked the real thing gets suppressed?"

Does Jeremy's ability to count letters fall under the category of OCD, synesthesia, or a simple party trick? Obsessive-compulsive disorder is an anxiety disorder. Synesthesia is not. Therefore, it would make sense that, if it were OCD-driven, it would change in intensity as Jeremy's anxiety levels changed. But his ability to accurately count letters never changes. This leads me to think that it may be a form of synesthesia.

Jeremy first recalls counting letters from a very young age. He reports that as he was learning to read, he saw each word associated with the number of letters in that word. He learned to read the word "house" and pictured the number five. Taking that one step further, he sees the number five as red, as do I. It's not much of a stretch then to believe that he can rapidly add up the letters as a person is speaking. The only time he is wrong is when he mentally misspells a word, which of course messes up the count. In any case, numbers have never been difficult for Jeremy. He earned a perfect score on the math portion of the SAT. So there are some strange connections to mathematics here, too—more things we don't understand.

FLUID OR STATIC?

I often wonder if the color associations I make with my synesthesia have any bearing on the colors of the auras I see around people. What I am learning but still am unable to interpret is that, while the color of a person's aura may change, the colors for a number or day of the week are fixed for me. For example, I can look at Mallory and see a green aura in the morning and a blue one in the afternoon. However, when I hear or see the number five, it is always red. The synesthesia colors are constant and unchanging. Aural colors are never constant and can turn on a dime. Still, I do think these two abilities are connected somehow. I personally believe that whatever internal capacity compels me to associate color with certain things can also somehow make allowances for the moods, feelings, and health that affect humans. And yet, that same capacity within me knows that five is ever five and Monday is always Monday. Both are red to me and immutable in the quantity they represent and their unchanging place on the calendar.

The synesthesia has begun to latch onto other qualities in my sphere. It now actually reaches further than letters, numbers, and days of the week. Recently, for example, I found that when I hear the names of different subjects in school, I associate them with color. Math is red, history is blue, science is green, and so forth. I'm not sure whether the synesthesia is reaching deeper into me, or whether I'm just becoming more aware of its reach. Has it always been stable since I developed it, or is it intensifying? I don't know. In any case, the colors are not nearly as spectacular as the otherworldly colors of the Garden, but they do saturate the palette of my life. No more simple and sharp black and white for this girl. Hues flow together for me like watercolors now. Regardless of their intensity, this ability allows me to see my world awash in a glorious rainbow of colors.

5

TRYING ON THE NEW AGE

*I think that ordinary people who are placed in
extraordinary circumstances find themselves pushed beyond
their limits, and learn new truths about themselves.*

—JODI PICOULT

As time has gone by, I have gradually found comfort in my newfound capacities. The lightning strike happened half my lifetime ago. I have now lived as long with these abilities as I did without them. But accepting them has been a very gradual process. It took years after the lightning strike and near-death experience before I could admit to myself that the powers I had developed were not just figments of my imagination, that they were real. I was as skeptical as anyone else. I really tried to suppress what in my prestrike life I would have called crazy. But the facts simply wore me down. So did the convictions of the Garden. I have now accepted and adapted to these inexplicable enhancements to my daily life as best I can. I think I've done pretty well.

What finally changed me was knowing in the marrow of my bones that what I had perceived and received in the Garden, and what I had come to know since then, were incontestably true and real. The harsh dichotomy between this certain knowledge and the cruel dismissal that I had previously heaped upon such stories made for some internal conflicts that were difficult for me to resolve. In the end, though, I find it is impossible to deny the profound knowledge I was given or the abilities that I had manifested in and around it.

Naturally, I looked for confirmation from others, particularly from those who might know something about these things and so might be able to help me. My correspondence for six years with Dr. Bruce Greyson helped for sure, but Dr. Greyson lives in Virginia, while I am in Texas. I also needed to talk to someone face to face. It took me twenty-five years to find someone who was willing and able to help me in person with my near-death experience. It was then that I met the Reverend John Price, an Episcopalian priest in Houston who works with people who have had near-death experiences. He published a book on the subject in 2013.[3]

After seeing a story about the Reverend Mr. Price and his book in the *Houston Chronicle*, and realizing that he lived in Houston, I emailed him and told him how much I needed a clergyperson to listen to my story. He was kind and supportive each time we met. It was that acceptance and listening that helped so much. It was such a relief for me to finally talk to someone, face to face, who understood that a transformation had taken place in me. He helped me to understand that I was not alone in my experience. People from all walks of life have near-death experiences. This priest lent credibility to my near-death experience, something I had searched in vain for when I tried to speak to my own clergy about my experiences. I explained to him that I had tried repeatedly to talk to four different rabbis at my synagogue about my near-death experience. They were kind to me, but they were also mostly dismissive. I could tell they were uncomfortable with the topic. I confess that I was, and still am, hurt and angry that I could not turn to my own congregation's religious leaders for answers and support.

I still wonder why those rabbis I sought out didn't look into the topic and try to help me. In recent years, I have found a wealth of information inside (and outside) the Jewish tradition that would have been of significant help, had I known where to find it and how to integrate it into my own life and experiences in the modern world. Jeff treats some of this material in Part Two of this book, both in his discussions of the comparative study of religion and in his conversations with and readings of his professional colleagues in the field of Jewish studies. The simple truth is that people of *every* faith have near-death experiences.

Accordingly, I feel strongly that those who lead and guide these faith-based communities should have some knowledge of the topic in order to be of spiritual help to those who need it. A person should never have to leave a religious leader's office feeling worse about a matter of great spiritual urgency than when she or he went in. This happened to me repeatedly, and there is no excuse for that. When a congregant goes to a rabbi with a spiritual crisis, and the rabbi is unfamiliar with the topic, my feeling is that the rabbi should learn something about the subject in order to spiritually advise that individual. That, after all, is their job. In my experience, clergy who don't take a few minutes to do a little research on this topic do a great disservice to the people who look to them for guidance and spiritual support. In Reverend Price, I was fortunate to find the support I so desperately needed, but other people who are looking for help processing their near-death experience may not be so lucky.

HEAVEN IS "NEXT DOOR"

While there is very little that I find inspiring in attending services in a synagogue, or any structured religious environment for that matter, I have encountered one relatively obscure prayer that actually means something to me. This prayerful meditation appears in a slim little paper prayer book at Congregation Emanu El in Houston, Texas. Oddly, the passage is the only one in the book that is cited as "Source Unknown." During the course of working on this book, I found the source of this beautiful prayer. It is paraphrased from a sermon given in St. Paul's Cathedral in London on May 15, 1910. The sermon, given by Henry Scott Holland, followed the death of King Edward VII, whose coffin lay in state in Westminster Hall.[4]

What speaks to me about this gem is that it illustrates that death is not final. It suggests that when people die, they are not gone. There is continuity. They are still *right here*, in a kind of room next door. This fits perfectly with my own experience of the afterlife and my subsequent conviction or knowledge that heaven is not some distant place but exists right here, right now, with us on Earth. It is simply in a different realm or dimension that we cannot see. Our loved ones are never truly gone. I find it wonderfully comforting to know that this is actually the case, that it is true. Here is the passage as it appears in the Congregation Emanu El prayer book:

Death is nothing at all. I have only slipped away into the next room. I am I, and you are you. Whatever we were to each other, that we still are. Call me by my old familiar name, speak to me in the easy way in which you always used. Put no difference in your tone, wear no forced air of solemnity or sorrow. Laugh as we always laughed at the little jokes we enjoyed together. Play, smile, think of me, pray for me. Let my name be ever the household word that it always was. Let it be spoken without effect, without the trace of a shadow on it. Life means all that it ever meant. It is the same as it ever was; there is unbroken continuity. Why should I be out of mind because I am out of sight? I am waiting for you, for an interval, somewhere very near, just around the corner. All is well.[5]

It was my correspondence with Dr. Greyson and then my meetings with Rev. Price that helped me finally become aware of just how much we already know about the subject of near-death experiences. I now know, for example, that there are thousands of case studies of the phenomena in question, and that in many of these case studies people display odd after-effects and newfound abilities after a near-death experience, much like my own. It has become very apparent that I may be different, but I am by no means alone. Publications from a respected psychiatrist (Dr. Greyson) and a well-regarded Houston clergyman (Rev. Price) on the subject of near-death experiences went a very long way in helping me understand that I am not crazy, that I am indeed quite sane.

A HEALER IN HOUSTON

It was through my great-aunt and great-uncle that Mom came to know Nancy.[6] My great-aunt and uncle were kind and very spiritual people who had sought Nancy out because of her reputation as a healer. They introduced Mom to Nancy, and then Mom brought me to meet her.

Nancy lived in Seattle, but she would come to Houston for a week each month to tend to her patients here. Nancy was a naturopath. She worked through a modality she called energy healing. She would assess the auras of the people who came to see her and determine through a person's energy what course of treatment to pursue, which meant which and how much of the vitamins and herbal supplements she sold were needed to enable the person to return to health, or so she claimed.

The first time we met, in 1989, Nancy told me that she knew I had psychic abilities. I was enraged, furious that someone was able to see through my hard and carefully constructed facade and dial in to something inside me that I worked so hard to obscure. She was as eager to speak with me about my abilities as I was to avoid the topic. She saw them as a gift, much like her own, but I could not disagree more. I wanted to yell at her and tell her to mind her own business. "No, I am as normal as anyone!" I shouted in my mind.

After we left, I railed at Mom for insisting that I go with her to meet Nancy. This was the first time I had been called out by anyone, and I was one angry, busted psychic. "Why can't you just accept that you have abilities?" Mom asked as we drove home. "You know you do." I told her I didn't want to discuss it. I made sure that my sulking and fuming made our quiet ride home most unpleasant.

Every month Mom would see Nancy when she came to Houston. Many times she took Dad with her. She'd tell me that she was going. While I pretended to be dismissive, I was, in fact, intrigued. I decided to look beyond the supplements Nancy was selling and to focus more on her energy healing and aura work. At that time I had only just begun to perceive auras, but I suspected that the energy I was seeing had the power to heal. I am not sure why I felt so sure of that, but it made sense to me for some reason. Perhaps it was the huge jolt of energy I had received via the lightning bolt that opened me to the notion that energy had powers beyond the visible. Or perhaps it was the near-death experience itself. Either way, I was intrigued.

Around 1992, I noticed a small area of skin on Mallory's back that looked like it might need medical attention. She was two years old at the time. I immediately took her to the pediatrician to have it looked at. He assured me it was nothing. However, being the worrier I am, I was not buying the wave of my trusted pediatrician's hand. I recanted my doubts about the merits of Nancy's mode of healing and made an appointment for the next time she was going to be in town. This was to be only the second time I went to see her.

Nancy palpated my baby girl's aura and then recommended herbs and vitamins to the tune of several hundred dollars. I politely refused.

As Mallory and I were leaving, Nancy repeated what she had said to me three years earlier, "You really need to do something with these abilities you have."

"What do you suggest?" I shot back. "What do you think I need to do, Nancy?"

"You need to be doing psychic readings for people."

I laughed at the thought, said goodbye, and left.

A PSYCHIC IN SEATTLE

But that brief interchange with Nancy planted a seed. I had toyed with the idea of possibly doing psychic readings, or channeling, for a while. After all, it was so easy for me. I could simply look at someone and know quite a bit about him or her. And if I spoke to them for a few minutes, I could receive all kinds of information. Personally, I had always been skeptical about this type of thing—until I found I had the ability to do it myself. Ever since my near-death experience, I have been able to tap into other people's spirit guides. These were the companions I saw people with in the Garden. I also discovered that if a person posed a question to his or her spirit guide, I could sense the response. It was this capacity that Nancy was referring to when she urged me to put my abilities to work.

I had many misgivings about doing any type of psychic readings or channeling work in Houston, however. I hesitated to have my children labeled as the kids with the crazy psychic mom. I worried that it could damage my husband's business if word got out that his wife was doing psychic readings. Three years passed. My children were still very young, we were a respectable Jewish family, my husband headed an accounting firm, and I simply could not bear the thought of people thinking of me as anything but normal. Because even then I still doubted the psychic abilities of others, I worried that people would make fun of me, just as I had always internally mocked those who were like I was now. I could not have my children stigmatized or known as the kids with the crazy mom. Nor could I run the risk of my husband's ultraconservative business being damaged by his wife being labeled as nuts. Nope, doing psychic readings in Houston was not going to happen.

It was not that I had misgivings about my ability to do psychic readings. I knew that I could. Easily. After mulling it over, I called Nancy. It had been three years since I'd last seen her, when she'd planted that seed in me. "If I were going to do this, I can't do it here in Houston," I told her. I explained my reasons.

"Come to Seattle five days a month, just like I come to Houston. Use my office. I'll even line up people to see you to get you started. You can stay at my house. Let's just try it once and see what happens." Her offer couldn't have been kinder or more generous. And I couldn't come up with a single reason not to give it a shot.

Until, that is, I told Barry what I was thinking. I explained to him that I had decided to leave him with the kids for a few days in order to perform psychic readings in Seattle. He was incredulous. "Going where to do *what?*" My send-off from home was not exactly a warm one. Mom, though, was very supportive of my decision to give this a whirl. She even went with me to Washington state to act as my receptionist.

When we got to Seattle, Nancy had people lined up to meet with me. For five days, I had eight or nine people scheduled each day for hour-long appointments. They paid me well and by the end of the week I had earned a substantial sum. The only downside at first was that I was so exhausted. I wasn't prepared for the physical toll it took on me to sit hour after hour channeling information that had meaning only to other people. (I generally had no idea what it meant or why it was being given.) Mom was the key here, bringing me food and drinks throughout the day to help me keep my strength up.

I loved earning money. I loved it because, for the first time in our marriage, I was able to make a significant contribution to our finances. I loved that people were willing to pay me for what was so easy for me to do. But something was wrong. It was like I was getting paid for just breathing, and it bothered me. I kept telling myself that doing psychic readings could not be the reason I have these abilities. I could not have been struck by lightning and had that amazing near-death experience just so I could tell women that their husbands were cheating on them. I felt I was missing the point of whatever it was that I was supposed to be doing.

The abundance of money made my arrival home much more pleasant than my departure had been. Barry's take on it was that I should make this Seattle trip every month. Barry was happy. Nancy was happy. So I scheduled my second visit to Washington state for the following month. People whom I'd seen the week before had made appointments to see me again the coming month. I wasn't bullshitting them. I was passing along real and accurate information. Over the next couple of weeks, I heard from many of them that what I had told them had, in fact, come to pass.

When I went back the following month, Nancy had scheduled more appointments for me than I had hours in the week. People had told their families and friends about me. My schedule was packed. I even had a waiting list in case someone cancelled.

One of the people I saw that second trip was a young woman who walked with a cane. She had not had a session with me the previous month. The moment she entered the room I could sense her disease and dis-ease. I immediately knew she had ALS, and that the disease would literally torment the life out of her. Everything about this unfortunate woman told me of her coming demise. Every hint of her being—her aura, her palpably depleting energy—told me that she did not have long to live. She wanted my insight into her health. I did not want to tell her what I saw. Despite all of my earlier accurate readings, I worried inside, "What if somehow my perception this time was inaccurate?"

This would be a turning point for me. My knowledge of what this woman was facing seriously deflated the image I had of myself as a psychic. Suddenly, this was no longer a walk in the park for me, an amusing and lucrative pastime. Who was I to tell this poor woman that her life was almost over? It was not my place. For the remainder of the hour, I evaded her health questions and gave her answers like, "You will be fine," because in heaven I knew she would be healed and happy. Because of these internal dialogues, I reasoned that I was not really lying to her, but I felt terrible that I was in fact misleading her. I redirected her health questions as best I could to information about her children.

That night Nancy asked about my session with the woman and what I had told her.

"She has ALS," I said. "She's going to die soon."

"Yes," said Nancy. "I know that. Did you tell her?"

"No," I said.

"Good. Her husband has come with her to see me. He told me that they have stopped all conventional treatment for the disease. What you have to tell her is what I tell her, that she is going to get well."

"Nancy, I can't do that. I can't do this anymore." I finished out the week and concluded my short career as a psychic in Seattle.

Such dilemmas did not simply disappear, though. Just because I sense things about people that they may not know about themselves, am I obliged to tell them what I foresee if it is a bad or negative premonition? Of course, if it is a loved one or close friend, I will take the risk and say something. But a total stranger I pass on the street? Who am I to upset other people's lives, especially if I might be wrong?

FLIPPING THE COIN

Okay, so I can see auras and precognize events before they happen. I don't know why I have these abilities, and my cluelessness about how to put them to use frustrates me to no end. If I could understand this, I really and truly think my life would be much easier, or at least more sensible. Is it possible that writing this book and getting the fact out there that there *is* an afterlife is what I am supposed to be doing with these unearned gifts? I don't know. But I do know that writing this book in Houston feels much more "right" than doing psychic readings in Seattle.

The lightning strike itself was not a revelation. It was a single natural event that brought on my near-death experience. Or is it more complicated than this? Toss the coin and tell me: Was it the purely natural phenomenon of lightning coursing through my body that is responsible for these aptitudes? Or do I possess these powers because I returned from death and had what we now call a near-death experience? What is "natural" here? What is "supernatural"? And is there really any difference? My metaphor of the coin toss gives away what I think. I think we are talking about two sides *of the same coin* here. Heads, and it is all natural. Tails, and it is all supernatural. But it is really the same coin seen or experienced in two different ways.

Whether it was the lightning strike or the near-death experience (or both), these abilities have been part of my life ever since. And they *have* been like revelations, at least to me. Each new ability unfolded and made itself known to me as situations arose that demanded my attention. I don't think that by preconceiving a plane crash that I somehow caused it to happen, but I do believe that we can know about things before they happen, because, in some sense, they have *already* happened in the future. In any case, however we understand these things, the simple fact is that I have the ability to know about things before they happen or just as they are happening at great distances. This is a kind of revelation or prophecy. It certainly does not feel "normal" to me.

It was explained to me in the Garden that my having been struck by lightning and the abilities that I have been given as a result were all planned. I have written earlier that I came to these abilities gradually. Both statements are true. I was told about some of these abilities in the Garden, and some came then, but others manifested later. For example, the sudden understanding about the nonlinear nature of time was something I was taught in the Garden. I possessed this knowledge then and there. But I was not told, nor did I realize in the Garden, that I might later experience this understanding in dramatic ways. I was not told about the later precognitive nightmares, for example. I only came to know about them as they happened. Another way to put this is that in the Garden, I was given the understanding; in my life after, I experienced the practical effects of what I now understood.

In the Garden, I remember questioning the timing of my actions in relation to the lightning strike. What if we had waited ten more minutes to leave the house? What if we had left earlier? What if we had had a flat tire on the way? What if we had stayed in the car to ride out the storm? What if?

As I have come to understand things, I now believe that the reason for the lightning strike was to help me, to really make me understand that death is not the end of life. I have also begun to reckon with the complexities of free will. I now know that had I not been struck by lightning on September 2, 1988, it would have happened on some other day. All the "what ifs" I can come up with no longer apply, because what was going to happen was going to happen. My guide in the Garden told me that, free will aside, the lightning strike event and all the things I can trace back to it were going to happen, regardless of what actions I may have taken on my own. Being struck by lightning was "in the contract" before I was born. I don't remember signing anything, of course. It's a metaphor. I may question whether or not such powerful events are preordained, but the only adequate "answer" may well be in the owning of them all, that is, in the acceptance of what the ancients called "fate."

In fact, I do question the idea of fate or a preordained future, because I like to think that everyone has the ability to exercise some control over his or her own life. I have to confess, though, that the events that have come to define my life since the strike, and especially the precognitive nightmares, have taken some of the strength of that conviction away from me. I am no longer so sure. As I will explain a bit in my next chapter, I truly believe the future is already "there," somewhere ahead of us "here." The future has already happened, just like the past. Certainly, I couldn't have made the lightning hit me or conjured these abilities myself. They happened to me. I didn't choose them. I don't know if I own them, or they own me.

Maybe the point of this is to communicate that there is more to our world and to ourselves than how we live and what we happen to know at this present moment. Maybe the point of this is to show us that there are mirrors behind and in front of our present in which we can see not just self-reflections but also actual images of who we are and what we are capable of. I really do think that the ability to know as I have come to know is inherent in all of us. We are all wired with the capacity to animate those abilities.

I also believe that every one of us has the physical ability to interact with the energy surrounding us and to do things that many people presently belittle and laugh at, exactly as I, in my own ignorance, once did. But if everyone has the ability to interact with this living energy, why must it be such a dramatic and painful process? Why not simply flip the switch, painlessly? Perhaps this is not always necessary. Jeff tells me that many psychics, or what he calls paranormal prodigies, come to their gifts naturally and effortlessly, while for others it takes a serious injury, illness, or near-fatal accident to trigger or awaken the newfound powers. Perhaps this all happened in my case in order to get my attention, to slap me awake, as it were. I was certainly fast asleep. I was not told why we humans don't gravitate toward greater interaction with energy. But then, I didn't know to ask that question at the time. What I know now, though, is this. I know that if we did interact more with the energy surrounding and suffusing our world, a greater number of us would understand that there's more to life than we ever imagined, that there is, in fact, much, much More.

6

THE LAYER CAKE OF TIME

But time is yet another of God's creations, and
as such, it has a life of its own.

—REBBE MENACHEM MENDEL SCHNEERSON

Suppose time is a circle, bending back on itself. The world
repeats itself, precisely, endlessly.

—ALAN LIGHTMAN, *Einstein's Dreams*

I mentioned earlier that one of the things I came to understand in the Garden involved the nature of time. I also explained how my later precognitive dreams gave me actual experiences or confirmations of what I had been taught about time. There is really no way around it. Since the lightning strike and near-death experience, I have been able to see *through* time, as if it were somehow transparent. I have thought a great deal about this. Who in my situation wouldn't?

I like to think of time and space as a layer cake of infinite proportion. The layer cake gives me a suitable metaphor to describe what I have been taught and have experienced. The middle layer of the cake is right here, right now. It is what we call the present. One layer above the middle is the future, and the layer above that is the future beyond the future—the future future. The layer just beneath the middle is the past, and the layer below that is the past before the past—the past past. Somehow, I am able to slice through these layers of time and space. I wish I had the ability to stop wherever I choose, but I don't. However, here is the key point. All of these bands or layers of the cake are already there, and they are infinite. And the events in each layer are all happening independently of the events in the other layers, but yet *simultaneously.*

Of course, that is confusing. It is confusing because we are used to thinking about time as a kind of straight flat line that we never leave, not a layer cake with different dimensions through which we can move. But what we perceive to be "now" in this layer cake of space and time is simply a snapshot of one infinitesimal point in time and space. As we move forward, the present becomes the past, and the future becomes the present. Since I am no physicist, the best way I know to describe this is that time is "cyclical." Time actually bends back on itself. The space-time continuum actually looks to me like a layer-cake arc that never ends. Things that will happen in the future happened in the past and are happening right now. Or to make it a little less confusing: since everything is happening at once, the same things are always happening in the past, in the present, and in the future. The trick is to find where in space they are happening all the time in a kind of endless cycle, to find that dimension, that layer in the cake, and then slice through to it.

When manifesting my abilities of precognition, I am simply slicing my way through layers that are all already there. The past, present, and future cannot be considered separate or different from one another. Any distinction between past, present, and future is made by where in space an event is, in what dimension of time that event is "happening." In the Garden I learned that all of time is an everlasting present.

Before my lightning strike I was about as straight a believer in the linearity of time as the next person. Like the White Rabbit in *Alice in Wonderland,* I fretted about time, rules, and stricture. I progressed along a clearly demarcated line of time, from the past to the plodding present to who knows what in the future. But when I emerged from the rabbit hole, my line of time was now multidimensional. It was no longer a line. *Time had heft.* I could burrow from wherever I was "now" into an expanded dimension of time and space and see what was happening already in the future.

I slice through the present due to energy that I do not understand and slip into the future. Not every detail is given to me, though. I cannot tell you who will occupy seats 20 and 21 in row F at tomorrow's baseball game. I *can* tell you they have already done it, are doing it right now, and will do it again tomorrow in other dimensions of the layer cake. The ability to move around in this cake is highly selective, and I am not the one doing the selecting. Someday, I hope that I can learn how to harness and navigate this slipping and sliding, but for now I have no control over where I land.

DREAMS THAT ARE NOT DREAMS

The slipping through time that I do, then, is not of my choice. Neither, unfortunately, are my precognitions. The distinction between my dreams and precognitive nightmares is the level of control that I can exert over them. In dreams, I am generally able to instruct myself to look away or close my eyes. I can tell myself that this is a dream, or to wake up. Once awake, I *never* remember my dreams. As soon as my eyes are open, the dream is gone. I can tell myself, "That was just a dream," but I cannot for the life of me remember what it was.

My precognitive nightmares are *totally* different. In those I am careening through scenes in which I am a witness to something happening in the

CHANGED IN A FLASH

world without the slightest ability to affect or influence it. The knowledge that I consciously have in this expanded state of mind, during the dream event itself, tells me that it is not a dream. As much as I want to do so, I am powerless to awaken myself or look away, and powerless to change anything taking place in this nightmare scenario. Something, some "energy" (I really do not know how else to describe it), will not allow me to wake up until I have seen the motion picture in its entirety. When I awaken, I feel great relief at being awake. But I can also recall every detail of what I was shown. These are some of the ways that my precognitive "dreams" (nightmares really) differ dramatically from my regular dreams.

There is also the "rush" or "power" of the precognitive nightmares. These truly spirit me away, as if I were on a runaway horse. I become short of breath. My heart races. The vision behaves and feels like a wild animal with a mind of its own, running off with me in unknown directions. I am carried away, and not in a good or pleasant way.

On many such occasions, I have said to myself in the vision: "Oh, shit! This is one of the plane crash nightmares. Wake up! Wake up! Wake up! Just open your eyes and it will all stop." But to no avail. There is an energy force that will not allow me to awaken. Even as I am struggling with the vision of some horrific scene, I am simultaneously receiving information. I know in the vision that once I receive whatever information I am supposed to be given, I will be able to open my eyes and make it stop. Whatever it was that I saw is seared into my memory. I do not have the luxury of forgetting the terror and destruction that I see.

Many of these rampaging nightmares appear to me in color, but not always. In one instance I will describe later, I clearly saw a red car that had plunged through a broken segment of a bridge. But in another, everything took place in black and white.

Very rarely do I have a precognitive vision while I am awake, although these too have happened. I discussed one such waking "hit" earlier, when I described being in the car with my husband, Matt, and suddenly knowing about an earthquake taking place in western China. This is actually a very interesting example. At that moment, the knowledge of a natural disaster came to me. It was not an image or a few frames of some movie-like visual perception; that is, it did not appear as a dream. It was simply a piece of information about an event that had been communicated to me with absolute certainty.

Clearly, this was not some trick played by a sleeping psyche. I had been very relaxed for several minutes before the vision came, but I was fully awake. I do suspect, though, that had I been sleeping when the China earthquake came to me, I might have been able to see and recall more details than I was able to articulate while awake. I have noticed that my mind needs to be as blank as possible in order to receive the full vision. My state of consciousness matters very much. It is generally only in a state of relaxation that the energy comes. When my ordinary mind is going a hundred miles an hour, it is impossible for the necessary energy to penetrate my thoughts and take over and show me a precognitive event. It is much more likely to happen as I sleep. For me, sleeping is about giving up control and letting go. It is also about letting the energy in.

To say that these perceptions or precognitive visions have lives of their own is as close as I can come to affording them the energy or presence of a living being. I cannot repeat this enough: I do not invite them. They occur to me unbidden. And when I receive them, they are as real to me as the freeway we were driving on that evening I knew about the earthquake in China.

I know that I have been writing in the abstract here. Consider a few concrete examples.

The 1989 Loma Prieta Earthquake

I am a lifelong Texan. Earthquakes are not of any realistic concern here. But there I was, in one of those nightmares, walking down a sidewalk in a city that I knew to be San Francisco. In my nightmare, I saw "snapshots" of damage from an earthquake. I saw that the sidewalk was split open as if it had been unzipped. I also saw a police officer peering over the edge of a broken section of the San Francisco–Oakland Bay Bridge, where cars had fallen through the break to the level below. A photo of the scene, which appeared in the news, is exactly the image I saw two days *before* the earthquake happened.[7]

This nightmare occurred on October 15, 1989, about a year after I had been struck. Two days later, the earthquake hit. The Bay Area was rocked by a powerful quake that broke the Bay Bridge and killed scores of people. Although I had already had smaller precognitive nightmares, this was the first large-scale precognitive event that I experienced. Somehow I *knew* that I had received the information due to the "energy." Had some kind of magnetic or electrical field related to the earthquake somehow reached my subconscious? Was there a subtle physical channel here?

I do not have any hard evidence that would prove to doubters that I really had this precognition. I did tell Mom and Barry about it. Barry took it as just a bad dream and promptly forgot about it. We have cousins who live in the Bay Area, and the precognition had me shaken (no pun intended) and worried for them. I wanted Mom to call and tell them to leave town. Although she tried to reach them before the earthquake happened, they did not connect until after it had struck. I did not want to call them myself because I was still very new to this and very unsure of myself. I was afraid of making a fool of myself. Although I wanted them to know it might happen and leave town as a precaution, I didn't want to be the idiot who cried wolf if nothing happened. Today, thirty years down the road, I would not hesitate to call and warn them to leave. I am much surer of myself now and have a somewhat proven track record.

But this does present me with an ongoing moral dilemma: What about strangers? Do I have a duty to warn the entire city of San Francisco if I feel a huge earthquake is going to strike there? As many times as I have been accurate in my precognitive visions, I have also been off—by a day, a week, or even a month. Or because the dreaded event fortunately never happened. Clearly, I cannot, and should not, alert an entire city to evacuate based on a precognitive nightmare. But what about loved ones? Is that a different story? This moral dilemma extends to almost every precognitive nightmare I have had. What should I do? What should I have done differently in the cases I discuss below, if anything? It is a very real problem for me and causes my stomach to twist into knots every time I have a nightmare.

US Airways Flight 1549

In January 2009, Matt and I were vacationing in Jerusalem. We had spent the morning of January 15 walking up and down the cobbled streets of the Old City. Jerusalem is a magical city. With its ancient white limestone edifices and its strong sunlight, even in winter the city gives off a glow that seems to touch all who visit. I remember where we ate lunch that day. It was in a restaurant across the alley from our hotel just off Ben Yehuda Street on the second floor of a two-story building overlooking Jaffa Road. I recall feeling a crackling energy, but I figured it was my surroundings. There is a very unique energy in Jerusalem that is perceptible to many people.

Even while on vacation in such a special place, it takes very little encouragement for Matt to be persuaded to relax and take a nap, so we headed back to our hotel in the early afternoon right after lunch. I was tired too, but the real reason I wanted to get back to the hotel was because I felt a precognition coming on. I felt like I was on the cusp of having a vision and wanted to be near our laptop in case something came to me that I needed to write down. I was a mass of buzzing energy and dog tired all at the same time. We got back to the hotel at about 2:45 that afternoon and decided to rest before dinner.

It helps for me to be in a quiet place where I can close my eyes and receive the energy of the precognition. When we got to our room, I retrieved the laptop from the hotel room safe. Matt stretched out on the bed to take a nap. After I turned on the computer and placed it on the nightstand close to me, I also stretched out on the bed to catch some winks. It couldn't have been more than a couple of minutes before I was awake and typing myself an email describing the precognitive vision that I'd just had. I had just been on the cusp of falling fully asleep when it happened.

Emailing myself these visions when they occur was something I had only recently begun to do. I never thought these emails would be seen by anyone other than me, or people very close to me with whom I chose to share them. I just wanted to create an electronic trail of evidence for *myself* that my sanity was intact. If I was to continue to be God's radio receiver, I wanted to make sure that I could show myself evidence of the events that I was receiving.

It is important to note how I phrased that last sentence. I intentionally wrote the words "show evidence" rather than "prove." There is a difference for me. I think we can have good evidence without that evidence rising to the standard of proof. I realize that I cannot prove that my visions are precognitive. All I can do is share the emails as an interesting collection of evidence that suggests or points to the reality of precognition without quite proving it. It may not be "proof," but it is "evidence." I am not naive enough to think that by documenting my precognitive visions any and all doubters will be convinced, but I am hopeful that this will at least help some readers, particularly those who have not already made up their minds about the world we live in, the kinds of beings we are, and how we are wired in to the future.

Below is a copy of the email I sent myself that afternoon in Jerusalem. To protect my privacy, the email address has been changed (here and elsewhere in this book). My hasty keyboarding awakened Matt. He had assumed we were going to sleep through to dinner. He winced when I told him that I had a plane crash nightmare and had sent it to myself. I was a bit worried, because we were going to have to get on a plane to fly home in the next few days.

FROM: Elizabeth Krohn <NDEexperiencer@gmail.com>
TO: Elizabeth Krohn <NDEexperiencer@gmail.com>
DATE: 01/15/09 at 2:57 PM IST

Mid-size commercial passenger jet (80–150 people) crashes in NYC. Maybe in River. Not Continental Airlines. Not American Airlines.

It is an American carrier like Southwest or US Airways.

"OK. What did you see?" Matt asked.

"It's really weird," I said. "I saw this plane and it was sitting, kind of floating, on water, and there were people standing on the wings of the plane."

"This may be one that you miss," he said. "Airplanes are heavy. They "float" like a rock. And people standing on the wings? ... You saw people on the wings of a floating airplane?"

"Yes," I said.

"The physics of that are impossible. I'm going back to sleep," my skeptical, tired husband said. "Impossible." And he was quickly back to his nap.

I knew the scene in my mind was implausible and as far-fetched as Matt considered it to be. I was torn. And yet the inner conviction of the reality of this event had more weight in my mind than my rational understanding and honest doubts.

It was 2:57 P.M. in Jerusalem when I emailed myself. The time difference between Jerusalem (IST, Israel Standard Time) and New York (EST, Eastern Standard Time) is seven hours. So 2:57 P.M. in Jerusalem was 7:57 A.M. in New York. Matt and I had our naps and then a nice dinner that evening. It was at breakfast in the hotel restaurant the following morning that Matt nearly choked on his *shakshuka* (a common Israeli dish made of poached eggs in tomato sauce) and pointed at the television in the dining area.

"Oh my God!" he shouted. "Look!"

I turned and saw my vision of the day before captured for the world to see: an airplane bobbing on the Hudson River and people standing on its wings. We both were more than a little upset and could not finish our breakfast.[8]

At 3:31 P.M. New York time, US Airways Flight 1549 piloted by Captain Chesley B. "Sully" Sullenberger had landed on the Hudson River after the aircraft had plowed into a flock of geese shortly after takeoff. This was about seven and a half hours after I sent myself the email. Miraculously, there was not a single fatality among the 155 passengers and crew.

TransAsia Airways Flight 235

Early on February 2, 2015, we were at home and sound asleep when I had another of my nightmares. I awoke and emailed this to myself:

FROM: Elizabeth Krohn <NDEexperiencer@gmail.com>
DATE: February 2, 2015 at 5:52:15 AM CST
TO: Elizabeth Krohn <NDEexperiencer@gmail.com>
SUBJECT: Plane Crash

Passenger plane with propellers. Plane is white. Foreign airline—maybe Asian. Crashes in a big metropolitan city right after takeoff. Right wing of plane is pointed straight up right before crashing. Most on board killed, but some survivors.

Sent from my iPad

This tragic vision came to me a day and a half before the actual crash of TransAsia Airways flight 235 on February 4, 2015. While fifteen passengers did survive the doomed takeoff, forty-three lives were lost. A camera in the dash of a car on the ground recorded the crash in progress. The left wing of the propeller-powered craft is perpendicular to the ground, and at about ground level. The tip of the downward-pointing left wing struck a cab on the bridge as the airplane cartwheeled into the Keelung River near Taipei, Taiwan.[9]

The Japan Earthquake and Tsunami of 2011

On March 11, 2011, a massive earthquake and tsunami hit Japan. The magnitude 9.0 earthquake struck at 2:46 P.M. JST (Japan Standard Time), a mere eighty miles off the east coast of Miyagi, Japan. Readers may recall that this was the tsunami that instigated a major nuclear accident at a power station along the coast. Almost twenty thousand people died in the disaster and its aftermath. The tsunami was so enormous that the wave actually reached the coast of Antarctica and caused a portion of the Sulzberger Ice Shelf to break off its outer edge.

At 3:48 A.M. CST (Central Standard Time) on March 10, 2011, I suddenly awoke from a deep sleep and wrote the following email to myself:

FROM: Elizabeth Krohn <NDEexperiencer@gmail.com>
DATE: March 10, 2011 at 3:48 AM CST
TO: Elizabeth Krohn <NDEexperiencer@gmail.com>
SUBJECT: EARTHQUAKE! And Tsunami

In Japan again. Terribly powerful earthquake. Terribly terribly terribly powerful! Like a 9.0 maybe. And then a tsunami that wiped out villages. Thousands dead.

Sent via BlackBerry by AT&T

Taking into account the time differences between Japan and Houston, this email was sent about twenty hours before the devastating earthquake and tsunami occurred.

The Soccer Team

Each case is quite different. Here is a more complicated example of a dream that turned out to be very accurate, that is, that reflected an actual plane crash, but which I wanted to retract or not count, since the crash happened before the dream. One interesting feature of this dream is that it occurred while we were working on this book. I sent Jeff and myself this email immediately after I wrote it:

FROM: Elizabeth Krohn < NDEexperiencer@gmail.com>

DATE: November 29, 2016 at 1:52:17 AM CST

TO: Elizabeth Krohn < NDEexperiencer@gmail.com>

CC: Jeffrey Kripal

SUBJECT: Plane crash

Smallish plane. Fewer than 100 people on board. Several may have survived. Crashed in South America. Bogota? Probably somewhere in Colombia. Athletic team on board.

Sent from my iPhone

A few hours before this email, around 9:00 P.M. CST (Houston time) on November 28, a chartered plane carrying a professional Brazilian soccer team crashed near Rionegro, Colombia, near the large city of Medellin. Seventy-seven people were on board. Six survived. It would be all over the news the next day. I had everything correct: the size of the plane, the relative number on board, the fact that some had survived, and the country where it happened. I even knew that an athletic team was on board. Still, I did not want to count this as a precognition, since my dream took place after the historic event.

I had trouble getting back to sleep after the nightmare. I wondered whether I tuned in to that plane crash because I had a stepson who was living in Medellin, Colombia, at the time. I can never see a rhyme or reason as to why I pick up on some tragedies and not others. I played around on the internet for a while, hoping to get back to sleep. Nothing was in the news yet about a plane crash, but I could not sleep. I was just so certain that it was coming. Sure enough, at about 4:15 A.M. I started seeing news reports of the crash. So I sent Jeff this email in the middle of the night.

FROM: Elizabeth Krohn <NDEexperiencer@gmail.com>
DATE: November 29, 2016 at 4:20 AM CST
TO: Jeff Kripal
SUBJECT: Disregard last email

It happened, but before I sent the email. :(. I woke up and sent the email at 1:52am but the plane had already crashed a couple of hours earlier. Sorry....

Sent from my iPhone

Jeff told me that he was happy that I sent him the emails, and that the fact that the crash took place a few hours before the dream hardly took away from the clairvoyant nature of the dream. It simply eliminated a precognitive element from the case (although, as it turns out, this might not be exactly accurate, as Jeff will explain in due time). He asked me if I knew about the Brazilian crash before I went to bed. I did not. The crash had not yet happened before I went to bed. He thought it was a striking commentary on our culture and worldview that I did not want to count it because of this fact, as if seeing an event thousands of miles away in my dream was any less extraordinary than seeing an event before it happens. I had to agree.

7

THE LESSONS OF THE GARDEN

Tell me and I forget, teach me and I may
remember, involve me and I learn.

—BENJAMIN FRANKLIN

There is no particular order to the things I have come to know since I was in the Garden. I have, however, come to understand that the general direction that much of this knowledge takes me is along paths that are remarkably parallel to places described in texts of the Asian religions, especially in their more mystically oriented expressions.

I am not now, nor have I ever been, a member of or believer in any structured religious doctrine, except for the pallid brand of Reform Judaism in which I was raised. The only remotely religious texts I have ever read are parts of the Torah (the first five books of the Bible), in English, and so long ago that I can scarcely remember anything but some of the stories.

When I write, then, that I have come to recognize some similarities between what I learned in the Garden and what some of the Asian religions teach, it is only because people who are well versed on the subject of religion have told me so. My coauthor of this book, the inestimable

Jeffrey Kripal, has said that a part of what was given to me in the Garden is very close not only to Asian religious traditions, but also and especially to Kabbalah, the mystical tradition of Judaism. I find this all comforting, to be honest. These similarities are for me further testimony to the fact that I am sane. As I have come to learn, I am not the only person on the planet who has attained, or in my case, been shocked into receiving this knowledge.

Jeff has also told me that thousands of years of human effort—by people too numerous to count—have been expended in the search for the knowledge that popped into me, seemingly effortlessly and immediately, during and following my near-death experience. If it seems that I gloss over such effort in describing some of my experiences, like the ease with which I can see the auras surrounding people, it is because that ability is so natural to me. I don't mean to diminish these abilities in any way. I am only a conduit for them. I can make no claims about their exceptional nature, and I certainly can't take credit for them. This would be like the radio taking credit for the song playing over it. I am not the song. I am the radio transmitting it.

VOLTAGE, VISITATION, AND VISION

Over the course of our conversations, Jeff has encouraged me to clarify my understanding of the relationship between the lightning strike, the Garden, and the new capacities. He has also asked me to be more specific about exactly how I received the new understandings about things like the nature of time and reincarnation. Was I told these things in the Garden by my spirit guide there? Did I think these things out afterward as conclusions of the Garden experience, or of my precognitive nightmares? Do I simply believe these things but am claiming them as things I actually know? Or what?

These are difficult questions, as the kind of knowledge that I am trying to express here is extraordinary. It did not come to me like other forms of knowledge. I did not learn it like I have learned other things. I just knew it. In my near-death experience, I did not receive what I know now as one revelation at a time, like individual droplets of water. Rather, everything came at the same time. Somehow, being on the receiving end of one of nature's most powerful emanations of energy, a lightning bolt, gave me the ability to comprehend everything *all at once.*

My experience was a single process, but I think we can tease out three different components, all of which together made me who I am today. There is the lightning strike itself, that is, the *voltage.* There is the knowledge that I received as a visitor in the Garden, that is, the *visitation.* And there are the ways I use that knowledge now, that is, the *vision.* Certainly there would be no visitation or vision without the voltage, but I do not think these are simple by-products of the voltage.

I do believe, however, that my becoming a receiver of knowledge of things previously unknown to me is somehow related to the voltage. I have read accounts of lightning strikes on others who have had similar experiences. I am thinking in particular of Dannion Brinkley.[10] The details of our strike experiences are different, of course: where we were at the time, how we were struck, and so on. It is in the changes that took place within us afterward that I find so many parallels. Compare what you read in my account with others like Brinkley's. You may be surprised to learn, as I was, that the appearance of strange abilities is not at all uncommon after a lightning strike.

The lightning strike had other physical effects on me—literally electric or electronic ones. I cannot wear a battery-powered watch, for example, as watches do not work for long when I wear them. Matt gifted me with a beautiful wristwatch shortly after we met and was miffed when I didn't wear it. This was before I felt comfortable enough with him to share the story of my lightning strike and subsequent tales. I had some fancy footwork to do to help him understand why I cannot wear a watch. I still have it, of course. It sits in our safe-deposit box waiting for the wrist of some young lady who is not electrically or electronically challenged.

I have also been through four Fitbits (wrist-worn activity monitors), each of which fritzed out shortly after I put it on. Additionally, I cannot tolerate a TENS (transcutaneous electrical nerve stimulation) unit, a device that sends electrical impulses into areas of the body to relieve muscle aches, because the current causes unbearable pain throughout my entire body. It's also not uncommon for light bulbs to burn out as I walk past them.

One night recently there was a bad rainstorm in Houston with a lot of lightning. As I walked through the kitchen, two light bulbs blew out with a pop as I walked under them. I left the kitchen to get some new bulbs from the laundry room where we store them. As I entered the laundry room, another bulb popped. I suspect that the lightning from the rainstorm somehow supercharged my already overcharged body. Many times when I try to change a light bulb the new bulb will pop just as I screw it into the socket. Similarly, I cannot touch the sheetrock on the walls in my own house without shocking myself with an audible pop, and usually with a visible spark. The use of earbuds with my iPad or iPhone is physically painful. I have been through numerous pairs. I dislike using microwave ovens—I don't know why that makes me nervous. And the thought of ever needing a pacemaker for medical reasons simply terrifies me.

None of these are pleasant experiences. And yet, without the high-voltage strike that occasioned my near-death experience, I would not have made it to the Garden. Without that bolt of electricity, I don't believe that I would have had the expanded circuitry needed to absorb and process the knowledge of the Garden. I wouldn't have been able to tune in to the frequency of the channel that was to impart that same knowledge to me during my visit. I know these are metaphors, but they are getting at something very important. Somehow, the voltage was necessary for both the visitation and the vision that it produced in me.

I think that the knowledge gained through the visitation is responsible for my comprehension of many things now. The visitation resulted in a vision. In particular, the way that this knowledge came to me, stacked on top of the intense stimuli I experienced in the Garden, helped redefine my sense of time. This is the "all at once" aspect of my experience that is so important, and so unusual.

As I explained earlier, I continue to question whether my vision (my abilities and knowledge) comes from the voltage (lightning strike) or the visitation (my near-death trip to the Garden). Does my ability to see auras arise from the fact that I was electrocuted? Was my brain somehow rewired or fused? Or does this ability to see auras come from the fact that I have visited heaven? How about my ability to sense that an inanimate object is haunted? Or to dream the future? It is difficult, really impossible, to say which of the events activated the "on" switch in me. But does it ultimately matter? I understand that others might ask different questions and want to know different things, but what my visit filled me with was not scientific knowledge or anything that can be learned here on this plane through the usual senses. What the visitation finally gave me was vision.

I know I am groping for words here (Jeff asks hard questions). All I can say is that I have encountered forces that were beyond me, that were not part of my thinking before I was struck by the lightning. What struck my umbrella and traveled through me was a shocking welcome to a place I had no idea existed and for which I had no real context. The Garden was, and is, a place where the energy that struck me with such force is mediated but does not dissipate. Nor is it subject to any lessening or entropy. Big words and seemingly scientific jargon aside, I know no other way to say it: this energy is *alive* and *eternal*.

ALL KNOWLEDGE ALREADY EXISTS

Another lesson I received in the Garden is that knowledge, like energy, can neither be created nor destroyed. All the knowledge that there is already is. Knowledge, however, must be discovered. It is like an onion with an infinite number of layers. One revealed bit of information uncovers the next. While there is no end to it, it is already complete.

The most significant discoveries that have advanced the human condition are but a scratch on the depth of knowledge that exists. My understanding of the depth of knowledge and our need to discover it is that this process is something like mining, and that this mining is the purpose or meaning of our existence in this world—what we are meant to do. If everything known were accessible in this middle layer of the present, there would be no momentum for human progress, no reason to live. The point of our existence is to learn, to gain this knowledge, which, again, already exists, like the rich ore or diamond deposits in the ground. Through the process of mining for knowledge, the soul learns and can progress. This process of mining or seeking knowledge is the key. It is the teacher from which we learn to peel back the next layer of the infinite onion.

REINCARNATION AND THE EVOLVING SOUL

One of the main lessons I learned through my conversations with God, or what I believe to be God, is that the kernel of every being is a spark of eternal light, a spark that derives its existence from an energy that permeates our universe, that is, from God the eternal light. Despite the many connotations that the word "soul" conjures, calling this spark the soul gives it a meaning to which most people can relate. In the Garden I learned that this soul-spark is a flourishing, evolving force. It seeks its own course and is programmed to persist like a plant that grows in the direction of the sunlight. Like a plant, the soul also requires nourishment in its cultivation and evolution. Each person must nourish his or her soul if it is to progress. Each human being is an incarnation of this eternal spark.

I also came to understand that souls tend to cycle back and reincarnate with souls they have been with before in other life cycles. Their reasons for recycling back with the same souls vary. Perhaps they are soul mates. Perhaps they have some unfinished business. One thing I know as certain as I know my name is that the first time I held each of my children in my arms and looked into their eyes, two things crystallized for me. First, I knew there was a God. After all, who or what else could have created such perfection? And second, each baby seemed familiar to me, as if I had known him or her in a different place and time. As I gazed at each of my newborn children, I wanted to say, "Oh, it's you."

As it seeks its evolutionary path, each soul will journey through many manifestations or lifetimes. With each incarnation, it has the opportunity to grow and progress, or not. The evolutionary path is not straight. At times, it even makes sharp turns that render the soul's progress stagnant. As the soul evolves and experiences more lives, it also gains additional opportunities for growth, progress, and learning.

Life in this present realm is like school. We are here to learn, to acquire knowledge. Through these means, our souls ultimately progress to the point where their evolution is complete and it is no longer necessary to return to this place where we all currently find ourselves. The primary mechanism or process through which the soul advances is reincarnation, which is what gives our souls infinite opportunities to advance. Without the numerous and various lives we are afforded the ability to live, we would not have the means to learn the lessons and make the advancements that are necessary. This remains one of the clearest and most profound lessons I received in the Garden.

PARANORMAL POWERS
AND THE EVOLVING SOUL

Events initiated by the lightning strike and the near-death experience that followed have made a much more direct path for my soul toward whatever destination it has in mind for me. I think that the speed of its evolution has been accelerated through these means. I believe this to be the case because, prior to that fateful day in 1988, I was a different person. Something in my soul clearly changed … or evolved. However we understand these things, the fact that I survived my near-death experience allows me to know things that I will not encounter or feel again until the death of my body frees my soul.

The strike, the going to and returning from an otherworldly beautiful Garden, the burns on my feet, and these troubling precognitions—none of this was my idea. The likelihood of a person being struck by lightning is about one in a million in any given year. If the bolt is what initiated or catalyzed all of this for me, the odds of my soul doing this on its own are miniscule to none. Each year, only about 310 people in the United States, out of a total population of about 318 million, get such an "opportunity."[11] And most of those struck, of course, do not have an experience like mine. And many do not survive. So the odds are even smaller.

The understanding that was given in the Garden does not make me faster, smarter, richer, or better in any way than someone who does not comprehend the place of his or her soul along the evolutionary spectrum. What I believe is simply the result of my experience. It is not anything I earned or deserved. Moreover, even with the distance my soul appears to have traveled, I still don't know how often I'll have to loop back around and inhabit this realm again.

Each soul advances at its own specific pace. Each possesses the inherent capacity for advancement, but the speed of progress varies. The deployment of paranormal capacities like precognition, clairvoyance, and the ability to read another soul might catalyze the progress of a particular soul. But none of this is automatic, and such powers do not guarantee moral maturity or spiritual wisdom. In other words, one can manifest such abilities and not be at all spiritually evolved. We all have these abilities, after all, and we are all in school learning how to use them. But I do believe that it is possible to make great strides in short order through a near-death experience.

I have written above about incarnations. By this I mean that your incarnation today is the tangible human form that you see in the mirror. The soul within you and the soul within me have been in bodily form before. Those previous bodily forms died, after which our souls took on new bodies in new incarnations. When dates on these particular incarnations expire, we will move on to the next. Again, this was one of the most emphatic lessons I received while in the Garden. I was told that the decision to reincarnate or not is not fully that of the soul to make. The soul does have a say in its reincarnation, though. I was helped to understand that it is God, who spoke to me in the Garden, who situates the soul in the starting gate. In other words, God makes the decision about whether a soul reincarnates again or not. What the soul can decide is what the next life will be like and when it will take place. What the soul needs to learn in order to advance itself will be the strongest determinant as to where and when it settles in its next bodily incarnation.

So did I choose to return and get struck by lightning? I asked this question in the Garden. The answer I received was, "Yes." I knew that I was to be struck by lightning before I arrived in this body. I did not know when it would happen, but I knew it would. I knew, and I chose to run with it. I also asked whether I knew about the physical and sexual abuse I would endure as a young child at the hands of the teenage babysitter. The answer I received was again, "Yes." It was explained to me that I was aware these things were going to happen to me, and yet I chose to return because this was all going to help me get to where I needed to be.

I have thought a great deal about this. I now believe that through the horrors of my abuse I learned how to leave and return to my body, first in the dissociative states I came to use in the sexually abusive situations, then in the out-of-body flight of the near-death experience. Basically, I learned in the abuse what I would later use and optimize in order to survive the lightning experience. This skill, I believe, is precisely what made it a near-death experience and not a death experience. It was as if my childhood trauma was a kind of training ground for the moment I would be struck by lightning, go to heaven, and then decide to return to my earthly body. At least I had practiced leaving *and* returning. I already knew how to do it.

THE SPIRIT GUIDE

What I have recently learned is that in many forms of Hinduism, Buddhism, and other Asian religions, the goal of the reincarnation process is to attain a state where one no longer has to reincarnate and can "jump out of the system" of birth and death. This end or purpose is variously described in these traditions as the goal of "liberation," "release," or "enlightenment." This is not exactly what I was taught in the Garden. In a metaphor that is easier for me to absorb, I was told that the point of reincarnation is *to graduate,* but that this "graduation" comes with a duty or calling. More specifically, I was told that one's soul, having slipped into a stream of frictionless movement in concert with the force that permeates everything, "graduates" and becomes a beacon and companion for others on the path.

If you'll recall, in the Garden I saw new arrivals, always accompanied by another presence or spirit. I understand now that these beings who were welcoming the newly departed were individual facets of the same gem, that is, the Source, or God. My understanding is that each of these companions is a graduate, a soul containing a spark of God, a soul who does not need to return to this realm. I believe that my understanding was accelerated because of the lightning strike. I also believe that this helped me to realize that my companion in the Garden was a part of God, the Source. All of the companions are to be considered as parts or pieces of God, as they all contain his spark, just as our souls do here on Earth.

What happens to a soul once it has "graduated"? The reward, to the best of my knowledge and understanding, is that after so many incarnations, the accomplished soul becomes a spirit greeter and guide for those souls that have been released from their corporeal selves. Such greeters or guides are no longer among the living. This was just something I understood instantly when I was in the Garden.

I believe that my experience of the Garden has uniquely positioned me to understand and now communicate these lessons. I am not dead, and I still have much to learn. Therefore, I do not qualify as a spirit guide. However, my return from the Garden and the abilities with which I am endowed as a result of my brief visit there make me a woman who is not quite of this realm either. I share in both worlds. I am here, but I was also there.

This was not always the case, to put it mildly. The woman who crossed the parking lot in the rain did not care about anything having to do with "soul," unless the term applied to food or music. That woman was deaf and blind to everything I am trying to communicate here. I am no longer that woman. Without seeking it, I received the knowledge in an electrifying instant that many people spend years trying to obtain, and yet never find. I was infused with the understanding instantly upon my arrival in the Garden that the goal for the perfected soul is to become a guide to those who have recently touched down in their own personal Gardens or heavens. There is great comfort for me in knowing that my own sliver of the eternal source of energy will live on in this new life and form, as a spirit guide one day, I hope.

That speck of the eternal that I perceived in the people I met with in Seattle knew I was there. There was interaction between us, between the two eternal sparks, but not, please note, on a personal or conscious level. The conveyance of the information was extracted from that person and passed to me by, for want of a better term, his or her own spirit guide.

Spirit guides are the greeters at the gate for the recently departed. They become active participants in service to the Source. They also often intervene for a soul in this life. It was with these spirit guides that I spoke in my Seattle sessions. When one of the people I met with eventually dies, the same spirit guide who spoke to me will greet and escort the person's soul to whatever version of the Garden serves best as their unique heaven. I believe that my ability to get in touch with a person's spirit guide is due to my near-death experience.

I should add that in my own experience there was no "near" to the event. My near-death experience was real. I understand that there is no way to know whether or not I was clinically dead, whatever that means in a situation like that. But in my own experience I died. I saw what I saw. I learned. I returned. Obviously, I did not stay dead. And when I made the choice to come back from the Garden, I had just enough information in me both to confound those who would doubt and to provide a source of humor for the mockers. But I also had the peace of mind that comes from knowing that what I believe to be true is, in fact, true. There is nothing anyone can say that would convince me that what I experienced was a twist of nature, an odd blip. I am convinced that it was an intentional, preordained event designed to help me understand the ways in which time, space, and energy interact. This is what matters to me now: not what other people think but what I know to be true.

8

ON GOD, RELIGION, AND SPIRITUALITY

Religion is a system of wishful illusions together with a disavowal
of reality, such as we find nowhere else but in a state of blissful
hallucinatory confusion. Religion's eleventh commandment is
"Thou shalt not question."

—SIGMUND FREUD, *The Future of an Illusion*

Congregation Emanu El in Houston is a Reform Jewish synagogue that I have attended all my life. There is much that I love about the congregation. Five generations on both sides of my family have attended Emanu El since its founding seventy-three years ago. The names of my parents and grandparents are inscribed throughout the building in thanks for the generosity of their contributions. It is my family connections— the weddings, funerals, baby-naming ceremonies, and other life cycle events—that keep me so closely tied to Congregation Emanu El. It is not the religious aspect of Judaism that holds me there.

My mother's parents both immigrated to the United States as teens. Mom's mother, Minnie Duval, came from Poland. Her father, Jean

Duval, was born to French parents in Salonika, Greece. My maternal grandparents were from different Jewish cultures. Fortunately, northern and southern European Jews had immigrated to Houston, and by sharing social and religious surroundings, they could bridge the differences between themselves as Jews from different traditions and fortify their new standing as Jews in Christian America.

It was the Jewish community in Houston that afforded my grandparents and many other Jews the sense of dignity and integrity they needed to build a life among strangers in a new land. Congregation Emanu El served as the anchor for my grandparents' nascent Jewish American identity. They met their friends at the synagogue. They all pitched in and volunteered. They helped make the congregation a warm refuge for people like themselves.

My father's parents were both born in America. Dad's mother, Francine Greenfield Rosenthal, was born in Louisville, Kentucky. His father, Max Greenfield, was a native Houstonian. Both came from similar Jewish cultures. They also found their religious and social home at Congregation Emanu El. My parents, and so many of their friends, met each other at Emanu El and grew up there together.

The congregation has a wide corridor down one side of the building. On the walls of this corridor hang all of the consecration and confirmation photos of each class that has gone through the religious school at Emanu El. I can start at one end of the hall and see crinkled black-and-white photos in picture frames of my mom and dad as confirmands in the 1950s: beautiful, proud, young Jews. As I move down the hall and peer into the open doorways to the offices of various administrators, I can picture in my memory my Grandma Minnie talking and laughing with her friend who sat and worked at that desk in that office decades ago.

Then there are the photographs of me. There is the little five-year-old girl dressed in her consecration dress who had no notion of the abuse she was about to endure. There is the photo of me as a sulky, unhappy sixteen-year-old confirmand who had recently suffered many years of sexual abuse. Further down the same hallway are the photos of the next generation, including my children—Jeremy, Andy, and Mallory—and soon there will be photos of my grandchildren, all part of my rich history with this building and this community.

Passing the open door of Feld Hall, the social hall, I peek in and can still see in my memory my paternal grandmother, Grandma Francine, a professional actress and makeup artist, performing on the stage in a fundraiser for the congregation. This building, this Houston institution, holds the collective memories of my family, not to mention the physical records of my family's history. Future generations will be able to look through the Emanu El archives and find all sorts of information about us, including our interests and our connections to one other. My history here runs deep, as does my love for the place. More photos of my family members hang on the walls at Congregation Emanu El than on the walls in my home.

GOD AND THE RELIGIONS

Having sat beside someone I believe to be God on the bench in the Garden, and having held my newborn children, gazing into their already familiar faces, I know beyond any doubt that God exists. Yet, what I have always struggled with is the gross mismatch between what I know to be God and the dogma of organized religions that claim to speak for God. What was revealed to me in the Garden is that God's guiding light is indivisible, and that it illuminates *all* of humanity with the *same* light. There is no evil dark enough or plentiful enough to snuff it out. The disbelievers cannot doubt sufficiently to diminish it. I can see very clearly now that any denomination, religion, or mode of belief that claims a particular doctrine to be the sole, exclusive path to God is both delusional and selfish.

My discomfort with organized religion does not mean that I am not proud of being Jewish. I am, tremendously. The history of the people to whom I belong is long and tragic. Several of my male ancestors were rabbis. They are interred in Israel. When I travel there, my connection with the land is more than simply spiritual. I can point to those specific places on a hillside cemetery in Safed where my connection is physical, where my rabbinic ancestors are buried.

Figure 8.1: Rabbi Eliezer Greenfield (1854–1930), Elizabeth's great-great-grandfather and a highly respected rabbi, is buried in Safed, srael a few steps away from the grave of Isaac Luria. Luria is considered to be the father of contemporary Kabbalah.

I am coming to learn that in the persistence of the spark that is in everybody and in the layer cake of time that I have tried to describe, there are mystical traditions that come from sources far more ancient than I. I know that there are traces in my understandings of traditions like Jewish Kabbalah and Buddhism, and no doubt others, too. So what of this Judaism? What of my Jewish roots?

The Torah spells out what Jews believe to be the word of God. Throughout it, God speaks both directly and through symbols. The word of God has given humanity so many good things, and we have employed these to construe a moral world in which love abides and the path is peace. This is the good stuff that I learned as a child in Sunday school and had reinforced in the Garden.

I never get crossways with this foundational message. For me, the rub comes when the believers of one stripe of religion maintain that their conduit to the eternal is the only path, and that all others are spurious. What we will all find out when we die is that we all graduate to the same Source. There may be intermediaries, whom we have been taught to expect, that await us in our respective version of the Garden: perhaps Jesus, or a panel of heavenly judges. But whoever forms our own welcoming committee and pairs up with us in this place of everlasting love, I believe we will all wind up in the same place. I have so much trouble buying in to the notion of doctrinal exclusivity when I know all rivers lead to the one Source.

My love of Judaism comes from the comfort I derive in knowing that at my synagogue I am surrounded by generations of my family—both physically and in spirit. When I go to services, I draw warmth from simply listening to the familiar hymns and prayers much more than when I feel forced to participate. Just being within earshot of them tells me that I am part of something greater than myself.

MATTERS OF SPIRIT AND THE FAILURE OF POLITICAL RELIGION

I do not recall the politicization of my religion being such an issue when I was growing up or, for that matter, when I was a young adult. However, Reform Judaism has increasingly become a force for secular change. For so many, Reform Judaism is egalitarianism in a tallit. That is an inside joke of sorts. The tallit is the traditional shawl used to cover oneself while praying in synagogue. Jews do work for freedom and social justice. We marched alongside the leaders of the civil rights movement in the 1960s as they protested exclusion and unfair laws. Indeed, if I were to point to three aspects of Judaism that I think Reform Judaism has come to hold the strongest, I would put these, in this order, as (1) social justice, (2) ritual and religion, and, lastly, far below these first two, (3) spirituality.

In my opinion, Reform Judaism has become so heavily focused on social justice that it doesn't even matter if you maintain Jewish mores, observe the Sabbath, or probably even believe in God, so long as you work toward *tikkun olam,* the repair of the world. Some Jews go too far. Reform Judaism has become a political organization—a far, far cry from what I feel religion should be. Where is the spiritual component?

The ritual dimension of Judaism—what I think of here as "religion" that most people would recognize as such—can be a complete immersion for those who want to become involved with it. This aspect might be satisfied by going to services, studying the Torah, and following the minutiae of the rules that govern the conduct of traditional Jewish life. So long as one keeps the maxims and follows the customs, this part of Jewish life may be fulfilled and fulfilling, if that is what the person is seeking. Because so many of these rules command so much time and make so many demands on what one eats, how one dresses, and when one rises and lies down, most Reform Jews do not hew too closely to the majority of these rigid rules. Myself definitely included.

The third aspect of Judaism, what we call today for the lack of a better term "spirituality," is the one that I find most absent from Reform Judaism. In the face of tragedy, hard times, or personal need, it has been my experience that Reform Judaism comes up dramatically short in this category. When I was tragically struck by lightning and had a near-death experience, it took me twenty-five years to find any spiritual understanding or religious confirmation of the experience at all, and this from an Episcopalian minister. I know that my experience defies the spiritual tenets of most Western religions. The number of near-death experiences that took place, or at least were reported, during the time that the scriptures of the two Western monotheisms I know at all (Judaism and Christianity) were written was no doubt miniscule.

The paucity of near-death experiences in the texts that an aspiring rabbi, priest, or minister learns in rabbinical school or in the seminary appears to my jaded eyes to relegate the discussion of spiritual phenomena to a tiny corner of the body of work that establishes the tenets of most religions. It is these venerable bodies of scripture and the centuries of commentary on them that, at least in my observation, most clergy are trained to discuss and argue endlessly. I mean no ill in generalizing this, as I am sure that not all religious schools of learning are equally dismissive. But this has been my take on the subject.

My near-death experience and subsequent spiritual awakening are something of a curveball to those who are trained to swing at only those questions and matters that come at them in the strike zone of their training and tradition. For years, I took personal umbrage at the lack of understanding and interest that my questions and concerns seemed to elicit from the rabbis I sought out. I now choose to believe that it was the sheer distance of my anomalous experiences from their experience and training that silenced the rabbis whom I approached. It was not necessarily a dismissal of my plight, although it felt like that each and every time I met with one of the rabbis. They simply lacked the tools to make sense of my experience, and so, to their discredit, they didn't even try. In this respect, I have to say that most trained clergy are like everyone else: they only comprehend what learning or experience has taught them. And even if they are schooled in faith and belief, they cannot hold to be true what is beyond their professed doctrines or their own limited experience.

I don't know what other brands of religion have to say about it, but the religious leaders of my tradition sort of exclude us humans even as they talk about eternal life. God is everlasting, and our souls come to be bound up with God at the end of the day, but what this means is never made clear. What I now know is that death, the binding up with God, *is not the end.* We are also everlasting, as we each have a spark of God's energy within us. We *are* that spark.

HASIDIC JUDAISM VS. REFORM JUDAISM

Adherents of Hasidic Judaism (a much more conservative and strict branch than Reform Judaism) seem to be more aware of matters of the soul than members of any other sect of Judaism. My understanding is that the Hasidic movement was founded partly to emphasize and integrate mysticism into Jewish life. Their care and concern for me are palpable when I am in their midst. In my experience, Hasidic Jews are kinder toward fellow Jews than those in other sects. When I attend any Hasidic gathering, they seem genuinely happy that I am there. The same cannot be said of the other branches of Judaism. "Welcoming" is not a term I have ever associated or heard anyone else associate with Orthodox, Conservative, or especially Reform synagogues.

Classes available at Hasidic *shuls* (the Yiddish word for synagogue), particularly through the Chabad-Lubavitch tradition, focus more on

Jewish mysticism and involve intense discussion of Kabbalah, the Jewish mystical tradition. Although my son Andy is now a Chabad rabbi, I am simply not familiar enough with this tradition's complexities and nuances to address its teachings. (Jeff and his Jewish colleagues do this later in this book.) I believe that some Chabad rabbis who have studied Kabbalah and its central text, the Zohar, regard the latter text to be on an equal or near equal footing with other Jewish holy texts.

I know that the journey of the soul is very important to Hasidic Jews in general (Chabad in particular), and that the doctrine of transmigration or reincarnation is also a common one in particular mystical schools and texts. The seriousness with which the soul and its many lives are taken in Chabad gratifies me. To know that in Judaism there is a branch of the tree that regards matters of spirit and soul with such earnestness makes me understand that the intensity with which I hold what I know to be true is significant in the Jewish tradition as well. One only needs to know where to look.

I only wish that the Reform rabbis I approached for help had bothered to explore the Jewish mystical traditions or had at least known where to look for answers to my questions. Had any one of them taken just ten minutes to Google "near-death experience in Judaism," not only would it have helped me much sooner, but reading even one of the millions of Google results would have served them well over the years. They would then be poised to help other Jews who might approach them with similar questions, if such individuals felt they wouldn't be shunned for doing so. I was definitely shunned. I most likely will always feel hurt and angry about the dismissive way my plea for understanding and help was repeatedly ignored by my own Reform rabbis.

The reader might ask (and it is a valid question) why I don't renounce my Reform Judaism for Chabad. The answer is simple enough, though obviously conflicted. While I know that Chabad sees the afterlife and the soul's journey much more clearly and correctly than Reform Judaism, the everyday demands of a Chabad lifestyle are simply not compatible with my beliefs. Chabad Judaism believes quite literally that the Torah is the word of God, and that all of it applies to modern-day life. I find that the Torah is a wonderful guide on the virtues of living a clean and honest life, but that it does not apply literally to numerous instances of twenty-first century life.

Examples to which I am referring include things such as the use of the internet, the sterile conditions of a circumcision, or the use of electricity on the Sabbath. I believe that people should be free to make their own choices about what to eat, what to wear, what to say, when to pray or commune with God, where to work, how many children to have, when to have sex, how to have sex, and whom to marry. And, while I feel that people should have the *freedom* to do the above, I feel we have a *duty* to ourselves and to our children to take care of ourselves. This includes not introducing germs unnecessarily to our babies during a surgical procedure (anything touching anyone during any surgical procedure should be sterile) and not walking around unsafe neighborhoods in the middle of the night alone (because one will not take a cab or drive a car on the Sabbath). I also feel that women should be treated at least as well as men and not be relegated to the kitchen or the back corners of the *shul* far from the Torah (so as to make room for the men to be up front).

I could go on here, but the point is made. Any religious teaching that tries to tell me these things and attempts to control my lifestyle or makes me feel subservient to men is simply not for me. I must admit that this leaves me in quite a quandary. Those traditions of Judaism with which I most identify because of their spiritual teachings on the afterlife and the soul are precisely those traditions with which I cannot identify because of their teachings on women and how to live in the modern world, some of which are simply not safe.

I feel pretty certain that I will always maintain a membership at my Reform synagogue. Most of my family is there. My history is there. My lifestyle does not suffer there. No one tries to control my decisions or actions. Yet, sadly, there is no spiritual component there for me. And while I might find the spiritual nourishment I need in Chabad, the lifestyle there is counter to my comfort and beliefs. There is a little something for me in both worlds, even if I am also uncomfortable and a misfit in both worlds. For me, it is a problem with no foreseeable solution. Hasidic Jews will not relax their rigid and sometimes dangerous way of life because they feel God has commanded them to behave the way they do. And I don't foresee Reform Jews ever giving the attention and credit to spirituality that would allow me to feel comfortable there.

This is particularly sad, because I know that sharing my knowledge and message from the Garden that *death is not final* would bring immense comfort to so many bereaved and frightened fellow humans. If only the clergy had any interest in researching, learning, and supporting their congregants when faced with spiritual issues they are unfamiliar with. If only they would listen to and support their fellow Jews without being so dismissive. Perhaps then even they could learn something new, while helping to spiritually support the people they are charged to help.

LOOKING BACK:
EVERYDAY APPLICATIONS FOR
WHAT I KNOW TO BE TRUE

The ridicule that I may be subjected to as a result of "outing" myself with this book is a risk I am willing to take. I simply don't care as much as I once did about what the critics, skeptics, and disbelievers will have to say about me. Many who express doubt will be those whose minds are molded in the rigor of scientific inquiry. These are brilliant people who will never be convinced that what I have put forth has any foundation in reality.

Until they die, that is, and experience it for themselves.

For all their brilliance, and I say this with total respect for how the results of their mode of thought have advanced humanity, their understanding, in my opinion, remains unevolved. To my way of thinking, the conviction they maintain in the exclusivity of the scientific method does not so much diminish their innate ability to plug in to the energy of the universe as it dampens their desire to admit to the reality of such energy and our natural access to it. The overwhelming physicality of life on this plane—the tangible, the painful, the provable—deters many from reckoning with the capacity of the eternal within them. This is *eternality*.

I have been to a place where words are scarcely able to describe where I was and what I learned. Words are tools and, like other tools, when they fail at the task at hand, they need to be supplemented to make them work. Eternality is the quality of the eternal that resides within us all.

Think of this quality as an endless river that flows strongly and powerfully in some and not so strongly in others. Contained and unacknowledged, this energy is a dormant source of significant human power. I am not suggesting that those who have accessed this power are able to run faster than a speeding bullet or are able to leap tall buildings in a single bound. I am suggesting something else, namely, that this same ability to be in contact with this inner flow, channeled most directly by enough people, has enough power to eradicate the greatest fear of every human being on the planet: the fear of death. We cannot eradicate death, but we can eradicate the fear of it.

If I had to narrow down everything I learned in the Garden to three key takeaways that people could use every day, they would look like this:

1. Everyone is loved. Intensely.

2. No one need fear death.

3. There is tremendous comfort in knowing that *there is More.*

Everyone is loved, intensely. To feel the unspeakable love I felt in the Garden is breathtaking. It is also comforting, energizing, empowering, and healing. We have all been hurt by life at some point, but to know that we are loved without question or end goes beyond any medication or therapy known to humankind. To feel that love when your soul separates from your body makes you know you are truly home.

It is fair to say that I no longer fear death. I do still fear pain, of course. And I do fear that those I leave behind will miss me terribly, just as I miss my loved ones who have passed. But I do not fear the actual moment of death itself. I have been through it, and I know there is nothing to fear. As for the pain, I had no pain, none at least until I came back. The lightning strike did not hurt. Leaving my body did not hurt. And the two weeks I was gone were totally free of pain. It was my decision to come back to this realm that opened the door to the physical pain of the burns.

Getting struck by lightning, of course, is not the same as having a long, lingering, painful illness or gradually losing one's mind. Thankfully, I cannot personally address that pain, and I pray that I—and everyone I love—will never have that firsthand knowledge. That pain I do fear. And I will always fear losing someone I love very much. That gaping hole it leaves in your heart is unbearably painful at times. But the actual moment of death and what follows it? Nothing to fear.

The knowledge that death is not final, that you will be back, that you will see loved ones again, and that they may even contact you after they die is all very comforting. As I have explained earlier, I believe that we cycle back with the same people in different lifetimes. Your beloved mother in this life may be your daughter in another.

I only recently came to understand how all this knowledge might profoundly help people. Allow me to end with this. I met a woman at a work seminar whose husband had died the previous year. We got to be friendly. Over lunch, she told me how much she was still suffering from the loss of her beloved husband. She had not slept soundly through one single night since his death. She rarely left the house. She had alienated all of her friends. Her religious leader had told her that her husband was "in a better place," but such platitudes, however sincere, remained abstract and unconvincing to her. Because of my near-death experience, I was the first person to speak with her with complete conviction. I could honestly tell her, "I've seen that place. I have been there. And it is *so much* better."

Recounting my experience to her and describing the love and peace that permeated the place where her husband was now was tonic for her. She called me a week later to tell me that the day we spoke was the first night she slept through the night in the year since her husband had been gone. She also was making social plans with friends to meet for lunch. The comfort I was able to bring her by giving her a firsthand account of the fact that *there is More* and that death is not the end of consciousness was very gratifying for both of us.

I sincerely hope that this book can be of comfort to people who have recently lost someone dear or who themselves may be afraid or suffering. If so, I think that my abilities will have borne much greater fruit than they did when I employed them in Seattle. There is so much more to life than what we see. Death is just a blip, a tiny point on the continuum. I pray that this is what I should be doing, that I should share my firsthand knowledge of these truths. I hope that by reading about my experience many people are able to find comfort moving forward. All is well.

PART TWO

How We Are Changing the Afterlife

Whoever lacks the capacity to put on blinders, so to speak, and to come up to the idea that the fate of his soul depends on whether or not he makes the correct conjecture at this passage of his manuscript may as well stay away from academics.

—MAX WEBER, QUOTED IN JONATHAN GARB'S
YEARNINGS OF THE SOUL

READING AS EMPOWERMENT

All dreams follow the mouth.

—BABYLONIAN TALMUD

The point of this second half of the book is to read—as in *to interpret*—what Elizabeth has just written. This is not some optional, "merely academic" exercise, as we say in our lazy moments. As I have signaled above with the ancient saying from the Babylonian Talmud (an important commentary on the Torah or Hebrew Bible held to be especially authoritative by a number of Jewish traditions), the meaning of a dream or dream-like vision (in this case, Elizabeth's near-death experience) depends on its later retelling and interpretation: "All dreams follow the mouth."[12]

What does this mean? It means that the message of a dream, what it most wants to say, is not in the dream itself but in the later interpretation or "reading" of the dream, which often, please note, is performed by someone other than the dreamer in contexts ranging from the ancient dreams of the Bible to the modern dreams of the psychotherapeutic session. The dream dreams or the vision envisions in enigmas and symbols because it wants to be thought about, talked about, and interpreted. It wants to be integrated into our personal and public lives. Such a "reading" thus completes and fulfills the purpose of the original seeing. Freud, a Jewish intellectual fluent in traditional Jewish modes of interpretation, saw this especially well. He wished to minutely engage the dream "like a sacred text," as he put it.[13] He called this entire process, from the visions seen in the night to the interpretive talk of the morning and day, the "dream-work." It was all one process for him. So it will be for us here.

I recognize, of course, that Elizabeth's near-death experience and subsequent precognitive nightmares were not exactly dreams as we normally use that hopelessly inadequate word. Still, as I will explain below, they definitely engaged the same imaginative capacities that ordinary dreams do. Moreover, the precognitive visions took place in actual dream states. Clearly, there is a profound relationship between vision, dream, and paranormal power at work here. The heavenly vision of a near-death experience, very much like a dream, comes to us as a text, as a story that wants to be heard, read, and pondered. But it all depends on us for its eventual meanings and force. It all depends on *you*.

I mean this all quite seriously. The lightning bolt *wants* to be interpreted, *wants* to be integrated into Elizabeth's life, and, through hers, into ours. In some real way, these acts of engagement and interpretation are extensions and expressions of the strike itself. By taking this second half of the book seriously, then, we learn to incorporate and integrate into our lives that which struck Elizabeth with such force. Following Freud, let us call this entire process, from the lightning strike in the parking lot to you sitting wherever you are sitting reading this page, our shared "vision-work."

Once we understand this, we can also understand why Elizabeth feels such a strong call to write and speak about her experiences in public. She even once mused with me that perhaps the purpose of the lightning strike and near-death experience was this—our book. Perhaps, she wondered, this is what she was called to do. I too suspect that this very book was somehow intended, that it is one distant rumble of that original thunderous strike. Through this book, the lightning strikes us all, empowers us all so that we too might be "changed in a flash." These marvels, then, may not have been just for Elizabeth. *They may have also been for us.*

This is certainly why I agreed to work with Elizabeth. I want to be a safe conductor, not a complete insulator, of the shocking energy that changed her forever. Still, none of this integration will be easy, even if one is "struck" by a book like this one. No one, including myself, can simply accept Elizabeth's story and make it fit into an already established worldview. There is no such established worldview, at least not in modern Western civilization. We need conductors and insulators. We also need transformers to "step down" the energy so that we can think calmly about it and perhaps even conduct it into our daily lives. Otherwise, our feet will get fried and our shoes will get blown off.

That, anyway, is what we are about in this second half of the book. We are about the vision-work. We are about capturing the lightning and conducting it through our words, thoughts, and imaginations in ways that we can integrate into our own lives. We are about a kind of reading empowerment. Are you ready?

Be careful how you answer that. This work is weirder than you think. It is not just about interpreting or making sense of someone else's vision or dream. As I will repeatedly remind you, the vision-work is also about *actualizing* that vision-dream, making it "come true," as we say. It is as if the near-death experience is waiting for us to activate it. By reading it, by interpreting it, we make it possible. We make it real.

It is not, then, that there is some singular correct meaning, buried like a treasure, that is waiting for us to uncover with the proper tools and a good treasure map: "Dig here, and now you are done." No. It is more that, as we engage the vision or the near-death experience with all of our cognitive and imaginative capacities, some of its potential meanings "pop" off the page and become more and more real in our own worlds. It is as if there is buried treasure *everywhere,* and which treasure we find depends on where we choose to dig. It is as if we are reading Elizabeth's story inside the story, and changing that story as we read and interpret it.

I know that sounds a bit odd. All of this will become clearer in the pages that follow, which are all about describing and activating "all of our cognitive and imaginative capacities." More specifically, I will be exploring how to think about Elizabeth's story in ways that answer the questions that I know are in the reader's head about now. I know this because I have lectured about this material in public on many occasions, and I have heard the same questions over and over again.

More specifically, I want to provide some (1) historical contexts, (2) cross-cultural comparisons, and (3) interpretive strategies from both the Jewish tradition and the comparative study of religion that I think will help the reader, and Elizabeth in the process, better understand her extraordinary experiences and so come to entertain the possibility that these are not only real and important capacities of our human species but might well signal something of our human futures—what we might yet become. It is one thing, after all, to have an extraordinary experience. It is quite another to integrate it into one's life, much less to propose its value to an entire culture, which is exactly what publishing a book amounts to.

◆ ◆ ◆

There are two things to underline up front, before we begin. The first involves my own professional location and explicitly comparative perspective. The second involves the central idea that I want to get across through these pages. These two things are in fact related.

First, it is important to note that I am not Jewish. In the language of the tradition, I am a Gentile. In my own understanding and self-naming, of course, I am not a "Gentile," as this label implies the primacy, authority, and perspective of the Jewish tradition, none of which I hold or share. In my own understanding, I am nothing more, but also nothing less, than a human being trying to figure out "religious experience" in *whatever forms* we find such a human mode of being in history, including in and after the lightning strike that instantly changed Elizabeth Krohn. Professionally speaking, I am a historian of religions, which you are free to translate as someone who specializes in the comparative study of religion, "comparison" here being a paradoxical intellectual-spiritual act that seeks to sympathetically enter and so understand any and all religious worlds while granting final authority to none.

Ideally speaking, the comparative quest may be about the whole of human religious experience, but it understands perfectly well that it can only arrive at such an understanding through a careful and long look at individual religions and figures. Ideally, at least, *it understands the whole through the parts and each part through the entire whole.*

Accordingly, my commentary is deeply informed by the work of my colleagues in Jewish studies, an important subdiscipline within the modern study of religion (that is, one of the parts). Following their leads, I have sought to locate and contextualize Elizabeth's visions and experiences in the specific currents of the Jewish tradition from which I have come to think that they are in fact arising: what we call the Kabbalah (the Hebrew means "Reception" but is usually glossed as "Jewish mysticism") and the Hasidic traditions (an important mystical current within many forms of modern Judaism), all of which are themselves in deep conversation with the Torah or Hebrew Bible (what some Christians think of as the Old Testament but which no Jewish person would understand as such, since the adjective "Old" presumes something coming that is "New") and the writings of the ancient rabbis who produced over many generations the grand commentaries on the Torah, collectively known as the Talmud.

I have referred multiple times to all of these Jewish textual and interpretive traditions in what follows. I have also sought out here the critical readings and responses of my colleagues in Jewish studies, whose work I have in fact read and engaged for my entire professional life.[14] Still, nothing I write below should be construed as speaking for any of these Jewish traditions or for these colleagues, or, for that matter, for Elizabeth herself. My voice is my own, and I own it as such, even when it is "ventriloquized" through a biblical, ancient, medieval, or modern Jewish source. Please remember that.

Most of all, please do not try to tame the danger of the comparative quest—that radical spiritual orientation that seeks to appreciate all and prioritize none. Such a quest comes with real gifts, but also with real costs. Do not underestimate either.

Such a comparative quest is also behind the single big idea driving this second part of the book. Sometimes this idea is working in the background. Sometimes it takes center stage. But it is always this: *We are changing the afterlife.* Not individually, of course, nor entirely consciously, and certainly not overnight, but we are really and truly changing the afterlife. Which is another way of saying: We are changing ourselves. This is my own version of the rabbinic saying, "The dream follows the mouth," which we might render here as: "The future shape of the afterlife will follow our present interpretations of the near-death experience." This is what I mean when I claim that Elizabeth's near-death experience empowers us all.

This is the deepest secret of what I am about to express. I am not trying to be cute or clever, nor am I simply playing with a metaphor. I mean to signal the truth that, as you engage this book, as you activate its pages and interpret them for yourself, you are helping to shape what we and our ancestors (who, as we will see, may well be us, too) will encounter when we all die. In and through this reading, you are really and truly helping to change the future of the afterlife.

In this same empowered spirit, I will encourage you to move away from the simplistic notion that near-death experiences are passive clicks of some mental camera that somehow give us an objective and universal picture of the afterlife that we will all see as such. I do not believe that. The near-death experience, I will argue, is much more interesting, and much more exciting. It is more like a 3-D virtual reality display or super-movie that we are all writing, coding, directing, and acting in together over our generations. Basically, the afterlife is a true interactive science fiction film of astonishing intensity, laden with very real psychic special effects, and projected by, through, and in the light of consciousness itself, which appears to be anything but fiction.

If that last line is confusing, so be it. Welcome to the second half of the book. May you understand that line before you finish this book. Or before it finishes you.

9

"THAT'S NOT FICTION"

Science, Religion, and Science Fiction

Some of the best and most popular science fiction writers
of all time had jaw-dropping paranormal experiences, and that's why
they wrote the stories they wrote. It's the paranormal that produces the
science fiction, and then the science fiction loops back and influences
the paranormal.... The whole history of religions is essentially about
weird beings coming from the sky and doing strange things to human
beings ... historically, those events or encounters have been framed as
angels, or demons, or gods, or goddesses, or what have you. But in the
modern secular world we live in they get framed as science fiction.

—JEFF IN BRAD ABRAHAMS'S *LOVE AND SAUCERS* (2017)

There is another way to frame our reading practice here. We could say
that the interpretations that follow are all designed to do one thing: make
the impossible possible. By this I mean to suggest that we are after a set
of new perspectives, a new way of looking, that can change, *instantly*, the

meaning of a set of otherwise unbelievable events and so render them not only possible but plausible. What makes certain kinds of human experiences impossible, after all, is not those experiences (they happen all the time), but our assumptions that they cannot happen. Put simply, the problem is not the events themselves. The problem is us.

To make the impossible possible, then, you first have to figure out what makes the impossible so impossible in the first place. You have to figure out what we are (falsely) assuming to be the case. If you can do this, you can also figure out why we keep ignoring people like Elizabeth Krohn, and why even she long wondered if she might be "crazy." As it turns out, there is a rather blunt reason for this ignoring and for this self-shaming in the modern world, and that reason is the conventional materialist interpretations of the otherwise wonderful discoveries of modern science.

STUDYING THE STARS AT MIDDAY

Here is the gorilla (and bully) in the living room of our conversation: classical materialism, that is, the belief that there is *only* matter, and that this matter, deep down, is lifeless and devoid of mentality or mind. "Up here," where our forms of awareness work, there appear to be life and mind, but these are all surface illusions that disappear as soon as we go "deeper down" and discover the "real" nature of reality, which is entirely material, completely dead, and utterly mindless. In this model, human minds are nothing more than extremely complex illusions of brains, which are themselves purely material and entirely restricted to bodies and skulls and their most immediate physical surroundings, which are accessible only through the physical channels of the senses. No leaving your body here (you don't really have a soul). No precognition (you are stuck in time). No clairvoyance (you are stuck in space). All of that is, by definition and in principle, meaningless and impossible. It can't happen.

If you want to take Elizabeth's experiences seriously, then, the first thing you must do is address this classical materialist interpretation of science. There is no way around the gorilla. There is only a way *through* him. So let us stand up and address the bully directly.

Here is how I stand up. First, I take Elizabeth's experiences to be real in the simple sense that they happened, and that she and others experienced them as such, directly and indirectly. That seems patently obvious, and I see no reason to deny this or sweep it under the proverbial rug with magical spells like "anecdotal" and "coincidence." Second, I make it very clear that I am not especially interested in proving or disproving these events. I am more interested in something more basic and, frankly, more to the point: querying and questioning the assumptions that are made but seldom examined as such in this call for "proving" or "disproving" these events that happen all the time.

After all, what any such "proof" or "disproof" amounts to is forcing a human being's experiences into the protocols of a very specific way of knowing, that is, into the youthful methods and models of modern science, which are barely a few hundred years old at the moment (the word "scientist" was not even invented until the early 1830s). The assumption being made (but seldom acknowledged as such) is that anything that cannot be measured, controlled, and replicated in a laboratory or formalized in a mathematical formula must not be real, must not be true, must not be important. The simple truth is that Elizabeth's experiences do not, and cannot, meet these protocols. They cannot be measured. (What exactly would you measure?) They cannot be controlled. (What are you going to do? Electrocute her and see what happens?) They cannot be replicated. (The nightmares come unbidden and unwanted.) But this does not mean that they don't happen, or that they are not real. It simply means that they do not play by the rules of the scientific method.

So what?

The gorilla is confused now.

There is something more basic still to say here. As shocking as it sounds to our present cultural instincts, it needs to be said that science is simply not the best method to engage and understand paranormal experiences, since these experiences are all about precisely what conventional science presently denies—the fundamental reality of consciousness itself and its presence and role in the physical world. "Objectivity" is the goal of science, and to get to that objectivity one has to erase any and all "subjectivity." One has to deny the reality and centrality of the subject, of consciousness itself, in all that one knows. *But paranormal events do the opposite:* they reintroduce the subject back into the object; they are elaborate displays of the mind's power over or within matter or "objects." That is why they are so vehemently denied by conventional science. That is why they are, supposedly, impossible.

The conclusion is obvious. If you are going to use a method designed to study only objects to study phenomena that are about subjects, things are not going to go very well. You are going to end up studying something that you have no real way of studying. You are going to deny what is staring you right in the face, or behind your face.

The gorilla is mad now.

I often use an old analogy here. It goes back a few centuries to the early nineteenth century and maybe further still. Writers have long noted that shoving extraordinary phenomena into a conventional scientific box is rather like insisting that one can only study stars at noon, and then telling us that, obviously, no stars exist since none can be seen at midday. I would add one little twist to this parable. I would add that, all the while we are told that there are no stars in the sky because we cannot see them at midday, we are also forgetting that the sun (in this analogy, our waking forms of consciousness, including the form of consciousness that does the science) is actually a star. We are denying that there are stars, ironically enough, *because such stars are completely outshined and temporarily rendered invisible by such a star.*

So it needs to be said bluntly and up front: the assumption that the only way to know the truth or the world is through the present scientific method is not an established fact and, as such, cannot itself be proven. It can only be assumed. It is *a belief,* and a rather naive one at that. My own position is that this same belief is not only naive but flat-out wrong, and that most anyone who works long enough and honestly enough with people like Elizabeth Krohn will eventually begin to see this. I did.

I go further still, though. I actually think that the future of human knowledge will pivot on how seriously, and how creatively, we will be able to study and understand such forms of human consciousness as part and parcel of reality itself, as real and as important as a photon or a tiger. These experiences are anything but tangential fluff or pseudoscientific nonsense. They are signs of or echoes from the future of knowledge itself.

This, anyway, is the perspective from which I write below. As a historian of religions, that is, as someone whose job it is to think historically and comparatively about religious experiences, however, wherever, and whenever they appear, it is not my job to prove or disprove anything to you with the scientific method. Rather, it is my job (1) to locate and contextualize a set of religious experiences (in this case, those of Elizabeth Krohn) in a broad and specific historical framework; (2) to compare these experiences across space and time to others like, and not like, them; and (3) to reflect on these comparative acts in order to arrive at some better model of what they might tell us about "religion" and, ultimately, what they might express or signal about the human condition and our actual place in the cosmos.

Put differently, my job is not to force-fit Elizabeth's experiences into our present scientific frameworks or, for that matter, into any particular religious system, be it hers or anyone else's. My job is to take her experiences as serious signs that these frameworks are much too limited, and then to work out, way out, from there to something grander. Alas, we will never quite get there. But we can point. We can guess. We can listen.

If, then, "belief" is about assenting to some past truth or religious worldview, and "proof" is about assenting to our present truth and scientistic worldview, neither is the point here. The point is to "imagine" the human from the future, much like, I can only observe, Elizabeth's near-death experience and precognitive dreams model for us.

EMPOWERMENT: READING AND WRITING AS PARANORMAL PRACTICES

Part of this imagining the future involves thinking about writing and reading in new ways. Actually, reading and writing *are* our main methods in these pages. There is no laboratory, no multimillion-dollar machines or equipment here. There are no statistics or numbers. But there are words to read and stories to imagine. As outrageous as it might seem, *reading and writing are the primary ways that we are changing the afterlife.*

I know how counterintuitive that sounds. I know that many people think that reading is always a banal mechanical act and that writing a book is about sitting down and recording some already established piece of experience or knowledge—a bundle of reliable memories, a stable set of data, a collection of hard facts. You know what you are going to say, so you sit down and say it. In this model, the author is like a tape recorder or video camera. She has recorded something objective with the senses, and now she is going to inscribe it into a document. It is that simple.

Except that it's not. That is not how it actually works, at all, not at least with books like this. It is much stranger than that. It is more that the book comes to be while *and because of* writing it, as if the book writes itself and the author in the process. One writes. One works. Yes. But one is also written. One is also worked on.

And it gets stranger still. It is also the case that the very acts of writing and reading about paranormal events often conjure the appearance of more paranormal events. Strange things happen when one writes and reads about strange things. Such practices somehow make the impossible possible. This is why I have often described writing and reading about the paranormal as paranormal practices in their own right. That's because they are, or at least can be.

Scholars of comparative religion are very familiar with these feedback loops and the mysterious, largely unconscious manner in which texts, particularly religious texts, routinely interact with their writers and readers to empower them, to change them in a flash. They are well aware that the act of an interpreter interpreting a text will also involve the act of the text interpreting the interpreter. It is seldom a simple, straightforward, or "objective" thing, which is another reason that the scientific method and the ideal of pure objectivity will not get us very far here—that is simply not how things work in this domain. Sorry. Get over it, gorilla.

This circularity is even more extreme, more twisting, when the "text" one is reading and interpreting is about an extreme or anomalous experience, like a near-death experience that wants to be interpreted, wants to be engaged, wants to mean something new and be spoken in the public arena, wants—there is no other way to say this—to change the afterlife for all those who will read and consider it. It hardly surprised me, then, when the writing of this book had all sorts of effects in the lives of its two authors. On the simplest of levels, this was quite obvious during our conversations in the ways that my questions and comments affected Elizabeth's answers and own self-understanding. Her interpretations of her own experiences sharpened and shifted as we talked and as I explained to her this or that idea from the study of religion. My understanding of those same ideas sharpened and shifted as well, of course, as I now saw them anew through the prism of Elizabeth's experiences. I saw new things. At the very end, all of these mutual effects took on an explicit paranormal form when Elizabeth essentially dreamed my ideas and, in the process, cognized a number of historical details about my hometown and the deaths of my maternal grandparents. You will see.

TO A SCHOOL FOR MUTANTS

I have seen this human mirroring and self-creation work its magic so many times that I have taken up the role of facilitating it. In the fall of 2016, I invited Elizabeth and her husband Matt to the Esalen Institute in Big Sur, California, where I often teach and work. There I introduced them to a collective of scholars and scientists who work on anomalous experiences. As codirector of the institute's Center for Theory and Research, I regularly help plan and host these private symposia.

As part of these five-day events, we organize a Wednesday evening event for the Esalen community, during which the group in session shares what they are addressing and exploring in their conversations that week. I asked two of our participants to represent the collective for the evening: Elizabeth and Whitley Strieber, the science fiction writer who has written explicitly about his own abduction experiences and with whom I have also written a book.[15] Whitley and Elizabeth both told pieces of their remarkable stories to about 100 people in the room that night.

Whitley seemed at peace with his gifts and experiences, although they have been exceedingly bizarre (go read his books, if you don't believe me). He seems to routinely interact with another plane of reality or hidden dimension that is different from the one most of us know and experience. Elizabeth does as well, of course, but she seemed more uncertain, more anxious about what it all meant. She seemed more, well, *conflicted.*

Esalen being Esalen, the audience responded in kind during the question-and-answer session that followed. They focused in on Elizabeth, with many of those in attendance offering their specific advice about how she could learn to better accept and integrate her gifts into her life. Whitley would also offer his own advice after the event. He explained to Elizabeth why he thought she only dreams of plane crashes and natural disasters: because she is being called to help those people move on to the other world from this one.

The takeaway, for Elizabeth anyway, was this. Before this week at Esalen, she had only seen her abilities and dreams as a curse, as a form of pointless suffering. One can well sympathize with this conclusion. I mean, really, what is the purpose of dreaming of people dying in a plane crash, and then hearing about their deaths the next day in the news? But now she was beginning to hear and think otherwise. She was beginning to see, or at least consider, these capacities as gifts, as a set of charged skills to be used for the benefit and welfare of others.

As a bit of context, I should add that this was hardly the first time that such stories and advice were offered at Esalen. The institute was founded in 1962 to intellectually explore and nurture through practice and community what it calls the "human potential," which one could easily gloss for our own purposes here as "paranormal powers like those of Elizabeth Krohn and Whitley Strieber." Esalen, then, is not just a place one goes to talk about such things, although that is very much a part of the nurturance, support, and development, too. One also goes there to *practice* the powers, and to learn from others how to integrate these human potentials into daily life on various related personal, social, and political levels. Esalen leaders, for example, have been deeply involved in Russian-American relations for more than four decades now (they sponsored Boris Yeltsin's trip to the United States in 1989), and much of the early work was explicitly focused on parapsychological themes.[16]

Similar fusions of intellectual understanding and paranormal practice spilled over into the symposium itself. During the conversations, which got very academic and technical at times, Elizabeth kept talking about seeing everyone's auras in the room, including the aura of Jeremy Stolow, an academic colleague who was writing a book on the history of media, photography, and auras! Jeremy was very generous about Elizabeth's observations and took all of this in humorous stride. He had encountered aura seers before, for sure, but never while delivering an academic talk on the history of auras. This fusion of the academic and the visionary in the same room was clearly a first for him, and for many of us.

The same was true of Whitley's participation in the symposium. During one of the presentations by a physics colleague, Harald Atmanspacher of Zurich, he appeared to be asleep. We all assumed as much, as did Harald, who tried to rouse him into a conversation.

"I am not asleep," Whitley replied firmly. "I am trying to leave my body." The comedic timing was perfect.

But he was also being perfectly serious. In a previous Esalen symposium that Whitley attended with me, he in fact did experience leaving his body, during the night this time. As he reported to us in great detail the next morning, he flew across the country toward the dawn, which was just rising on the East Coast, and visited a university campus there. As he described specific details of the campus (the buildings and what was hanging on the wall of one of the faculty offices), two of the attending scholars recognized it as their own campus and department through some bizarrely specific details. Whitley later visited the same campus at the invitation of these colleagues and confirmed a number of details of his out-of-body flight. I should add that before he left for the East Coast in his out-of-body trip, Whitley tried to visit me in my room, which was just across the hall from his. But I could not be woken from my slumber. Typical. I am dull like that.

Because of moments like these (of which there have been too many to recall or recount), I often refer to Esalen as a real-world Hogwarts, of *Harry Potter* fame. I am indeed a "Muggle" in relationship to the fantastic beasts and magical world in which individuals like Whitley and Elizabeth routinely live and act. If you have not read the books or seen the movies, a Muggle is an ordinary human being who does not have access to the magical world and abilities that the students of Hogwarts take as second nature, despite the fact that it is all "next door" in another dimension of the same super natural world in which we all live. My deep slumber and inability to see Whitley in his second body was Muggle-like in this mythical sense.

In other moods, I sometimes describe Esalen as a real-world School for the Gifted, that is, a school for mutants, as in the *X-Men* films, where psychically gifted individuals can come for support, guidance, and human community in a world that only shuns and rejects them, or worse. Given the fact that Esalen and the X-Men were created at the same time (1962–63), and given the long history of evolutionary spiritualities at Esalen, that is, ideas and practices that explicitly link supernormal abilities to evolutionary processes, this particular mythical reference is eerily precise. I am only half joking when I invoke such references, then. The mythical language actually comes closest to the actual truth of things. Mutants exist. So do magicians. If you don't believe me, well, that's because you're a Muggle. That's because you are not a mutant.

PSI-FI: RELIGION AS PRACTICED SCIENCE FICTION

I am speaking mythically, of course, but also perfectly seriously. This same deep resonance between science fiction and the paranormal was the main theme of my book *Mutants and Mystics*.[17] There I argued that much of science fiction is based on the actual paranormal experiences of the psychically gifted writers and artists who have helped create this particular genre (hence my opening epigraph). In other words, there is an invisible experiential foundation to what we now call science fiction, and this invisible baseline is spiritual in nature, if in a nontraditional or very modern way.

Because of the specific talents of the individuals in whom such extraordinary events erupt (that is, professional writers and artists), these paranormal events are not "believed"; that is, they are not treated as a confirmation of some past religious worldview. But neither do such artists seek to "prove" them; that is, they do not try to reproduce them in controlled, reliable, and measurable ways. They are not professional scientists. Rather, these writers and artists do what they do. They *create* future worlds. More practically speaking, they transform their paranormal experiences into fiction and film, which is to say: into mystical art and modern myth. This process is so well known that some writers have invoked a playful pun and referred to sci-fi as psi-fi, "psi" being the word (drawn from the first Greek letter of the word *psyche* for "soul" or "mind") used by parapsychologists to posit some shared force or presence behind all psychical phenomena.

Once this metamorphosis from private paranormal experience to public work of art is accomplished, these works of film and fiction then enter the public mainstream, where they powerfully inform the imaginations and intuitions of countless individuals on both conscious and unconscious levels. From there, they then shape the subsequent paranormal experiences of others, some of whom speak or write of them in public, and the process starts all over again. Around and around it goes, and where it stops (or begins) nobody knows.

It is simply naive, then, to say, as the dogmatic debunkers often do, something like, "Well, these visions and encounters are clearly based on the science fiction stories of the time." True enough, but the reverse is also true, namely, "Well, the science fiction stories of the time are clearly based on the visions and encounters of those who wrote them." The arrow flies both ways. The snake swallows its own tail.

Science fiction, of course, is hardly the first genre about strange beings coming from the sky to do strange things to human beings. Human beings have been experiencing such things and telling such stories as far back as we can see, and these stories are, yes, always framed in the cultural narratives and natural science of the place and time. This *is* the history of religions.

Elizabeth's near-death experience and subsequent life events are no exception to this general pattern. They clearly have something profound to do with what we have come to call "religion." But what is religion? And how are we to think about it in ways that are sensitive to a particular person's relationship to a particular religious tradition? Elizabeth, recall, loves her Jewish community but has serious problems with much Jewish belief and practice, even as she displays in abundance all kinds of special powers that have long, long histories in the religions, including and especially Judaism and its mystical traditions. Any definition of religion we want to take up has to be supple and sophisticated enough to embrace both the big picture and all the little pictures. Moreover, it cannot paper over anything. It cannot just cheerlead for religion. It also has to say, "Now wait a minute...."

I want to suggest one such definition here. It is not mine. It was conceived by the late sociologist of religion Martin Riesebrodt, who described religion as a "legitimate form of science fiction." What he meant by this is that religion is "a complex of practices that are based on the premise of the existence of superhuman powers, whether personal or impersonal, that are generally invisible." In Riesebrodt's model, a practice or belief is religious precisely to the extent that it enables human beings to "make contact" with a source of superhuman power. Elizabeth and the lightning strike (not to mention Esalen and the human potential movement) resonate perfectly with Riesebrodt's description of one form of such religious contact: "activating superhuman potential that slumbers within a person."[18]

I want to take up Riesebrodt's definition here and reread religion, and especially modern forms of spirituality, as "practiced science fiction" aimed at just this actualization of the "superhuman potentials" that slumber in each of us, with some of us, like myself, alas, slumbering deeper. I propose this definition with the understanding that (a) this "practiced science fiction" might well express something very real and very important about the world we live in, including the actual presence and power of these superhuman potentials, and (b) just because something is expressed fictionally does not mean that it is not real or true. Fiction in fact might be the *only* way available to us at the moment to express future truths that have not yet taken on any stable cultural or conceptual forms in our religions and sciences, that is, in our respectable public institutions. Science fiction, in essence, allows the paranormal to slip through our censors and thought police, be they religious or scientistic.

I also recognize, of course, that using a word like "fiction" might offend, as individual believers do not understand their beliefs as "fictional." I do not want to blunt this edge, however, as I think that that edge is important. This is my "Now wait a minute...."

I see no honest way around this. After all, if we are going to respect and take seriously *all* forms of religious belief and experience (and that is precisely my calling and job as a historian of religions), then we must treat each and every specific religious belief system as fictional in the simple sense that no particular religious system can be literally or absolutely true (since this would render nonsensical and false every other religious system, which would make it impossible for us to take *them* seriously). We must also recognize that every specific religious belief system *is* fictitious for anyone living outside of it. It simply is not true for such a person. We may be polite and not say this, but this is the actual case of things: every religion is fictitious for anyone living and thinking outside of it.

I understand, of course, that nearly all traditional religious systems want to insist on their own absolute and literal truths and dismiss or demonize every other religious tradition. But that is not my goal or perspective here. Like Riesebrodt, I compare religions. I do not pick one over all the others. And comparison thrives not in a literalist approach to religion but in a symbolic approach, that is, an interpretation that understands the religions as mythical and ritual systems that claim to communicate transcendent truths through images and stories that express cosmic truths without themselves being literally true. Religion, here at least, is *a kind of fiction that communicates truth, not a fiction that is nothing but fiction.* Please hold onto that paradox. Please sit with its inherent ambiguity. Do not try to resolve it; that is, do not erase the fiction for the truth or the truth for the fiction. Hold onto both at the same time. As Elizabeth learned in her near-death experience, *nothing* is black and white. Everything is gray. So be gray.

Such a both-and approach is perhaps best captured by something Elizabeth once said to me after I had loaned her a copy of Mircea Eliade's paranormal novel *Youth Without Youth*. Eliade was one of the most celebrated scholars of comparative religion of the twentieth century. He towered above the field. He was also a well-known literary figure in his own Romanian culture. This particular novel, his last, is about an aging Romanian intellectual named Dominic Matei (Eliade was quite old and suffering from severe arthritis when he wrote this novel). Dominic is decrepit and depressed, and he is on his way to commit suicide on the evening of Easter when he is struck by lightning in a sudden rainstorm behind a church while holding an umbrella. A "fiery cyclone" appears above his head and lifts him off the street in a spectacular display of power and light. But the strange strike does not kill him. The lightning in fact initiates a whole series of profound transformations in Dominic while he recovers in a hospital.

Many of these mysterious transformations are paranormal in nature. He can hear people's thoughts. He has dreams of the near future, of the next day, for example. He experiences a spiritual double or guardian angel that appears throughout the novel at key points and who informs him that the extraordinary events of his life are not accidental. His eventual love interest, also struck by lightning, also possesses paranormal powers. She had been traumatized, almost killed, in a terrible storm that involved heavy lightning and falling boulders. She remembers her previous lives, one of them as a Buddhist in ancient India.

When Elizabeth returned the book to me, I asked her what she thought of it. She was immediate and blunt: "That's not fiction."

But, of course, it is.

And yet it is not, since Eliade was convinced of the reality and fundamental importance of paranormal powers.

And therein lies the irreducible paradox of religion as practiced science fiction.

"I AM THE SCREEN"

There are other modern ways of getting at the same spiritual paradox. Riesebrodt's definition of religion as a legitimate form of science fiction, for example, comes with a number of further gifts of insight and new direction, some of them no doubt unintended. One of the most important of these is how it provides us with a very powerful metaphor through which we might balance both the fictional components and the potential reality of the near-death experience through a single image: *the image of projected light in a movie theater.*

This is a very subtle point that requires the reader to hold in tension the fundamental ambiguity of the near-death experience (and, really, almost any extreme religious experience): the simultaneous presence of fiction and fact, of illusion and reality, of trick and truth. I have, of course, just introduced this paradoxical structure of religious experience above, and I will return to it below, when I treat the key role of the religious imagination, but an initial thought experiment and set of images are more than apt at this juncture, again around our psi-fi theme.

It is really quite striking how often modern near-death experiences, or modern visionary experiences in general for that matter, invoke the imagery of film or television to describe their details. Elizabeth once said to me: "I am the screen to a movie when the visions occur." In a similar technological metaphor, another near-death experiencer speaks of the common "tunnel of light" that pulled him inside and out of which emerged "a man made of light that I think was Jesus." The human light-form showed him his entire life, whose scenes emerged from a "wall of light that looked like a television that I could actually step into if I wanted."[19] One could go on here for pages and pages recounting other modern religious experiences coded in film or television frameworks. Such film and television metaphors are so common, of course, because of the centrality of those mediums in modern life.

But they are also commonly used because the analogies work so well, perhaps, we might speculate, because the visions themselves *are* biotechnological projections of some sort, intensified and activated by the innate but rarely expressed biochemistry presumably released by the traumatic moment and its life-or-death needs. The latter possibility is suggested by the fact that the hyperrealistic visions catalyzed by the sacred plant cultures of Latin America are highly reminiscent of near-death experiences. Many of these visions are induced or catalyzed by a particular psychoactive plant molecule called DMT or dimethyl-triptamine, an entirely natural molecule occurring in many plants and animals, and probably in our own bodies and brains. Indeed, some psychopharmacologists and botanists have speculated that in moments of trauma and death our body-brains release DMT to induce vision and allow us to leave the body. The same sorts of visions can be had in the ayahuasca rituals with a specifically brewed tea. Interestingly enough, the visionaries sometimes call the result "vegetable television."

Let us take up this oft-used analogy of the living television or movie and think with it. Consider in particular a movie theater and its projection technology. What is a movie here? It is an elaborate display of colorful and carefully refracted light that is being projected onto a blank screen from up above and behind the audience. The viewing audience quickly forgets this, of course, and interacts with the personalities and events on the screen as if they were real, when in fact—forgive me—they are reel (or at least were: they are mostly digital now).

Please also note that a great deal of human work has gone into each and every second of each and every scene, but the audience forgets all of that as well, that is, until the credits roll and it becomes obvious that the last hour and a half took the labor of *thousands* of individuals spread out over *tens of thousands* of hours. What looked spontaneous and effortless on the screen was no such thing; it had, in fact, been constructed by so many intentional acts, skill sets, and physical and economic resources that we as individuals cannot process it all. The credits continue to speed by. The mind is boggled.

I once explained this model of the religious imagination to a fellow academic, Luis Eduardo Luna, an anthropologist and scholar of comparative religion who grew up in Colombia and who has worked with psychoactive plants and Amazonian shamanism for decades now. He laughed when I explained the metaphors of the 3-D movie and its long cultural credits running at the end. He laughed because his visions on ayahuasca are often 3-D in this precise sense (he can move around in them in a three-dimensional visionary space). He also laughed because he has often asked during his visions who or what is behind it all and how he is supposed to understand what he is viewing in three-dimensional space.

Luis has been given two different answers, in visionary form. In one, he saw a movie screen being held up by strange little creatures. He giggled as he described it to me. In another, he actually saw credits rolling by after the visionary experience was over! Obviously, the vision itself knows that it is a culturally written and directed movie, and it wanted Luis to know, too. Now we all know. For the historian of Western philosophy and mystical literature, such movie metaphors are not entirely new, and the particular arrangement of the modern movie theater is strangely familiar. Indeed, it eerily reproduces the setup of one of the most famous of all philosophical parables, often simply called "The Parable of Plato's Cave," since this story has come down to us through the ancient Greek philosopher Plato and involves a cave. The recorded or written story dates back to the early fourth century before the Common Era, that is, around 2,400 years ago. Plato's *The Republic,* the text from which we take the tale, is usually dated around 380 BCE. But the parable itself and the mystical and philosophical sensibilities it encodes are no doubt much older.

Plato uses the story to get across the profound difference between how the philosopher or visionary sees reality and how the common person sees it, or really does *not* see it. He wants to help us understand how we routinely mistake our sensory perceptions and commonsense assumptions for the luminous nature of reality as it really and truly is. We have opinions. The enlightened philosopher *knows.*

To demonstrate what he means, Plato describes a group of hapless individuals chained to a cave floor. Their chains are such that they cannot look back. Imprisoned in this position, they are made to watch simple shadow shows on the cave wall. These shows are created by the prison-keepers passing objects in front of a fire in the very back of the cave. Essentially, what we have here is a crude, ancient movie theater. Since this is all they ever see, the prisoners assume that reality is such a shadow show. That is all there is. Plato then describes one of the prisoners breaking free and climbing up out of the cave into the open air and brilliant sun outside. At first blinded and bedazzled, he nevertheless eventually adjusts his vision and sees, for the first time, the true nature of reality as beautiful and shining. He returns to the cave in order to tell his fellow prisoners about what shines just outside their dull, dark perceptions, but they reject him as crazy, as a dreamer, as a threat to their own stable and obvious sense of things.

But the truth is the truth, and the visionary can never be tricked again by the banal, boring shadows on the cave wall. He is different now, and he will never fit in again to the dark, dank cave. He does not just think or see what someone else wants him to think and wants him to see. He now *knows* the world as it is, not as it seems. And he is free.

WHY THE NEAR-DEATH EXPERIENCE FEELS SO REAL (AND PROBABLY IS)

The most important places in Elizabeth's story where I think the sci-fi or psi-fi reading works best are those moments in which she reflects on how her extraordinary experiences were both revelations of the way things really are *and yet are also visionary projections of her imagination.* Here is the paradox of religious experience again, that confusing mix of fiction and truth. And here again is where the metaphor of the movie theater and the projector works so well. This metaphor, after all, can help us to understand much more easily how and why a near-death experience feels "more real than real," and probably is, *even if* it is being expressed through a fictional, film-like narrative. There are at least three separate issues here: one a matter of *neurobiology;* one that we might gather under the rubric of *intensity;* and one that we can refer to as *the invisible projector.*

First, a note on neurobiology. It is absolutely crucial that we understand that *we are always living in a virtual reality display:* we are always projecting our own personal 3-D movies. There is no light inside our skulls. It is entirely dark "in there." And there is no color or sound or pleasure or pain "out there." The lit-up world you see and move through is an elaborate neurological display that is being constantly corrected and modulated by sensory input from the electromagnetic environment around you. (When we fall asleep and dream, these sensory inputs from the physical world cease, and so our internal displays get wild and fantastic, but the neurological processes are shared.) The colors you see, the sounds you hear, the warmth and cold and pleasure and pain you feel, the meanings you attach to different objects, including the different biological organisms interacting with you called "people"—*all* of this is constructed and then projected by your neurobiology.

You have probably heard the philosophical riddle: "If a tree falls in the forest and no one is there to hear it, does it make a sound?" There is actually a straightforward answer to this: "No." It does not make a sound. A sound, after all, is a relationship between an eardrum and an electromagnetic event or sound wave. We can speak of a wave here, but we cannot speak of a sound. No eardrum, no sound.

A little side note about the paranormal practice of writing and reading. Humorously, a half hour or so after I wrote those last lines, a tree fell just outside my window, not more than 200 feet away in a cemetery next to which we live. I distinctly heard the crash. Then a few hours later, a *second* tree crashed to the ground, not thirty feet away, just on the other side of our fence. The falling trees were getting closer, as if to catch my attention and underline a point. But which point? Then I took a walk in the cemetery. *Five* trees were now down. This was getting a bit ridiculous.

It was unclear when each of these trees fell, and in which order. I really have no idea. I never saw any of the trees fall (a fence on our lot line prevents such a view into the cemetery from the first floor where my home study is). But I distinctly heard one just after I wrote the lines above about hearing a tree fall in a forest. And I knew that all five trees had fallen very recently, as I walk our dog, Delilah, in that cemetery nearly every day. Of course, there were natural reasons why a tree might fall, like a rain-soaked ground, a subsequent freeze, and a strong wind that day, but still, the wind wasn't that strong, and *five?* But really, it was the *timing* that was so eerie (and so funny). That and the fact that never in my entire life had I heard a single tree fall naturally.

Maybe I am not a Muggle after all. Maybe I am some kind of unconscious psychokinetic marvel, a sleeping superwizard.

Okay, probably not.

Back to the neurobiology. We do not yet understand how this all works (including the falling trees answering to my line about the falling tree), but we do know that what you see is *not* what is there. We know that our senses, evolved to adapt, survive, and procreate, in fact pick up the smallest fraction of the electromagnetic spectrum of energy that is out there and that constitutes the physical world. The rest, even of the physical world, is entirely outside and beyond the reach of the evolved sensory system. Accordingly, the movie you are seeing and living in right now is a constructed fraction of the real. It is *not* the real.

Second, a note on intensity. It is impossible to read very far into the near-death literature and not encounter, again and again, the claim or description of what was seen as "unlike anything I have seen before." But, inevitably, the visionary *has* seen such things, here on earth actually, even if those things are put together in a new and striking way in the visionary afterlife, much as we do every night in our dreams with the stuff of our waking lives.

It is also the case in a typical near-death experience that the "colors are so much brighter," or that "everything just seemed so much more real." To return to our metaphor, it is as if the light of the projector has suddenly amped up, way up, and the movie screen has become psychedelic. Or, better, it is as if the visionary has moved from the simple technology of the movie theater into the 3-D world of virtual reality goggles. One can now move around *inside* the vision, *inside* the movie. Whatever visionary technologies are being activated by the trauma and extremity of the near-death experience, the show is *way* better.

The analogy is breaking down. Let us return to the movie theater. There is a reason that the near-death visionary display might feel so real, and this has to do with the invisible projector at the "back" of the visionary theater. Think of it this way. The characters and events on the movie screen are not real, *but the light is.* Moreover, the real source of the light will remain entirely unknown, since, to stick to our metaphor, the projector projecting the light remains "up" and "behind" the viewers. What happens in a near-death experience, I suspect, is that the dying viewer loses interest in the drama on the screen *and turns around.* What he or she "sees" (or becomes), of course, is the projected light itself. Hence the famous "tunnel of light" into which one is sucked or toward which one flies. The tunnel might well be the projector.

The 3-D display into which one nearly dies, then, is superrealistic, unlike anything a human being can experience with the ordinary senses. Still, it is not literally true. It is also actually not what is being encountered and intuited through the motifs of immortality, infinity, eternity, and unconditional love. What I think is happening is that the light of consciousness itself, now being increasingly released from its ordinary bodily restrictions and neurobiological reductions, is trying to reveal itself as it really is. The projector is attempting to reverse its projections. Still, it cannot yet do this. It cannot yet express itself as itself, since the person has not yet really died and so still exists as a movie screen, which is to say, as a projection. And so the light expresses itself to the visionary or human screen in the only way that it can: through more projections, that is, through symbolic and mythical terms within a kind of sci-fi virtual world.

This double truth (a very real light shining through a very fictional display) is why every near-death experience is different: because every human projection/screen is different. It is also why near-death experiences also seem so similar: because the light is the light before it is refracted through and "becomes" a person on the screen. Finally, it is also why the visionaries have a profound sense that they are encountering something superreal and superintelligent in, through, and behind the visionary display. They probably are.

10

"*NOTHING* IS BLACK AND WHITE"

The Double Nature of the Paranormal and Its Evolutionary Function

When I started writing about life after death, I had Plato in mind.
He was the founder of the academia, the man who formed the
institution that gave people MDs and PhDs and the like.

—RAYMOND MOODY, *PARANORMAL: MY LIFE IN*
PURSUIT OF THE AFTERLIFE

Whew. I must immediately remind my readers that the discussion above is about a set of metaphors, not literal facts. I do not think there is some kind of literal projector in the back of our heads, or that our internal 3-D worlds we (mistakenly) take for reality are actual movies. I think it is no doubt much more complicated than all of that. But we have to start somewhere. We have to start with our ordinary experience to understand our extraordinary experience.

We also have to be humble here. When we try to understand the history of visionary and clairvoyant experience, we are mere children drawing stick figures (not very well), trying to understand special effects that have been created by teams of billions over countless generations of evolutionary adaptation and cultural mutation. Extreme religious displays like those featured in the near-death literature are *way* more sophisticated than the most advanced virtual technology we have today, and likely will have for centuries. Ever heard of a visual biotechnology that can access information *from tomorrow?* Still, these primitive technological metaphors give us something.

The same film metaphors in turn rely on a set of actual and contemporary human technologies, in particular the very recent invention of photography, the still camera, the film reel or movie camera, and now, a mere yesterday, the world of digital photography, virtual reality, and computer-generated special effects. We understand these metaphors only because we have experienced all of these technologies and know something very basic about them as users. But here is one of the many implications of such an insight: as our technologies continue to evolve, so will our metaphors, and so will our understanding of our own psychic projections.

So too, the religion-as-science-fiction model is only one of many possible approaches into Elizabeth's exceptional experiences and the spiritual truths that emerged from them. I will pursue this "practiced science fiction" line of thought below, but I will also explore many others. None of these approaches should be taken as *the* way to understand or explain what Elizabeth "just knew." That is not my point. Each model is limited. Each set of metaphors has its problems. But each also gives us something that we would otherwise not have without that particular model or set of metaphors.

In effect, I am orbiting around Elizabeth's Planet of Powers from as many angles and directions as possible. Each view will give us a perspective and piece, but none taken alone will allow us to see the whole alien planet, and none, please note, will enable us to land on it. Most of us will have to die, or nearly die, to do that.

IT'S ABOUT THE FRAMEWORK, NOT JUST THE FACTS

This orbiting of the Planet of Powers and observing it from as many perspectives as possible is important for another reason. Human beings will seldom, if ever, accept a set of events for which they have no adequate framework. Give them that framework, however, that model in which the particular experience or claim makes some sense and so becomes plausible, and they will usually at least consider it. The true skeptic (that is, the thinker who is skeptical of *any* philosophical position, including scientific materialism) possesses as much integrity as the thoughtful believer here: each doubts or accepts the data depending on his or her own previously established framework. If the new data fits into that framework, it is tentatively accepted. If the new data does not fit into that framework, it is doubted or rejected. Again, the key is not the story or the historical facts themselves, but whether or not we possess a model or set of metaphors in which these can be accommodated and rendered plausible.

Here is a famous and simple example. For centuries, really until the nineteenth century, very smart, highly educated people considered it utterly ridiculous that rocks could fall from the sky. They rejected this notion as pure superstition, as naive folklore, as pseudoscience (okay, they didn't use that word, but it fits). They rejected such a crazy notion because they were working with a model of the universe that rendered such a thing wildly implausible, impossible really: it just couldn't happen. Rocks were heavy. They couldn't possibly exist in the sky. Given their framework, that all made perfectly good sense.

And it was perfectly wrong. Meteorites, of course, are not impossible at all. They are quite real. Although rare events, and exceptionally rare or simply nonexistent events for any single person to witness up close, they nevertheless occur all the time and have been reported for millennia, particularly in folklore and mythology, where they have often been given religious meanings. Once, however, astronomical observation began moving in a direction that was gradually changing how people thought of the cosmos, it became increasingly plausible and then obvious that (a) rocks do indeed fall from the sky, and (b) this makes perfectly good sense, given what we were learning about the nature and content of outer space. It was in this way that what was previously a fable became a fact, *but not, please note, because the phenomenon itself changed.*

I would propose that we are in a similar situation with streaking "meteorites" like Elizabeth Krohn. These individuals and experiences are rare, and they are often completely nonexistent within a particular person's immediate experience (hence the reasonable skepticism). Moreover, these experienced events cannot be replicated or predicted in any reliable way. They do not play by the rules of science. But they nevertheless happen, and all the time. The "rumors" are there. We have all heard them. The folklore is present and active, but it is mocked and made fun of, not unlike how intellectuals once made fun of people who believed that rocks fall from the sky.

For now it is enough to be open to the possibility that rocks really do fall from the sky, or, in this case, that people really do access information outside their local bodies and know things that are going to happen, or have already happened, in the future. Again, I am not going to "prove" any of this. I cannot. My analogy here, like all analogies, fails: Elizabeth's experiences are not rocks that we can all see and hold. They are not objects to measure or to put under a literal microscope. They are entirely invisible subjective experiences, which are real in the natural or super natural sense but not material in this hard rocky way. What I *can* do is provide you with different frameworks in which the facts of such experiences can make better sense and so become both plausible and possible. I can help you make the impossible possible.

First up—the modern, technological context of the "near-death experience."

THE NEAR-DEATH EXPERIENCE BEFORE WE CALLED IT THAT

What we now almost effortlessly call the near-death experience is in fact a modern, very recent expression, just a little over forty years old at the time of this writing. It was first coined and brought into broad use by a medical student with a PhD in philosophy (that is, by someone who knew both the humanities and the sciences). It was Raymond Moody, in his best-selling 1975 book *Life After Life*, who first brought the expression into contemporary use. He used it to describe a number of cases that he had either encountered in his medical training or read about in the literature. These cases involved people emerging from potentially deadly circumstances to tell remarkable stories of encounters with a pure presence, often experienced as a brilliant, beneficent conscious lightform (the light at the back of our movie theater).

It was not that such stories were entirely new. They were, in fact, written about in many different professional and historical venues before Moody arrived on the scene. Mountain climbers had long reported experiences of transcendence and of a doubled presence, often during falls or in the midst of grave danger. Widows had also long experienced the presence of their dead husbands shortly after the loss. And countless individuals had witnessed spectral or even physical forms of their loved ones around the latter's deaths for millennia in dreams, in waking visions.

Anthropologists from the late nineteenth century on had speculated that such encounters were one of the likely origin points of various
cultural beliefs about the separable soul and the ghost story. Numerous psychical researchers in Victorian England during the same period
were looking closely at analogues of the modern near-death experience.
They called them "veridical hallucinations" and "crisis apparitions." A
bit further back, in 1605 to be exact, the father of the modern scientific method, the English aristocrat Francis Bacon, was writing of various altered states that occur when the mind withdraws into itself in
moments like religious ecstasy or "near death." He was thinking in particular of the powers of "prenotion," or what we would today call precognition, that is, the same human potential actualized in Elizabeth after
her own "near death" experience.[20]

There were much older examples as well, of course. When Raymond
Moody, who had just completed a PhD in philosophy, was encountering
these cases in medical school, he could not help but think of the ancient
Greek philosopher Plato, the founder and iconic genius of the Western
academy and intellectual tradition. In his *The Republic* (the same book,
recall, in which the parable of the cave appears), Plato tells a story about
a soldier named Er who was apparently killed in battle, thrown on a
pile of corpses, and then came back to life days later to relate numerous
details about the afterlife and, in particular, the moral mechanisms of
reincarnation. The first Western near-death experience story, in other
words, was a reincarnation story, again like Elizabeth's. Hold on to that.

FROM JUDGMENT TO LOVE: THE PARABLE OF RAYMOND MOODY

It is often pointed out that there was no "hell" in Moody's book, and
that the Light appears as universally accepting and loving in the stories. This is true of a number of studies and books on the near-death

experience, actually. So too here, with Elizabeth's experience. As she stressed, the love she experienced was *utterly* unconditional: it did not require any particular set of beliefs, any ethnic identity, or any religion. That may be good news to many modern people, but it is pure heresy and very bad news in the context of the history of the Western monotheisms, where one's afterlife is generally conditional on following a religious contract or set of purity codes and moral rules, belonging to a particular ethnic or religious community, or holding to the correct set of beliefs.

Later research has complicated this positive picture of the NDE somewhat, as there are also "negative NDEs," that is, near-death experiences that are dark and terrifying. Twenty-one different studies put these at anywhere from zero to twenty-three percent of reported NDEs—a very large margin. Nancy Evans Bush, who has looked at the literature closely, estimates that the average rate is somewhere in the mid- to high teens.[21] We also recognize that these negative NDEs, due to their disturbing content, are likely underreported.[22]

These negative NDEs need to be considered carefully and compassionately. But we also need to be very careful not to use them to prop up some conventional belief system about "hell" and "judgment," as is sometimes done by conservative religious writers. This does nothing more than add trauma on top of trauma. In the words of Bush: "There is *no evidence* that these experiences are punishment for wrong beliefs or unacceptable or evil behavior, nor does evidence show that NDEs happen only to bad people," as some of the ultraconservative religious voices claim (since the total NDE literature is incompatible with their exclusive and literally damning belief systems).[23] In short, the occurrence of negative NDEs does not prove the existence of hell, anymore than the positive NDEs prove the existence of heaven. What they all *do* lead to is a rich meditation on the modern experience of the afterlife, the fundamental role of the imagination in shaping and reshaping these religious experiences, and the complexity of the human spirit, which can manifest itself as a heaven or a hell, as it were.

Regardless of where we land on these important issues, one thing is fairly clear: there is a very profound mismatch, gap, or disjunction between the NDE phenomenon as a whole and what one would expect to see or experience, given a particular religious worldview or conventional set of beliefs. This in turn matches what numerous researchers have found, namely, that there appears to be little, if any, correlation between a person's beliefs and the likelihood of having an NDE. Religious belief appears to be nearly irrelevant when it comes to predicting an NDE, although it does often shape the content of the visions once they get going, if seldom in complete or entirely predictable ways.[24]

I do not think this mismatch and unpredictability can be overexaggerated. *NDEs do not behave.* They do not follow our rules or our beliefs. As such, they are often fundamentally deconstructive of cultural forms but also creative and productive of new ones. At some point, we must come to terms with both the bright radicalism of these stories and the fierce resistance with which they have been and will continue to be met from those who are still committed to mythologies of judgment, anger, exclusion, and hell realms *or* to specific traditional images of heaven, most of them "guarded" by particular beliefs. We have to come to terms, someday, with the powerful ways that the NDE both affirms and denies what we believe, what we have been told.

Moody's own life and work can well function as a kind of parable for us here. It is seldom noted, but Moody himself has described in great detail how his *Life After Life* was met with anger and harassment from Christian fundamentalists, many of whom wrote him nasty abusive letters. As he tells the story in his autobiography, Moody's personal life was profoundly impacted by the same fundamentalist sensibilities, when his family and wife were deeply influenced by a man Moody had known in graduate school. According to Moody, this man was "declaring that God would let only the truly religious see a heavenly light and not some of the heathens I was interviewing. Therefore, he said, near-death experiences were the work of the devil. Which meant, of course, I was working for Satan."[25] This same man would also write a book against Moody, which contained deeply personal information that he could not have gotten anywhere other than from Moody's own family. The eventual result was the end of Moody's marriage.

I take this not simply as a sad story from Dr. Moody's autobiography, but as a clear sign that the near-death accounts are extremely powerful in their own right and are explicitly challenging some of the deepest religious sensibilities of at least some of our faith traditions. I take this as a clear sign that the near-death stories are really and truly changing the afterlife.

"NEITHER BLACK NOR WHITE": HOW TO THINK ABOUT THE PARANORMAL

The "near-death experience," then, is one expression that allows us to see things and listen to things that we otherwise might not. They make the culturally invisible visible. But they also can blind us to other things, just as any focus on a particular object in the distance renders everything else in view fuzzy and indistinct. The trick, of course, is to use many focal points, many new expressions, each of which gives us something while taking other things away.

Like the "near-death experience," there is another fairly recent expression that is worth being much more conscious about, since, if used with nuance, it can give us much. Unfortunately, if the same expression is used sloppily, it also can take a great deal away and end up erasing (mostly through pure embarrassment) exactly that which we want to understand here. That gifted but dangerous expression is "the paranormal." There is a very simple and elegant way to think about the paranormal. Let me back up into it, like this.

It would certainly be something of a relief if experiences like Elizabeth's were all mistaken perceptions, honest mistakes, or just bad pseudoscience. Elizabeth's experiences may be honest ones in this view—that is, she may well be telling the truth of her own experiences as best she understands them—but these experiences are entirely "subjective" or "mental" and have nothing to do with the "objective" world of objects and "physical" things out there. She is just dreaming of plane accidents because she is afraid of planes, and some of these dreams just happen to coincide with media events the next day. She is not precognizing anything. It is all just coincidence. No big deal. Sorry. End of story.

If, on the other hand, such precognitions are true in some sense—that is, if they are granting empirical information about the world through channels other than the five senses—then the implications are immense, not just for Elizabeth or the reader of these lines, but for the future of science and our conception of the human being and its limits (if there are any). In this case, we are left with a set of *subjective* impressions, garnered in a dream state no less, about *objective* events in the physical, historical world. Put differently, we are left with a situation in which "subjective" and "objective" cease to have much meaning, as if we have entered some strange cosmic state that is neither mental nor material but somehow expresses itself as both at the same time. Another paradox. Another both-and. And that's before we get to the embarrassing fact that time appears to be reversing itself, flowing backward from the physical future to Elizabeth's dream present.

As I explained earlier and will repeat again here, this both-and is a classic feature of mystical experience and expression around the world. Previous scholars of religion have thus written of the *coincidentia oppositorum,* that is, of the "coincidence of opposites" that defines so many religious experiences and their subsequent mythological framing. In his study of dreams in the Jewish tradition, for example, Elliot Wolfson writes of what he calls the "mythologic" of the dream, that is, the dream's ability to unite opposites and even "undo time." This is a mythical logic that the left hemisphere of the brain, which can only think in either-or terms and in linear, arrow-like time, simply cannot understand, and yet it remains very much *a logic,* that is, a way of thinking in images, narratives, and paradoxical images. In this same right-brained spirit, Wolfson recognizes the paranormal nature of dreams as symbolic "signposts" that represent the very limits of our ability to represent the world to ourselves. The paranormal, then, "does not represent a realm outside the universe, but its edge."[26] That is to say, the paranormal represents the human mind's furthest ability to represent in both-and or paradoxical terms that which lies beyond its own evolved, left-brained, either-or ways of thinking.

I fully recognize that all of this is confusing, and that these are, again, strange words. But that is precisely my point. The paranormal can *only* be confusing, since it is about a way of thinking and being that temporarily collapses the "mental" and "material" dimensions of the world that we usually succeed in keeping distinct and separate in our ordinary experience, language, and thought. But in this very confusion we have a very good and simple working definition of the paranormal, which goes like this: *the paranormal is an exceptional experience-event that temporarily collapses the mental and material or subjective and objective dimensions of our ordinary human experience and sensing.*

Hence a departed spirit (a mental or subjective event) rings a physical phone and fills a room up with smoke-that-is-not-smoke that both a wife and a husband can clearly see (a material objective series of events picked up by the senses). Hence a sleeping woman dreams (a mental or subjective event) about a future plane crash (a material objective event). Hence an author writes about a tree falling in a forest (a mental event), as five trees fall in his forest (all material events). Please note that the mental does not *cause* the material event. The mental and the material events *correspond* to one another, apparently to create a link, symmetry, or set of meanings in a particular moment for a particular person. The paranormal is all about *meaning* here, not mechanisms. That is another reason that science is not our best method here. Science knows nothing of meaning. That is a philosophical, literary, and religious question, not a scientific one.

Our normal experience of the world, of course, does not work like this. We experience ourselves as "in" our body somewhere, perhaps floating inside our skull. Actually, if you pay close attention to your form of awareness, you will see that it is really not at all clear that you are "in" your skull or are your brain, or that you are even all in your body. Still, that is what I think most of us assume, because that is what we are told, and it does bear some very rough and tumble relationship to our experience. In any case, this "I" "in here" is supposedly looking at the material world "out there." There are just two orders or dimensions of human experience, then—the mental "in here" and the material "out there." These are in turn somehow linked by the senses, although no one quite knows how that works either.

It's a real mess, if you just think about it for ten seconds.

Still, common sense continues to hold that these two realms are separate. There is a mental world, and there is a material world. As we have already explored, common neuroscience holds that the inner subjective experience is actually a sophisticated illusion produced by the material processes of the brain, and that there is actually only a single world—the material one. What a paranormal event does is offend *both* of these common positions. It collapses the assumed division of common experience. *And* it challenges the materialist assumption that the mental is only a function of the material, that is, that mind can be reduced or fully explained by matter. Within a paranormal event like a precognitive dream, the world "out there" seems to speak to or correspond perfectly to the world "in here," and—weirder still—the mind or mental realm appears to be everywhere and everything; it seems to be nearly omniscient and omnipotent, as if it knows everything and could do almost anything.

This, of course, is all totally outrageous—outrageous, that is, to our present common frameworks. Next thing you know a burning rock will fall out of the sky. Crazy, right?

Allow me to define the offense on the materialist side. In the conventional materialist picture, the subjective or mental realm is nothing more than a temporary product of physical processes in the brain. The mental is reduced to and explained by the material. When the brain shuts down, mind disappears. But such an "explanation" is really no explanation at all. It is an interpretation of the facts. It is not a fact. And it is an interpretation that actually doesn't work very well. Indeed, no neuroscientist has ever been able to show how such a remarkable transformation from wet, warm brain matter to the full-color, 3-D movie you are in right now might work. Not even close. They have been able to show in increasingly exquisite detail that subjective states of mind are *correlated* with or *connected* to brain processes, but this is a very long way from demonstrating that brain matter somehow *causes* consciousness. How that is accomplished remains an utter mystery in the materialist model, probably because it is simply not true.

This is one reason why conventional materialists and professional debunkers so vehemently reject experiences like those of Elizabeth. Apparently, they are not very sure of themselves. If they were, they would not lash out like they do. They would simply provide a better explanation for the same events and reported experiences. But they don't do that. They claim they don't happen at all. They then offer exceptionally lame, really fake explanations, which they invoke through words like "coincidence," "anecdote," and "hallucination," which at the end of the day explain exactly nothing and paper over everything. They might as well be chanting magical spells to ward off feared demons.

THE PARANORMAL AND PROCREATION

Conventional materialists are generally neo-Darwinians, by which we mean that they believe that evolution is random and without purpose or intent, and that every feature or characteristic that survives the long journey of biological evolution does so because it helps the organism to adapt to its environment, survive, and procreate. But this is exactly how paranormal abilities also often function.

As I have already noted, one of the obvious practical effects of Elizabeth's near-death experience was that it resulted in another potential genetic line—that of her daughter. It is an often overlooked fact that near-death experiences and psychical phenomena of all sorts often serve a crucial biological purpose: they enable people to survive dangerous situations and hence to procreate.

Such an observation is hardly original. As a historical example, consider the word "telepathy" and how it came to be. When the Victorian classicist, education reformer, and psychical researcher Frederic Myers coined the term telepathy in 1882, he sought to link it quite directly to both family bonds (hence the -*pathy* or "pathos" part, which was a reference to human emotion and love, particularly of a familial nature) and evolution (he absolutely adored Darwin). Myers believed that telepathy represents a clear evolutionary advance of human sensory capabilities.

This conviction was in turn grounded in a very specific model of the mind-brain relation. Myers became convinced, largely because of his massive ethnographic data on telepathic and other psychic experiences, that *a mind uses a brain,* and that the "human brain is in its last analysis an arrangement of matter expressly adapted to being acted upon by a spirit."[27] Put a bit more simply, "mind" or "spirit" is not something that is produced by a physical brain. A physical brain is a receiver or transmitter of mind that has evolved to "pick up" and "translate" mind, rather like a radio is constructed or designed to pick up and translate an electromagnetic signal. There were no radios when Myers was alive. But there were telephones and telegraph wires. Hence his coinage: telepathy, after "telephone" and "telegraph" (all from the Greek prefix *tele-* for "from a distance").

For Myers, and for many of his intellectual colleagues of the place and time, evolution is guided by conscious forces that have, over the course of millions of years, evolved their own biological and neural receptors. Their evolutionary language was more than metaphor. Myers is quite clear that the history of spirit communication gives witness to "the evolution of human personality," and that his work speaks "of faculties newly dawning, and of a destiny greater than we know."[28] He even suggests that humanity may be able to hasten its own evolution, writes of "a cosmic moral evolution," and openly encourages his readers to see that their greatest duty is to increase the intensity of their spiritual life and so come to recognize that "their own spirits are cooperative elements in the cosmic evolution, are part and parcel of the ultimate vitalizing Power."[29] If I may return to my personal myth, Frederic Myers was the original Professor X of *X-Men* fame. He was speaking and writing about mutants before we had the word or concept.

If something along these lines is the case, one of the things that one would expect to find in cases of telepathy is some kind of survival advantage. This, after all, is partly how evolution works. Organisms that can survive are the same ones that can procreate and pass their genetic lines on to the next generations. And this survival advantage is exactly what one does indeed find. One finds story after story of some telepathic communication allowing a loved one—usually a family member—to survive a near-deadly accident or a near-fatal situation. The paranormal saves lives, which, of course, are also genetic lines.

Here is an example of one such paranormal event, taken directly from my correspondence files, this one from an avowed materialist academic responding to my *Chronicle of Higher Education* manifesto, "Visions of the Impossible."[30] It is a perfect example of how the paranormal, mediated here through the imagination, is an evolutionary gift; how it is often supremely adaptive, indeed in this case literally lifesaving.

My correspondent begins by resisting my essay on the paranormal, but he then quickly and radically changes his tone when he gets to his uncle, who, he insisted, was the last person to exaggerate anything:

I'm the kind of guy who sees Paul, e.g., as a guilt-ridden persecutor of his own people who also suffered from temporal lobe epilepsy, or something similar. In other words, I'm one of those materialists you wrote your article for. However, I have a veridical hallucination of my own to tell you, or rather one that happened long ago to an uncle, in 1918 in the Meuse-Argonne sector of the Western Front.

My uncle was a Greek immigrant serving as a platoon sergeant in an Illinois National Guard regiment. His unit was dug in facing the west bank of the Meuse, and on this portentous night, as he told us over a poker game at a Thanksgiving family gathering some 60 years ago, he was observing the Germans across the river in a sandbagged firing pit (aka, "foxhole") ahead of the main trench line. The Germans were mortaring these positions sporadically to keep the Americans awake, and my uncle was keeping his head down among the random, distant blasts.

Then he heard a voice, a Greek voice, that he was sure was his father's voice. "Demetri, Demetri, get out of there."

My uncle shuffled down the communications trench to his platoon, which was filled with Greek immigrant boys, and asked them, "Have any of you guys been calling for me?"

"No, Sergeant Moskhopoulos," they all said.

All this time, my uncle had been telling us this story with his eyes down, looking at his cards. Now he looked at us all and said, "When I started to go back a shell blew up the whole place where I'd been.

After the war, when I went back to the family in Greece. I found out that day was the day my father [had] died."[31]

And so the genetic line was saved, as if by itself.

WE DIE INTO OUR IMAGINATIONS

The modern near-death accounts are made possible in their increasing number and depth by the advances of biomedical technology, which can "pull us back" from further and further into the death process. This might look like a minor observation, but it has major implications for how we think about the near-death literature as a whole. What we have in the near-death stories, after all, is essentially *a new mystical or visionary literature made possible by new biomedical technology.*

Note that the role of technology here is not a causative or productive one. You cannot turn a dial or hit a computer button on a piece of hospital technology and digitally "cause" an experience of an afterlife. Nevertheless, the same technology does appear to make such events more possible, *much* more possible. What we have here, then, is a technology of *retrieval* or *allowance.* The biomedical technology allows individuals to enter very deeply into the death process and then return from their otherworldly journeys and tell their tales.

The increasing number of such tales is having a real cultural and religious effect. With such observations, I do not mean to suggest simply that now we have many more stories and, oh, isn't that nice. I mean to suggest that these snowballing stories may well be "doubling back" on the experience of death itself and shaping present and future death experiences. I mean that *death and the afterlife are changing to the extent that we are envisioning and then experiencing both in new ways with the help of things like modern biomedical technology and a more inclusive and progressive social imagination.*

Let me put it this way. The English expression "to have a vision" is very helpful here, as it can mean two very different things. First, it can name a more or less passive process. "To have a vision" in this sense is to be given something, as in a dream. But the same phrase can also name a process that is much more active, that is about creating and projecting something and then working toward actualizing that projected vision in the future. Here, "to have a vision" is to make something actual that was previously only potential. As such, it is more akin to writing, directing, and then projecting a movie. When I refer to the modern near-death literature as a visionary literature and write of our vision-work here, I intend *both* meanings: something is received or revealed, and then something is created out of the gift. I mean to suggest that these revelatory visions of our own deeper nature are also projects that we must engage with and act on; that these need our attention and intention to fulfill their purpose; and that they are finally about us changing us.

We can think of the entire history of religions in this way. We can think of it all as a long series of science fiction movies—with the scenes painted on the walls (of the caves, of the churches, of the temples), and all of it inspired by countless and quite real super natural special effects (like precognition and auras). For thousands of generations, we have been born and then died into these running science fiction movies, changing the scenes and stories as we go, largely unconsciously and gradually, but sometimes dramatically and, seemingly, all at once.

Not surprisingly, the religions have always known something of this, if in a largely implicit, unconscious, or at least unexpressed way. This is why they have so richly supported and funded the arts, not for art's sake, but for the vision's sake. They understood very well that it is the image and the story that ultimately define a community's worldview and religious experience. We do not have to share any of those values or beliefs (that is, we do not have to believe their movies) to see that they may well have been on to something very important, namely, that it is the image and the arts that largely determine what we see and what happens to us in the death process and in the afterlife, at least in the "near-death" zones from which we sometimes return.

In short, *we die into our imaginations,* be these psychological, cultural, or religious. We die into our own personal and collective art, not unlike what happens to Robin Williams in the film *What Dreams May Come* (1998), where his character, Chris Nielsen, is killed in a car crash and ventures into the afterlife to find his dead wife, who has committed suicide. The afterlife, Nielsen discovers, is like an oil painting. He has died into an art world. He has died into the imagination.

If any of this is close to the truth, and I think it is, the conclusion is as obvious as it is shocking: if we want better death experiences, it would do us well to make better art. If we want to be in a better science fiction movie "there," it would serve us to make better science fiction movies "here."[32] Toward this same end, we might even decide to take up the modern near-death literature and create new art, i.e., new meditation and prayer practices out of it. We might use this literature and these reports to imagine what death might be like for us, or better, what we might want it to be like. By doing so, we could take more responsibility for our own visionary displays and work with them, as in a lucid dream, here and now before we die. We could not just "see visions." We could also "have a vision"; that is, we could possess a vision of the future and consciously act on it as our project. We could decide for ourselves which paintings we want to die into.

If we were *really* smart, we would also create practices that taught us that none of these forms of the imagination are literally true, that they are all "ours." We might then seek the artist behind all the art, the projector behind all the movies. We might even wake up from our own dreams of life and death, however real they might seem at the moment.

11

"I JUST KNEW"

The Alien Translator, Gnosis, and the Secret Powers of Interpretation

And Jesus said, "Whoever finds the meaning of
these words will not taste death."

—GOSPEL OF THOMAS, LOGION 1

In the previous two chapters, we looked briefly at the nature of "science" and "religion" and what they have to do with Elizabeth's experiences. In this chapter, I want to return to the "imagination," which we have already engaged through the metaphor of the film being projected from the back of the movie theater. I want to return in an attempt to dislodge from the reader's mind any notion that what is imagined is always imaginary. I want to take what I consider to be Elizabeth's instinctive understanding of the religious imagination and turn it into something more akin to a fully conscious and discussable model. Put a bit differently, I want to take up Elizabeth's precognitions and revelations and try to transform them into something the rest of us can think about and use—take a little lightning from the bottle/book, as it were, and put it to good use. I want to get a little sizzle and spark on the page.

In truth, the imagination is the secret of everything we are discussing in these pages. If we do not have an adequate understanding of the imagination, then we will not have an adequate understanding of the near-death experience, of ourselves, or of the afterlives we ourselves are dying into and constantly changing. The imagination is the ultimate framework that makes any event plausible or implausible, possible or impossible. It all hinges on *this*.

HOW TO TALK TO AN OCTOPUS

As a first attempt to think about the religious imagination, let us think of it as that organ or dimension of consciousness that gives us access to communications that can only reach us in symbolic or mythical form, that is, in fantastic images and strange stories akin to science fiction. The religious imagination is what acts as a medium or diplomat between us and that which is attempting to communicate with us (which may be some alienated part of us).

As a way of getting a handle on this, we might think of the source of these communications as the form of life and consciousness that, say, a dolphin, a whale, or an octopus possesses. How exactly would such alien forms of life communicate what they know, what they experience in the ocean, to us violent hairless monkeys up on that thing floating on top of the world? They certainly cannot use any human language, and we certainly cannot understand whatever languages or forms of communication they no doubt routinely use. What can they do, then? What can we do? Maybe most seriously of all, why would they want to communicate with us at all?

I am uncomfortably reminded of a bumper sticker I saw on the highways of Florida once: "If animals could talk, we would all be vegetarians."

That is no doubt closer to the truth than most of us are willing to admit. My brother, otherwise an omnivore, will not eat octopi—they are just too intelligent, too damn smart, too, well, *human*. They are squishy humanoids that live in the sea. He first told me this as I shamefully cut my steak knife into an octopus's tentacle on a seafood platter. I do not eat octopus anymore. Jerry ruined that one for me.

But octopi are certainly not alone in their intelligence and humanoid awareness. So maybe we don't want to communicate with the alien forms of life we eat every day either. But what if we did? Or what if they reached out?

FROM CONTACT TO COMMUNICATION

What we would need, of course, is *translation*. Their language or form of communication would need to be translated into ours, and vice versa. Perhaps we should distinguish here between *contact* and *communication*. Contact is fairly easy and extremely common (if often violent—consider the poor octopus on my plate). Communication, adequate communication anyway, is really difficult and very rare. We could have contact without such translation, but we could not have effective communication. There must be some kind of interface or translation process from one species to another for true communication to occur.

The way this works in the history of religions—which, true to our understanding of religion as practiced science fiction, we might imagine as one long history of "contact" and attempted "communication" between human and nonhuman or superhuman forms of mind and presence—is through revelation, symbol, and myth, that is, through overwhelmingly powerful irruptions into ordinary life that communicate in indirect and imperfect forms. Such divine invasions usually work through some altered state of consciousness in the recipient—say a meditative or trance state or a possession—and attempt communication with us through poetry, picture, and, above all, through story.

This is how these forms of mind attempt to get around our rational forms of thinking, how they try to "get in." Apparently, they cannot get in through our normal defenses, our everyday bounded sense of self, or our linear "sensible" logic. The container of the ego or body-brain (for the ego is modeled on the body) is just too thick and dense. But sometimes, when this bounded container is violated or compromised (as in sexual trauma or a lightning strike), these communications come rushing in, often, alas, to the great confusion of the recipient. They are confusing because such forms of mind and knowledge have to speak to the recipient in translated ways, and what they are translating makes little or no sense to the ordinary forms of knowledge that the ego knows and assumes to be true in its particular social surround and partial, sense-based movie world. The octopi are talking to the fisherman, and they make absolutely no sense—no sense *to the fisherman,* of course.

To make sense to the fisherman, such deep, watery truths must be translated into dry, landlocked terms that the fisherman can understand and process. The result is translation, yes, but also distortion. This double translation-distortion is essentially what one finds in the history of religious revelation. Such remembered events often likely encode actual anomalous events or extraordinary experiences, which are then subsequently expressed in elaborate mythical narratives and ritual reenactments that have been worked over and inevitably concretized or literalized over generations and then centuries.

Such mythical and ritual expressions (basically what we mean by "religion" today) need not be considered false, but it is quite dangerous to accept them as literally (and exclusively) true. Put differently, such revelations may well encode truths that are so complex and so subtle that they cannot be spoken or understood with ordinary language and reason. They are forms of octopi truth that the landlocked thinking of the crazy monkeys floating on top of the water cannot process and understand. They are forms of true science fiction.

If you ask how the ancients, or the moderns, came to their own stories, how they heard and saw them, I would say, "Well, often probably a lot like Elizabeth Krohn did, in extreme conditions and anomalous psychic states, like near-death and out-of-body experiences, which is to say: they heard them 'in the heavens.'" In the ancient world, by the way, the term "in the heavens" meant "among the stars." And here the ancients were being quite literal. They meant "up there." They meant something close to what we mean by "extraterrestrial" or "alien."

ARRIVAL

I wrote the bit above about octopi well before I saw the science fiction film *Arrival* (2016), which features octopi-like aliens communicating symbolically through inky language-circles, which, to the historian of religions anyway, look a lot like the calligraphy of Japanese Zen artists expressing the Buddhist teaching of emptiness. Elizabeth saw the film shortly after it was released in Houston the week after we returned from Esalen. She was so moved by it that she insisted I go see it, and that we meet immediately.

It would take me almost a week to get away from my duties, but I would finally see it as well. I too was deeply moved by the film, if for somewhat different reasons. In a previous book, *Authors of the Impossible,* I had been critical of the fact that the only culturally relevant framework for extraterrestrial contact was a Cold War one, that is, the alien invasion trope. This, of course, implies that what an alien presence is about, what it can *only* be about, is a threat to national security or an invasion from outer space. Just *whose* violence and invasions are we really talking about here?

I begged my readers to reconsider this and to imagine contact from the perspective of an anthropologist or a historian of religions, that is, as a contact between different cultures, mind forms, and languages and all that this might mean for both cultures. I also invoked mystical literature, religious symbolism, and, above all, literary forms of interpretation as the proper modes of intercultural translation between such radically different forms of consciousness. In short, I begged for *translation and communication,* not more bombs and fighter jets and macho military bravado.

Really? You *really* think that will work?

What so delighted me about *Arrival* is that Hollywood finally got it right. This was no silly shoot-'em-up space western, with Will Smith punching out an alien or the Marines rescuing Los Angeles from ugly extraterrestrial monsters. The military was present in *Arrival,* of course, but it worked only *by not working,* that is, by holding back. The military, for once in such a movie, practiced wise restraint. And when the haters of our fake propaganda news (you know who I mean) inspired some soldiers to carry a bomb onto the floating alien craft, the result was not an open war, but once again restraint, this time on the part of the wise aliens.

Even more telling, it was not the physicist Ian Donnelly (played by Jeremy Renner) who provided the goods to save the day. Rather, it was Louise Banks (played by Amy Adams), the expert linguist, the academic who specialized in human language and the subtleties of interpretation. The (male) physicist-mathematician was there for support and occasional insight, yes, but his forms of knowledge were minor and more or less useless. Pretty much everything relied on the intuitions of the (female) linguist and her willingness to be vulnerable and physically exposed to the alien presence. She took a stance that was anything but aggressive, military, and male. She literally took her protective suit off to stand before the tentacled aliens and communicate with them visually, physically, and even, we imagine, spiritually. She took a stance of communion.

Once such a stance is established and operationalized, the narrative plays out through a series of communications that are at first misinterpreted but eventually read correctly. *It is not guns and bombs that save the world, but communion, communication, and, above all, paranormal interpretation.* The octopi-like aliens, for example, spin an inky circle that apparently means, "There is no time." At first, the human team thinks that this means, "You are out of time. It is too late." But this is not what the aliens are communicating. They mean something like, "There is no such thing as time. Time is an illusion." Or as they put it, "All is one."

If there is any unifying message of the world's mystical traditions, by the way, that is it.

They also communicated the messages, "Louise has the weapon" and "Use the weapon." Yikes. That is what they seemed to say, anyway. But what Louise Banks possesses is not a "weapon." Again, that is the wrong interpretation. Rather, what she has is a "gift." And misinterpreting this single word—"gift" as "weapon"—could spell disaster for the entire planet, since the phrase "Use the weapon" seems to imply: "Use your nuclear arsenal. We are threatening you." But this violent military reading is *all* wrong. This is not what the aliens are communicating with their Zen-like circles of emptiness and enlightenment. The gift, it turns out, is Louise's paranormal ability to see outside of time, and in particular to see the future. Louise is learning to think and cognize outside of linear time. She is learning to accept as a precious gift what feels like a terrible curse. It feels like a terrible curse because throughout the movie she is in fact precognizing the early death of her own precious daughter, not yet born, from a rare and incurable disease. Significantly, we as viewers, caught in our own (false) assumptions about linear time, assume that these scenes are flashbacks to the past. But she is remembering the future, not the past. We don't get it, until we do.

Another kind of circle.

And this, it turns out, is the reason the aliens have landed, to teach us about the illusion of time. This is the goal of their global "invasion." In three thousand years, they will need our help, so they are giving us help now.

It is not difficult to see why Elizabeth was so moved, really deeply shaken, by the film. The fictional aliens are teaching us what she can already factually do—perceive forward along the timeline. In this sense, the aliens are correct: "There is no time." Like Louise Banks, Elizabeth Krohn too was learning to accept as a gift what she thought was a curse. This was essentially Whitley's message to her at Esalen the week before: "You are precognizing the plane crashes to help the dying transition. Use your gift." Eerily, Elizabeth's gift is the same gift that the aliens of *Arrival* brought to earth—the gift of the knowledge that at least some of us, as embodied forms of consciousness united with the cosmos ("All is one"), are perfectly capable of knowing something of the future ("There is no time") and using this knowledge for the good.

GNOSTIC FILM

Such films raise the question of what exactly these alien forms of mind are communicating and how they are communicating it. A number of writers have noted how modern science fiction film has been playing with the themes of illusion and reality and how we might recognize the illusion and move toward the real. Such modern commentators have also observed how the modern movie theater is an especially apt ritual space with which to do this. Indeed, this modern space replicates in nearly every detail the layout and potential purpose of Plato's cave discussed earlier (okay, except for the chains). My Rice University colleague April DeConick has been particularly eloquent about this in her book *The Gnostic New Age: How a Countercultural Spirituality Revolutionized Religion from Antiquity to Today* (2016).

As the title signals, April is most concerned with "gnostic" forms of knowing and seeing. *Gnosis* is an ancient Greek word whose verbal root *gno-* is related to our own English root *kno-*, as in "knowing." The word refers to immediate or direct knowledge, usually of heavenly or extraterrestrial truths or—and this is really important—of the innate and natural divinity of the human soul. These are truths of ultimate or cosmic import that, being direct or immediate (rather than external or indirect), cannot be expressed in typical sensory or objective terms.

Gnosis is simply not the kind of knowledge that one can derive from the senses mediating a physical environment. It is not information. It is not data. You cannot Google it and "get" it. It is not about knowing that there is a tree over there, or that so-and-so was born on such-and-such a date. It is not a knowing *about* something. It is a kind of knowing *by becoming that which one knows.* As with the paranormal, the normal division between the subject of knowing and the object of knowing breaks down or dissolves, but in an even more radical way. Finally, gnosis is a kind of knowledge that releases one from the common consensus reality and ushers one into a fantastically new sense of reality. This is why it is so often connected to what we think of as religion (though it need not be).

If such a gnosis or direct knowing cannot be communicated by the senses and does not involve the knowledge of some object or event "out there," then how exactly can it be communicated? How can it be shown? Significantly, gnostic forms of knowledge have most often been expressed in two different genres: in nuanced philosophical discussion, and in elaborate visionary, mythical, or symbolic frameworks, which is to say: *through images and stories communicating ultimate truths or profound meanings.* Plato's cave, of course, is just such a story illustrating a profound philosophical idea. But if you read the ancient gnostic scriptures, composed in the first few centuries of the Common Era and now widely available in many translations, you will see that they do much the same. You will also see that they read very much like ancient science fiction stories. Read literally, they are kind of crazy. Read mythically or philosophically, they are sublime.

This is one reason why an author like April DeConick has argued that the stories and truths of the ancient gnostic Christians are best expressed today in two related forms of popular cultural expression: New Age revelation and science fiction film. She plays out this idea through careful readings of classic sci-fi films (*The Matrix, The Truman Show, Pleasantville, Pi, Avatar*, and so on) and careful comparisons with ancient gnostic material, demonstrating in the process how both genres—one modern, one ancient—attempt to communicate very similar truths about the fiction of the world we think we live in and the beauty and power of the world we actually live in but cannot normally know.

As social robots, we live in a virtual reality display coded by those dark archons who wish to feed on us and so would keep us trapped and ignorant of our own unlimited powers (*The Matrix*). The carefully ordered and conservative world of a 1950s sitcom might seem to be all "black and white," but if we tapped into our deepest sources of artistic creativity, reading, and sexual arousal, we could turn it all into a brilliant, colorful world of creative freedom and productive disorder (*Pleasantville*). And so on. It is in this way that DeConick explains what gnosis is, not by giving it to us directly (she cannot), but by showing us what it looks like, thinks like, feels like in different sci-fi films.

All of this is directly relevant here. Much of Elizabeth's account of her near-death experience and its effects on her life fits very comfortably in such a gnostic framework. As she repeatedly says and now writes here, she "just knew." And the things she "just knew" included the cosmic truths of immortality and reincarnation, which are classical, ancient gnostic motifs. Her understanding of the soul as being a "spark" of the eternal light of God is also perfectly gnostic (and kabbalistic). Also especially relevant here is the dramatic ways that her gnosis showed her how illusory and mistaken her former assumptions about the world were:

"How could I be *so* wrong? I was *so* wrong!" She had stepped out of the cave of the skull and seen the sun.

Even her precognitive nightmares express a deep resonance with the ancient gnostics and their communities. Those communities, after all, were fascinated by astrology and divination, that is, in the star maps for understanding their place and purpose in the cosmos and the rituals for predicting or shaping their own futures. Our own modern model of what the cosmos is and how it operates may have changed dramatically since then, but individuals continue to be concerned about their futures and continue to receive uncannily accurate signals from the same. The gnostics continue to live among us, like the magicians and mutants.

BUT HOW DID SHE KNOW
WHAT SHE "JUST KNEW"?

There are some very big questions wrapped up in such thoughts, such as: How did Elizabeth know what she "just knew" in the near-death state and in the subsequent paranormal cognitions? And, more complexly, how are we to think about and coordinate the obvious symbolic or imaginal components of what she knew (that is, her visions of the Garden, the mountains, the bench, and so on) and the empirical, objective, or historical nature of her subsequent precognitions (that is, the precise visual details of the actual plane crashes), which were also clearly mediated by some form of the imagination in her dreams? In what sense was she in a 3-D synesthetic movie of her (and our) own making? And in what sense was she also stepping out of that movie into some kind of transcendent hyperspace or superplace?

Two observations seem worth making here. The first is that Elizabeth's near-death experience and subsequent paranormal cognitions appear to employ the same sensory and cognitive capacities of the human brain and body that our normal everyday experience does. We are clearly talking about a spectrum of sensory capacities here, not an absolute break with the senses. Hence she "sees," "smells," and "hears" in the other world. The landscape itself, although clearly alien, is also recognizably earthly.

The second observation is that, although such states appear to draw on the same sensory and cognitive capacities, they are clearly playing by different rules than our ordinary perceptions and cognitions. They appear less bound, more free, and, above all, much more vast in their reach and capacity. It is as if the human organism and its ordinary faculties have been suddenly empowered by some unknown force or energy. It is as if Clark Kent has flicked off his glasses and suddenly turned into Superman. He *looks* the same (except for that red and blue suit), but he's not.

We know that our ordinary capacities are mediated and modulated by the immediate external environment, our senses, and, of course, the computer-like, on-off firing of the brain's neurons. Our ordinary perceptions and cognitions are also, I hasten to add, *limited* by that same neurological hardware, which, as we have seen, has evolved to pick up only a very thin slice of the electromagnetic environment, what we call visible "light," "heat," and "sound." That same hardware is also always insisting on some kind of either-or framework. Either something like a near-death experience is all literally true. Or it is all imagined, imaginary bullshit. It is all "objective," out there. Or it is all "subjective," in here.

That sort of thing.

Maybe we think like this because that is how the brain works: with on-off switches. But this, of course, does not mean that reality works that way. It only means our (left) brains normally do. If those brains have evolved to survive and reproduce, and they have, it also means that they are put together to pick up only what is necessary for such survival and reproduction, *which means that they are also put together to be blind, deaf, and dumb to everything else.*

It is difficult to avoid the obvious next step here: the brain is more of a filter or reducer of reality than a total perceiver. It keeps out far more than it lets in. But what would happen if this filtering mechanism were temporarily shut down? What would happen if a person were somehow to perceive reality without the normal cognitive functioning of such a brain, say, in the moment of a potential death? What then? Would the on-off switches and the either-or thinking still be active and in control? And if something did get through this temporary fissure or gap, how would such knowledge be communicated to the person in that experience and afterward in memory?

Again, whatever Elizabeth was seeing, smelling, and hearing in the Garden was deeply informed by the human sensory system, since "seeing," "smelling," and "hearing" are all sensory capacities. And yet these events also went well beyond the ordinary limits of these particular sensory capacities. Hence the colors she "sees" were like none she had ever seen, and she "hears" the voice not as an external set of sound waves but "telepathically," within herself. She also finds herself with capacities that she did not have in her normal life. For one thing, she can float in the parking lot and synagogue, and she "flies" to another realm, apparently by mere thought or desire. She also finds herself in a place that does not exist on Earth. It looks like another planet altogether, with multiple moons or orbiting planets. (Or, as my colleague Brian Ogren suggested after reading her descriptions of these spheres, these look more than a little like the three uppermost *sefirot* or spherical "emanations" of the *Ein-Sof* or "Infinite" of Kabbalah.) It is as if all of her senses and capacities were working, but in a supercharged way. She is still human, but she has also become superhuman. *Everything behaves exactly as if it were taking place in a science fiction film.*

We cannot know the precise neurological state of Elizabeth's brain during the few seconds she lay unconscious on the wet pavement in the rain. We cannot even say if she was clinically dead. But we can certainly observe that, in her own experience at least, she had indeed died. She went. We can also reasonably suggest that Elizabeth's time in the Garden was modulated by some other order of perception and contact. For one thing, although she was unconscious "here" for only a few minutes, in her experience "there" the event lasted two weeks! The temporal stream had expanded exponentially, as if "now" had exploded and opened out into some kind of pre-eternal Now. For another, her multiple experiences and conversations in the Garden were filled with content and claims that could not have possibly been a function of her eyes and ears soaking in the rain in the grease puddle for a few brief seconds.

So how did she do this? More precisely, with what organs of perception and cognition was she perceiving and knowing? Elizabeth herself does not answer these questions. Why should she? These are my questions, not hers. But her natural language and her memories give us clues about how we might answer those questions now, standing well after and outside her story. Consider, for example, Elizabeth's reflections on how "heaven" will appear differently to different people, and that this is why the near-death state appeared to her as a Garden (because she loves manicured gardens). Or consider her reflections on the absence of her wedding ring in the Garden (that it signaled or symbolized her future divorce). Or consider her conviction that, although the voice she conversed with sounded exactly like her grandfather's, it was probably no such thing. It was probably God speaking to her through her grandfather's voice. Or consider the magical bench in the Garden that takes the shape of whomever sits on it (just as the afterlife does, as it were).

Such lines strongly suggest that Elizabeth was perceiving and thinking through what we call the imagination, that is, through that organ of perception that uses images and symbols to communicate truths to us that cannot be captured in typical or ordinary ways. For example, Elizabeth's observation that the voice sounded like her grandfather's but probably was not carries a remarkable human-but-more-than-human sensibility: something, or someone, is communicating with her, but not in its own voice or appearance. Rather, this presence is translating itself into terms and images that Elizabeth is prepared to process and understand, but the presence itself remains behind the scenes, as it were, just off stage.[33] Actually, since this presence also knew information that only her grandfather would have known, it must have also "been" her grandfather in some sense. What this scene seems to imply is some kind of superpersonality that takes on different personas but is in fact "above" or "behind" all of our personal masks. "It" has access to us, but we do not have access to "It." We are the masks that It wears.

In any case, the conclusion seems obvious: whatever we finally make of the near-death experience and subsequent paranormal cognitions, they were clearly mediated by the human imagination, that is, by the same organ that gives us things like dream, science fiction, and oh, by the way, religion.

THREE WAYS TO THINK ABOUT THE IMAGINATION

Everything, of course, depends upon what we mean by that word: imagination. Most people use it without having the slightest idea what they actually mean. Or they think that the expression always means the same thing to everyone, when in fact different people mean very different things by it. To speak bluntly, colloquial English and, with it, conventional secular society, are pretty dumb here, as they recognize no such distinctions and collapse all imagined things into imaginary things, that is, into the realm of the nonreal. This is simply wrong.

To take the most obvious example, Elizabeth is perfectly aware that she has ordinary dreams, and that these are mediated by her imagination. She has no trouble classifying these as "imaginary." She is also perfectly aware that she has nightmarish precog dreams, and that these too are mediated, like all dreams, by the imagination. But these are anything but "imaginary." She insists that these two experiences of the imagination are fundamentally different: that the former is "just a dream," whereas the latter is hyperreal, that is, literally seeing into the near future. Clearly, we need a better language or way of expressing ourselves here.[34]

Allow me to suggest a way forward. I see three basic options, to which we might assign the following three descriptive names: literalist, hallucinatory, and translational. I am pretending no neutrality here. I think the first two models, *when taken alone,* are deeply problematic, and that the third, *always in conversation with the first two,* pushes closer to the truth without ever quite getting there. Let me reemphasize that I am speaking here as a scholar of comparative religion. This is *not* a traditional religious model of the imagination, and it is not fully compatible with traditional Jewish modes of interpretation, including kabbalistic ones.

Here, then, are the three proposed models:

1. A *literalist model of the imagination* is taken up and adopted, often unconsciously, by many best-selling near-death experience books and many conservative religious believers. This model assumes that what the visionary is seeing is really there in some kind of objective, one-to-one fashion. In other words, *the image or story is entirely objective—it perfectly represents what is really there.* If a visionary sees flowing streams and blooming trees, then there are flowing streams and blooming trees in heaven. If a child sees Jesus on a white horse, then Jesus lives in heaven and has a white horse. And so on.

   Simple fair comparison can easily reveal this position to be what it is: deeply problematic. The basic problem here is that different people see different things, even those raised in the same general religious environment or community.

Many people in the death process, moreover, see (or at least remember seeing) absolutely nothing, regardless of the intensity and sincerity of their beliefs. Again, there does not appear to be any reliable, clear, or stable relationship between the presence of belief and the likelihood of having a near-death experience. I know that is difficult for some to hear, but that is what the evidence suggests at this stage.

If we still want to insist on an exclusive literal reading of the religious imagination, we are forced into one of two options: (1) either we conclude that there are many objective and perfectly real afterlives that different people experience differently; or (2) we revert to the deeply dubious practice of declaring some near-death experiences "genuine" and others "not real," or, worse yet, "false" or "demonic" (as Raymond Moody's colleague did) so that we can preserve whatever exclusive literalist view of the afterlife we ourselves happen to hold (usually, because we were born into it). And there is where the religious intolerance begins. To press the point further, there are social, moral, and even political consequences of this exclusive literalist model of the religious imagination, and none of them are good.

There *are* ways to preserve the experienced literalness or hyperreality of revelation or extreme religious experiences like the near-death experience, however. I have offered one earlier (at the end of Chapter Nine) and will offer a few more thoughts below.

2. A *hallucinatory model of the imagination* says, "No. It is not like that. Everything that the visionary sees is being imagined, is being projected by a dying brain. What the person is seeing is a kind of completely subjective or internal movie (which

is why it looks like a science fiction film), which bears no relationship to any objective or self-existent afterlife or other world. In other words, *the image or story is entirely subjective—it bears no relationship to what is really there.* It is all 'in your head,' as we say. This is why everyone sees different things: everyone brings different things to the experience of death." In this model, a near-death experience might serve all sorts of important psychological functions, particularly around calming the person down as she or he dies so that she or he may not die, but there is nothing else to any of it. Near-death visions are like hyperrealistic dreams, and nothing more.

This second reading gives us a great deal, including an easy ability to explain why every near-death experience is different: because people bring different life experiences and shaping influences to the events. Its gifts should not be underestimated or set aside lightly. It can include and understand *all* forms of religious visionary experience but, please note, only at a great cost: it must declare them to be culturally relative hallucinations with no bearing on the afterlife or our place in the cosmos.

Cost or no cost, the basic problem with this model is that it contradicts the honest experiences of those who have known such a near-death event. Such people know quite well what a subjective hallucination feels and looks like. They have all dreamed. They also know that what they have experienced in and around death is not at all like such a dream. They may be wrong, of course, about this. Near-death experiences may be superrealistic dreams. Therein lies the crunch.

The same model, of course, also fails us completely in providing a model of how one can accurately dream the future,

that is, how the imagination might actually perceive something down the timeline. The only response here is that such
dreams do not happen or are pure coincidences. That seems
altogether too convenient. It feels like a cop-out or a failure of
nerve.

3. A *translational model of the imagination* combines and moves
beyond the literalist and hallucinatory models and replies:
"Well, of course, what the visionary is seeing is based on her or
his life experiences. Of course, the display is being projected
by the individual along the manner of a dream. How could
it be otherwise, given that the human being is a kind of filter
or medium of consciousness? How can the medium be anything other than a medium? None of this, however, excludes
the possibility that the display being projected may also be
functioning as a translation of truths that cannot otherwise be
spoken or seen. Nothing here excludes the possibility that the
movie being projected is being projected by a real projector,
or that the movie might actually *mean* something."

Here, the image or story is neither entirely objective and
exclusively true (as in the literalist model) nor entirely subjective and exclusively false (as in the hallucinatory model)—
rather, the visionary experience is what erupts "in between"
the subject and the object to effect contact, communication,
or communion. In some profound sense, it creates or brings
about that of which it speaks. It is "literally true" in the sense
that it is actually communicating or transmitting something
profoundly real to the experiencer.

We have seen this model at work already, of course, in my
discussion of the science fiction movie analogy—the light

might be very real, even if the show itself is not literally true. We might also add here now: and there might be real and important messages coming through the story on the screen. The movie might actually mean something.

In this third model, a near-death event is a very special moment in a human life when the imagination functions in very different ways, when it becomes supercharged and functions as a special organ of knowing that no on-off neuron can handle. The imagination here is not a literal sensory organ seeing something perfectly objective, but neither is it simply a projector of subjective fantasy. Words like "objective" and "subjective" or "true" and "false" cease to have much meaning here. The empowered imagination collapses or fuses these two realms in the "in-between," a both-and realm that can only appear to the subjective ego as a series of fantastic images and strange narratives or stories that is nevertheless somehow ultimately real.

And the bizarreness of the imagery and narratives is itself significant. Such strangeness cannot be reasoned or explained away, since the strangeness *is* part of the message. Put another way, what the imagination as alien translator is communicating can only be bizarre and paradoxical to the subjective ego "seeing" into this both-and realm, an ego that assumes that the world is about simple subjects interacting with simple objects that never mix or really meet, that an event like a near-death experience must be either "literally true" or "literally false."

The situation appears to be fundamentally different with phenomena like precognitive dreams, where there is a close one-to-one correspondence between what is seen and what will really happen in the external, physical, historical world. Here there is very little translation going on. It is more of a direct seeing into the future along the temporal stream. Even here, though, if one looks closely, one will often recognize mistakes and translations. One will see the imagination at work behind the literal scenes.

Although it is hardly perfect, and although it will offend both the exclusive literalist religious believer and the dogmatic materialist, I personally see few problems with this third "in-between" option. It preserves the felt "literally true" sense of the experience (since the light in and through which the visionary is experiencing is indeed real, and since the message might in fact be true in some sense), but it also recognizes the constructed or imagined nature of the visions (since what the visionary is seeing is indeed being constructed and imagined in the moment and relies on vast, unimaginable amounts of human labor and creativity in the historical past).

It is very important to note in this context that one need not treat these three models as mutually exclusive of one another, that is, as if only one was applicable to a particular religious experience or event. A translational model of the imagination, for example, would feel no need to declare everything about every near-death or religious experience "translational." Maybe some of it, or a great deal of it, is hallucinatory and simply a subjective projection of the person seeing it. As the ancient rabbinic saying had it: "Just as wheat cannot be without straw, so there can be no dream without nonsense."[35] The second model, in other words, remains perfectly active.

There might even be something "literalist" about a particular near-death or visionary experience. Experiencers do observe and report empirical or factual details in their out-of-body states, from conversations going on at the time in other rooms of the hospital to the presence of a loved one in the afterlife who was not known to have died recently but in fact had. Perhaps there is even something "literally true" or "really real" about the visionary landscapes that are seen and cocreated by the visionary consciousness, even if the shapes and sense of these landscapes are not universally applicable to all human beings and all times. Again, the Light may be really real, even if the particular shapes it projects and becomes for a moment are temporary and unnecessary.

From a historical and comparative perspective, however, there is no good reason to accept any *exclusively* literalist interpretation of a religious experience (as a literal and absolute truth for all human beings in all cultures and times), that is, the first model of the imagination taken alone. This is where my model definitely breaks with most religious models of revelation, including the kabbalistic ones that preserve a firm sense of the exclusive literal truth of scripture that the comparative study of religion would firmly reject.[36] Such claims are rejected because these exclusive literalist readings simply fall apart as implausible when they are compared fairly and humanely to other similar religious visions and scriptures in other climes and times. I do not know how else to say this: *comparison spells the end of any and all religious exclusive literalisms.*

What comparison does not negate is the very real possibility that some religious truths may be closer to the cosmic truth of things than others.[37] Religious beliefs *can* be philosophically assessed. For what it is worth, my own sense of things here is that mystical systems that emphasize unity or communion between humanity (all of it), the cosmos, and the divine are generally much closer to the truth of things than public belief systems that emphasize ethnic, religious, or cultural differences and their attending egos and conflicts. In the end, I believe that all of our differences are expressions of a deeper and more fundamental sameness, that it does not even make sense to speak of differences without assuming some sort of shared sameness. Of course, we are a long way from seeing that, much less realizing it in our social and political lives.

ON DREAMS, VISIONS, PROPHECY, AND THE SECRET POWERS OF INTERPRETATION

So, clearly, not everyone is going to see Jesus. Or Krishna. Or a Buddha. Or a Jewish panel of judges. Or anything else in particular. And all of these beliefs that we will or must see so-and-so or such-and-such are functions of an insufficiently nuanced understanding of the religious imagination and how it actually works.

So how does it actually work?

Allow me to dwell for a moment on an extremely sophisticated model of the religious imagination as it has been explored and explained by a contemporary Jewish intellectual. Elliot Wolfson has been an especially close conversation partner for decades now. His recent work on dreams and prophecy in the Jewish mystical tradition, *A Dream Interpreted Within a Dream* (2011), is particularly relevant here.

I have briefly referenced Elliot's work earlier in my discussion of the paranormal. Let me return to his thought here in more depth, as it speaks directly to what I am trying to say in my own way. I am also doing this, I confess, because I want the reader to know that none of my emphases on religion as "true fiction" and on the religious imagination as a translational medium are unique to me. I want the reader to know that these ideas are quite common positions in the study of religion (I am not speaking for or about the religions themselves), particularly in their more esoteric or "secret" forms that are virtually unknown outside the academy.

In the poetic language of Elliot Wolfson (who is also a poet and a painter), every image of the divine, every religious symbol or sign is a "veil" that reveals only by concealing that which is behind the veil, and conceals that which is behind the veil only to reveal it. This is the inescapable paradox of "seeing" a God who cannot be seen: "My face cannot be seen" (Exodus 33:23). In the words of Wolfson now, when it comes to religious revelation, "there is no access to truth but through the guise of untruth."[38] Here is what he calls "the paradoxical notion of fictional truth."[39] This is what I was trying to get at above when I wrote of "translation-distortion."

All of this might strike the reader as confusing. I hope so. If you think you understand religious experience, much less "God," you most certainly do not. And how, please tell me, could it be any other way in a tradition that holds that God is beyond any and all images *and* in which human beings need images to think of and relate to this same unspeakable "God"? How could such human beings *not* use images that cannot be literally true?

Nowhere is this paradox more obvious than in the realm of the dream-space, a psychic hyperspace that in the Jewish tradition is explicitly linked to the experiences of vision, scriptural interpretation, and prophecy. The latter notion of "prophecy" certainly entails seeing the future, but it is also much more than that, as the category of prophecy also names the highest form of consciousness a human being can attain, an altered state of consciousness or "state of prophecy" through which God communicates to human beings in divine speech and enigmatic symbols. "Prophecy" in the Jewish mystical tradition, in other words, encompasses *both* what we today call precognition *and* what we think of as religious revelation or scripture, and all of this is understood to be possible because of a fundamental transformation of human consciousness via trance, channeled speech, or mystical ecstasy. Or, we might add, near-death experience.

The most common and humble experience of such altered states is the dream, a kind of nocturnal visionary event that everyone knows well. The linkages between dream and prophecy are acknowledged everywhere in the biblical, rabbinic, and medieval mystical texts. The Torah itself recognizes these linkages, even if, taken as a whole now, it is also deeply ambivalent about *which* dreams and visions to trust. The texts of the Torah, after all, both repeatedly warn the Israelites against "false" prophets and dreamers but also unambiguously describe God appearing to his own prophets in dreams and visions.[40] Joseph is the paradigmatic interpreter of dreams, both in Genesis, the first book of the Bible, and in later Jewish lore. And Joseph foresees the future as much as he interprets dreams. Indeed, the famous biblical story makes no sense unless we assume the possibility of precognition through dream images.

And then, of course, there is the famous scene in Genesis in which Jacob dreams of a ladder reaching from the earth to the heavens with angels of God ascending and descending on it (Gen. 28:12). Note that there is no real distinction made in the latter story between a dream and a revelation. The same positive assessment of dreams and visions is also apparent in the coming age foretold by the prophet Joel, when "I will pour out my spirit on all flesh; your sons and daughters will prophesy; your old men shall dream dreams, and your young men shall see visions" (Joel 3:1). And on and on we could go, citing both scriptural anxieties about and affirmations of "dreams and visions."

The Torah uses different strategies to affirm and deny the content of such altered states, particularly when they claim to be about God. One of the more common strategies is to affirm their auditory dimension and to deny their visual components, that is, to affirm what *can be heard* as opposed to *what can be seen.* "The blessed holy One said, Even though I have concealed my countenance from them, 'I will speak to him in a dream'" (Num. 12:6). Or again: "The Lord spoke to you out of the fire; you heard the sound of words but perceived no shape—nothing but a voice" (Deut. 4:12).[41] This, of course, is also what we note in Elizabeth's near-death experience. She never "sees" God, but she does "hear" him. This is a very Jewish, and very biblical, feature of her near-death experience.

The rabbis who interpreted the Torah for the Jewish communities over the centuries recognized the fundamental ambivalence of the biblical texts around dreams and visions. Sometimes they resolved these apparent tensions by suggesting that dreams share in the same ultimate source of knowledge and revelation that prophecy does but do so on a much "lower" level. They alternately framed the dream as "one-sixtieth of prophecy," as a "minor kind of prophecy," or as "the unripe fruit of prophecy."[42]

When the rabbis spoke of dream as "one-sixtieth of prophecy," they were thinking of dream as a kind of radiation of God six gradations "below" or "after" the highest level of prophecy.[43] We need not get into all of the nuances of these systems. The important point is that this model *both* distinguishes dreams from prophecy but also *links* them as sharing in the same ultimate source. Again, exactly as we see in Elizabeth's precognitive "prophecies" that occurred in very special dreams that were not dreams.

The rabbis had other reasons for considering dreams as minor forms of prophecy, including the fact that they often thought of sleep as a kind of mini out-of-body or near-death experience, since the soul was believed to leave the body during sleep. This was, in fact, an extremely common notion in the ancient and medieval worlds. In numerous mystical traditions, for example, sleep is "a partial simulation of the separation of body and soul" that takes place at death. In the rabbinic tradition, this same cultural understanding is expressed in the teaching that "sleep is one-sixtieth of death."[44]

You get the point by now.

Dreams were also sometimes prophetic in the popular sense of foretelling the future. The rabbis were hardly alone here. It is a very ancient understanding that dream messages often function as forms of prognostication, that is, telling the future. This conviction (and no doubt this experience) appears to be universal and very, very old. To stick to what we think of as Western culture, we can see this notion as far back as we can see in Western literature, for example, in the Greek epic writer known as Homer (eighth to seventh centuries BCE), whose writings recognized that most dreams have no purpose, but that some are different, that some do in fact see the future and indeed accomplish that which they foresee.[45]

The rabbis had a particular theory about why dreams are special forms of consciousness that can do things we cannot otherwise do in our waking life. Theirs was a model that sits well with our present neuroanatomical understanding of the brain as "lateralized" or split into a right and left hemisphere, with the right dominated by our intuitive and image-based abilities and the left by our rational, logical, and mechanistic thinking. When a person sleeps, they observed, the intellect that makes distinctions, that is, the rational mind, "is removed, and all that remains is the imaginative faculty."[46] In the modern framework, the intuitive and image-making powers of the right brain take over when the linear logic and mechanistic thinking of the left brain fall asleep. In a more modern metaphor, the former comes online as the latter goes offline.

And what of Elliot Wolfson himself? His thought and work clearly participate in these same medieval and modern mystical streams of Jewish thought, even as they also push well beyond them. Wolfson's corpus is immense and nuanced beyond measure. I cannot possibly even begin to summarize it here. What I can do is observe one deep current that runs throughout those three decades of writing, namely, the conviction that in the Jewish esoteric sources there is no final difference or distinction between the revealed scriptural text, the Torah, and the interpretations of that Torah advanced by the medieval mystics who activated the Torah in their writing, rituals, visionary experiences, and even in their conjugal beds (since they connected the secrets of scriptural interpretation and the secrets of sexuality). In the world of Judaism and Kabbalah, interpretation *is* revelation. Revelation *is* interpretation.

A single example might help here. The Gospel of Thomas passage with which I began this chapter is a perfect case in point, since Jesus, after all, was a charismatic Jewish rabbi (and not a Christian, as so many falsely assume). The stakes of "interpretation" could not be higher with such a passage. Here the correct interpretation of the secret gospel results in immortality: "Whoever finds the meaning of these words will not taste death." Interpretation here, of course, has nothing to do with "thinking" or manipulating data in a computer-like brain. Such a revelatory meaning depends upon the reader *sharing in the same mystical state from which the secret sayings were first uttered.* Their uncovered meaning *is* that state of consciousness. That state of consciousness *is* their uncovered meaning.

I can hear Elizabeth saying something similar about this book and these passages. She would say that she knows that we do not die, and that she knows this because she has experienced it. Her conviction about our immortality flows from her state of consciousness, which she is now trying to share with us in her story and this book: "Whoever finds the meaning of these words will not taste death."

Part of this Jewish reverence for interpretation stems back to the traditional Jewish teaching that there are in fact *two* Torahs: the written Torah revealed to Moses on Mount Sinai, and the oral Torah spoken by the rabbinic sages and commentators that continues down into the present. Text and interpretation constitute a single whole in this vision—one cannot be artificially separated from the other. Revelation is interpretation. Interpretation is revelation. The same conviction is also carried by the remarkable histories of Jewish learning, which orbit around textual interpretation or Torah study. Such learning does not see the sacred scripture as possessing one meaning or one message, much less a single literal one. Rather, the Torah is seen to be infinitely meaningful and always capable of revealing new meanings for new readers and generations. The kabbalistic teacher Moshe Cordovero taught, in the words of the historian of Jewish mysticism Jonathan Garb now, that "each soul has its aspect in the Torah that cannot be revealed by another, that enable it to reveal secrets known only to God."[47] In one expression of this conviction, it is even said that there are as many Torahs as there are Jewish souls.

The implications of all this for our subject at hand are vast and deep. But we have been exploring them all along. This intimate connection between interpretation and revelation is what I was trying to get at earlier when I wrote about the paranormal potentials of reading and writing, that is, how deep reading can bring about in one's life, even in the physical world, what one is reading about—a kind of conjuring or, more simply, "magic." I intended to whisper something of the same soul-making secret again when I wrote about how we are changing the afterlife through our decades-long engagement with the near-death literature, or when I wrote that near-death visions are like 3-D movies that morph and mutate as we engage them.

I am employing metaphors, yet I intend none of this as mere metaphor. I mean to suggest that, on some profound, hidden, largely unconscious level, this is how the world actually works—the social world, the religious world, the physical world, *all* of it. I cannot speak for Wolfson, but he seems to suggest something similar when he invokes quantum physics as an apt analogy for what he is trying to get at. Listen: "We may assume that ... the 'hyperspace' of the dream ... changes with each effort to interpret it, whether to oneself or to another—in line with the part accorded in quantum physics to the observer in determining the properties of an observable object."[48]

What Wolfson is referring to here is a particularly bizarre but well-known phenomenon within one standard interpretation of quantum physics whereby the "wave function" of a quantum particle is said to "collapse" and takes on a material certainty as a particle only when it is measured or observed.[49] Before that measurement or observation, the wave function is a smear of possibilities. It is an entirely invisible probability wave. It remains "physical" in some sense (since it follows the mathematical principles of physics), but it is not "material" in any way that we think of that expression. For example, one cannot say where the quantum "particle" is. One can only say where it might be with differing degrees of certainty. It is, in effect, many places *all at once*. At the moment of the measurement or observation, however, the quantum particle finally "appears" and takes on a specific material concreteness in space and time. There are no longer possibilities. There is a single actuality now.

And so Wolfson can write: "In the quantum world, if you interact with a quantum system, inevitably, you are also changing it."[50] If dream phenomena are quantum phenomena (and many writers have speculated as much), the implication follows logically: "the very supposition that the dream can be separated … from its interpretation must be jettisoned."[51] Here the interpretation is standing in for the measurement or observation that, in effect, collapses the wave function of the dream.

Wolfson then goes further still and suggests that the quantum analogy is not just an analogy; that the dream (and, by extension, the religious vision) *may well be a quantum process itself.* He turns to the psychedelic bard Terence McKenna, who wrote that, "the major quantum mechanical phenomena that we all experience, aside from waking consciousness itself, are dreams and hallucinations." Still within the same quantum register, Wolfson also writes of "nonlocality" in the dream (very roughly, the notion that quantum processes are not determined by their location in space and time) and a full chapter on the "undoing of time." The latter poetic expression refers to the ways that in the dream, time can swerve or even bend back on itself. Such phenomena recall for Wolfson "the reversibility of time affirmed by some quantum physicists and the related notion of a retrocausative causality," that is, the notion that on the quantum level the future might actually influence the past.[52]

It is very difficult to read such lines and not think of the empirical precognitive nightmares of Elizabeth Krohn. If these are not expressions of time swerving and looping from the future back into the present that is past, what exactly are they? We can debate, of course, whether or not they are quantum processes. That is another question, and I certainly cannot answer it. What I do know is this. I know that the quantum theories render plausible and even understandable what was previously unthinkable, even outrageous. They make the impossible possible.

And then it gets weirder (if that is possible). Wolfson quotes another scholar, Philip Alexander, describing how in one ancient rabbinic understanding, "the outcome of a dream is determined by the interpretation that is put upon it: its fulfillment—whether for good or for ill—is somehow activated by interpretation."[53] In other words, a dream does not have one meaning or possible outcome. Its meaning will be determined by how it is interpreted by the intentions and skill of a human being in the future. Meaning arrives *from the future* (as we shall see in another chapter with another author). Like the Torah, a dream or vision is many things at once, and what it comes to mean in a particular mind at a particular place and time will depend on that soul "reading" it. To switch to a more secular metaphor, the interpreter holds the cards, not the dream, and these cards can be played in any number of ways.

Wolfson puts his own cards on the table here: "Interpretation is an apparatus through which events in time can be molded."[54] Put more simply (and impossibly), how we interpret a dream or a vision (or a near-death experience) in the present might well determine how it appeared in the past and, of course, how it plays out and what it comes to mean in the future. We can actually influence the past and the future and so "undo time" by engaging our own secret powers of interpretation. We can shape our own lives, and deaths, from the future.

Sound like science fiction?

My point exactly.

12

"I CAN SEE ALL OF YOUR AURAS RIGHT NOW"

Electromagnetism, Conscious Energy, and Spiritual Illumination

There is nothing anyone could say that would convince me that what I experienced was a twist of nature, an odd blip. I am convinced that it was an intentional act to help me understand the ways in which time, space, and energy interact.

—ELIZABETH

Obviously, Elizabeth's life after the lightning strike has been riveted with exceptional events and the dramatic appearance of new psychic capacities, many of which are clearly related to ancient religious lore and now contemporary sci-fi themes. Some of these strange events and new mutant abilities have also been connected to electromagnetic phenomena: the dramatic lightning strike itself first and foremost, of course, but also the perceived energy fields around human bodies and the odd behavior and content of modern technology (a ringing phone, the popping light bulbs, and the malfunctioning electronic devices).

"I can see all of your auras right now." That is what she told a group of us in Big Sur in November of 2016, as we met for a week to try to explore just these kinds of perceptions and "bodies of light." Elizabeth was being perfectly serious and matter-of-fact with such a statement. She was not claiming any superior spiritual state. Indeed, she repeatedly told us that she had no idea what the different bright colors mean or why our auras looked so different. She was simply reporting her own perceptions, as if she were watching the sun dip into the ocean and change the colors of the sky as it disappeared (we did that, too). She was simply reporting on the electromagnetic environment in which she lives and perceives. This environment is different than the one we perceive (or at least I do), but it may be different only in that she can see things that we cannot.

Or perhaps it is more complicated than that. Perhaps it is the case that what she is "seeing" is actually a *combination* of an empirical or objective fact (a living electromagnetic field) and a psychospiritual interpretation (a colored, flame-like aura). In this model, a perception of some actual electromagnetic presence is being registered by her sensory system and is then immediately, unconsciously translated into the image of auras around each of us. Perhaps what she is reporting, then, is a *relationship* between her psychoneurological system and the invisible electromagnetic ocean in which we all bob and swim. Another translation.

I don't really know. What I do know is that "energy" is everywhere for her; that she perceives this energy as living and conscious; and that it is attempting to communicate meaning to her through its intensity, behavior, and colors. What it signals is not at all clear, again. The only color of whose meaning Elizabeth is certain is black. You don't want a black aura. If your aura is black, you are very ill and probably about to die, as we saw with her story about seeing the black aura of a relative. You don't really die, of course, but that is another story—the story of this book.

But even the "black aura" scene suggests a symbolic dimension and the activity of the religious imagination, since there is nothing in the natural world about the color black that would signal death. That is a *cultural* association, not a natural or objective one (and not every culture associates black with negative meanings, much less with death). So even here Elizabeth's imagination is no doubt at work, translating for her in her vision the very accurate, even empirical meanings she is picking up and interpreting in the environment. For her, black means death, and so when she picks up the truth of a person's physical state as dire or near death, she "sees" a black aura around that person. This may be her way of registering an accurate psychical cognition in a culturally relative visual or symbolic form. Another translation.

Obviously, there are many questions embedded in such moments that need to be addressed at this juncture. I write "addressed" rather than "answered," as I do not think that we have any clear answers at this point in space and time, and we are certainly not going to arrive at them in the next few pages. I think the most productive things we can do are: first, simply stop denying that these things happen; and then, second, engage them honestly, fairly, and forthrightly with all of our intellectual resources. Once we do these two things, I suspect new, and better, questions will emerge to lead us forward to future answers.

THE HISTORY OF RELIGIONS AS A HISTORY OF LIVING LIGHT

One question that keeps emerging, for me anyway, is the question of why paranormal events so often get connected to various languages of energy, and whether this energy has anything to do with the particles, waves, and physical laws that physicists study and describe. "Enlightenment" or spiritual "illumination," after all, are not always simple metaphors. Nor, I doubt, was Elizabeth simply being metaphorical when she described a glowing form that she followed after the lightning strike.

She is hardly alone here. Conscious lights, glowing bodies, spheres of intelligent plasma, altered states of erotic energy, visionary photisms, and electromagnetic effects are the very stuff of the history of religions. But what, exactly, do we mean when we refer to these experiences as "energies" or "light"? Are we speaking of the physicist's photon that can be mathematically modeled, or perhaps some unknown place on the electromagnetic spectrum? Or something related, but different? Or something else entirely? When the folklorist and medical researcher David Hufford asked Genevieve W. Foster whether she could have read a newspaper by the light of her own mystical experience, when for days "the world was flooded with light," she answered simply, "No." And, yet, there *was* light—beautiful, knowing, beneficent Light.

We have thousands of other accounts of altered states of energy. Electromagnetic effects within paranormal events span a broad spectrum (and may actually be a spectrum). People have long reported glows or odd lights around particularly gifted or "holy" individuals. Greek Orthodox Christian theologians have long written of the "created" and "uncreated" energies of God that can transform human beings into saints. Contemporary near-death experiencers (like Elizabeth) and ufological contactees commonly report problems with electronics—they cannot wear watches, or computers malfunction in their presence. Electric lights flicker in poltergeist events. Similarly, streetlights go out (or on) in the presence of a whole class of experiencers known as SLIders (for Street Light Interference).[55] Apparitions of various sorts (including of the Virgin Mary in Catholic cultures and UFOs in more secular contexts) occur in areas of high geomagnetic and seismic activity. Television sets fritz out in spectral or ghostly encounters. UFOs routinely stall or stop anything operating with a battery or electrical system—cars, tractors, or fighter jet systems. UFOs are commonly seen over or around atomic research or nuclear missile sites, military installations, and power lines, as well as while traveling in cars (that is, while sitting inside a very powerful electrical field produced by the automobile engine). Encounters of different kinds, from the ufological to the traditionally religious, often involve reports of "humming" or "buzzing," as if magnetic or electronic fields are involved. I am thinking, for example, of the "divine speech" of Jain liberated souls, which are said to buzz when they "speak," or the "buzzing" heard around the 1917 apparitions of the Virgin Mary in Fatima, Portugal, which also, by the way, featured lightning that was seen by the visionaries but not always by others present (who did hear the buzzing and a certain thunderous "roaring," though).[56]

"Radioactive" saints transmit superintelligent energies into others by their mere presence or through some ritual touch. Glowing or burning forms, subsequently interpreted as deceased souls in purgatory, have appeared to baffled Catholic visionaries for centuries.[57] People levitate (and are seen levitating by others), which suggests that the gravitational field is being affected by some temporary fantastic energy. Similarly, tables, or in one famous case a person (Daniel Dunglas Home), would float in nineteenth-century séances, a phenomenon that was sometimes accompanied by a palpable drop in temperature in the room, which suggests some kind of transfer of energy. The Virgin of Zeitoun, interpreted as an apparition of the Virgin Mary of Christian lore, glowed on top of a Coptic church outside of Cairo like some occult hologram for *thirty months* in the late 1960s. It was photographed multiple times and even became an advertised tourist attraction![58]

Indeed, if there is any single universal in the history of humanity's religious experience, it is energy and light, or perhaps better, Light. Such a history is literally filled with instances of human beings getting zapped, illuminated by mysterious lightforms, and receiving revelations or messages from humanoid figures emerging from some kind of glow, radiance, or lightform. The classic experience of the apostle Paul, who was struck by a light and a voice on the road to Damascus as he traveled to persecute the followers of Jesus, is such a case (the effects of which were unspeakably vast in Western history). But we could come up with tens of thousands of similar examples, if only we simply chose to invest enough time and resources in locating, describing, and classifying them. Elizabeth's vision of a floating, guiding glow immediately after she was struck by lightning is simply one example of this same global pattern.

The language of light and energy is clearly not just metaphorical in these cases, then, even if many of these events are subsequently interpreted in various culturally specific ways and so come to shine through the prism of the human imagination. To return to the double nature of the paranormal, and indeed of so much religious expression: How do we make sense of *both* this very real light or energy *and* the obvious cultural refractions through which it shines and takes shape in the various publics? How do we acknowledge the symbolic nature of these events (that is, the way they are clearly designed to create and sustain very different worlds of meaning), but also the simple facts that they sometimes literally shock (or heal) bodies, levitate bodies, and stop electrical equipment? How do we account for *both* their real mental *and* material dimensions? And what exactly does "real" mean here?

STRUCK BY COMPARISON: LIGHTNING LORE FROM THE BIBLE TO THE AMERICAN PLAINS INDIANS

One initial and very basic way to better understand Elizabeth's experiences is to place them in a larger comparative context, that is, to look for cases like hers in other cultures and times. As it turns out, we find similar stories and similar people pretty much everywhere we look, if only we will look (and if we know where and how to look). Elizabeth is not the complete freak she thinks she is. She is a weirdo only in relationship to our present materialistic assumptions and conventional public culture. Once we compare her experiences to those of other times and climes, she becomes much more understandable, even if she never quite becomes "ordinary" or "normal." Indeed, once we make this comparative move, we can easily see that Elizabeth is in good company precisely by being extraordinary, special, or set apart from the ordinary lot of us dullards, Muggles, and nonmutants.

Take, as a simple and obvious example, the key presence of lightning in her story. One could go to the Jewish tradition here, and in particular the Torah, where storms and lightning are said to surround the presence of God as a kind of natural cloak or hiding. But I know of no major Jewish stories or traditions that describe lightning-struck people as religious prodigies. No doubt, there must be some somewhere (there is something somewhere in any longstanding tradition), but their rarity and relative absence are significant, I think.

This absence, of course, is precisely what one would expect in a monotheistic tradition like Judaism (or Christianity or Islam) in which "God" is finally transcendent to the natural order, and the natural order is entirely created and separate from God, that is, is *not* God. Such "struck stories" imply, after all, that there is something sacred about the natural world *itself,* that it is not just there for us to use, that nature itself is *intrinsically* sacred, alive, and intentional. It is this same monotheistic imagination, I suspect, that is behind the assumption that the energies and lights of mystical or visionary experience can having nothing to do with the photons and waves of physics. They must be entirely different things, since "God" and "nature" are entirely different things.

But are they? I am not so sure.

Tellingly, probably the most common biblical association with lightning is as a form of punishment or threat, itself based on a number of passages spread throughout the Bible, both Jewish and Christian now.[59] Hence the common sensibility that one will "be struck by lightning" if one offends God. This was no simple metaphor. When the lightning rod was first invented in Europe, in the late eighteenth century, it immediately became the object of intense religious concern and condemnation. For centuries, religious preachers had used the regular occasion of church steeples getting struck by lightning as apt moments to call their people to conversion and to repent from their sins. But now there were rods that could catch the divine punishment and disperse it harmlessly to the ground. The new invention was roundly condemned as blasphemous, as another example of human hubris and defiance of God.[60]

Lightning is commonly used in the Bible to signal the hiding of God's nature and to invoke the human response of awe, or as a sign of God's wrath and punishment, but never (or very rarely) the bestower of special powers or divinity. There are a few important exceptions, however, where lightning or lightning-like light signals divinity. A column of cloud by day and lightning by night guided the Hebrew people through the desert in Exodus. The shining body of the Son of Man in the Hebrew prophetic book of Daniel and that of the mysterious angel that announces Jesus's resurrection in the Gospel of Matthew are both described as lightning-like.[61]

As is the thunderous, UFO-like vehicle of God that Ezekiel witnesses and is "abducted" by in the first chapters of the book of Ezekiel. Later in the Jewish mystical tradition, this whatever-it-is in Ezekiel becomes the focus and goal of a rich history of mystical practice, all aimed at encountering and entering the "chariot" (merkabah) of God, although the vehicle's descriptions in Ezekiel render it anything but a simple chariot.[62] Perhaps most relevant here, the strange Hebrew word in Ezekiel, hashmal, that is used to describe the "shining metal," "amber" color, or "gleaming bronze" of the supercraft, remains deeply mysterious. Even more significantly for us, when the Torah was translated into Greek and Latin, this same Hebrew word was translated into Greek as elektron and into Latin as electrum and is now used in modern Hebrew for "electricity."

The history of this strange word is hardly exhausted there. Indeed, this same electric word, *hashmal,* was considered *so* mysterious and *so* holy that the Jewish tradition tells a story of a child who happened on the book of Ezekiel in his teacher's house. Literary historian and critic Michael Lieb tells us what happened next: "There, the child decided to read the opening chapter of the prophecy. Arriving at that point in which the text mentions *hashmal,* and apprehending its meaning, the child was suddenly consumed by the fires that surged forth from the mysterious phenomenon."[63] As the story goes on, the rabbis subsequently sought to suppress the study of this strangest of prophetic books and restrict its interpretation only to the properly prepared and most advanced readers. We are back to the paranormal powers of language, to the ability of a text to manifest or make real that which it is about, and the shocking, here literally deadly, potentials of interpretation.

For all of that, it is very doubtful that Exodus, Daniel, Matthew, or Ezekiel intended to communicate a sacred understanding of lightning *as lightning.* For such an understanding, we really have to go outside the monotheistic traditions (which the comparative method encourages us to do) and into the indigenous cultures of the Americas, where, interestingly enough, we can easily find virtually all of the different teachings and experiences that Elizabeth received in the Garden and reported afterward, including the reality of reincarnation, the importance of premonitional dreams, and the ability to visit the world of the dead, that is, the world of the ancestors.

Here, too, we can find different oral traditions in which a person is identified as sacred or special by virtue of a lightning strike. Consider what anthropologists call the *shaman,* a word derived from a Siberian language whose precise meaning has been lost but is now alternately translated as "knower," "holy man," "medium," "sorcerer," and "wizard." There is *no* single "shaman" or single cultural way of being a shaman. The word is used today as a broad comparative term to describe any sacred person with special powers and recognized as such by his or her community, particularly in the indigenous or tribal cultures of Africa, Australia, the Americas, and Australia.

What is significant for us here is the fact that the shaman is sometimes identified or "chosen" by a lightning strike. He or she has literally been touched or elected by the heavens. Sometimes, like some ancient superhero (think Shazam or the Flash, both of which display a lightning bolt on their chests), a lightning bolt is displayed on the shaman's ritual garb. In one case reported among the Sudanese of Africa, the individual was "dead" for two days; that is, he became a shaman through what we would today call a "near-death experience." In one Canadian indigenous culture in British Columbia, the spirit itself is believed to come down in "in the shape of a stroke of lightning." Another Eskimo shaman received his power when he was struck by a "ball of fire," perhaps ball lightning. Among the Yakut of northeastern Russia, it is believed that the shaman's ritual drum, with which he enters into trance, should be constructed from the wood of a tree struck by lightning. In another indigenous culture, those struck by lightning are believed to be able to fly up to the sky (perhaps in an event similar to our own "out-of-body experience").[64] Dreams, by the way, are also incredibly important in both the callings and the clairvoyant, healing, and precognitive practices of shamans.

According to Lee Irwin, a scholar of Native American religions, such lightning lore is especially prominent among the native peoples of the Plains, where huge thunderstorms with multicolored lightning are not uncommon, as anyone who has grown up in the Midwest knows well.[65] The general religious notion here is that a person hit by lightning has been chosen by the spirits and initiated by the Thunder Being, who is usually imagined as a great eagle who hides in the storm clouds and is rarely seen. His eyes are closed, but when he opens them, lightning flashes forth. Note here how the natural world is not a cloak of God or a sign of God's wrath but *is* an actual physical expression of divinity.

There are also a number of Native American stories about famous medicine people or religious prodigies whose spiritual paths were initiated when they were struck by a lightning bolt. The power surge is believed to give the individual special *wakan,* that is, sacred or mysterious powers. Such powers might include what we call clairvoyance and telepathy. It might also enable them to commune with the spirit world. Other powers include an ability to read impressions from material objects (what is known as "psychometry" in the parapsychological literature) and the ability to hear distant voices speaking in strange languages, called "spirit talk."

Interestingly, there is also a tradition of "thunder dreamers," that is, individuals who have been selected by the deity Thunder to enact a contrary or countercultural lifestyle. These are the Heyoka, the sacred and powerful but "upside down people" whose actions often challenge social norms and pretentions. Heyoka may also be gender switchers, taking on opposite gender roles for a period of time and then switching back again. From a broader comparative perspective, I should note that gender fluidity and transgenderism are common markers of sacrality or holiness in the world's religions, not a sign of sin or mental pathology.

Overall, we might say that those hit by lightning in the indigenous cultures of the Americas are regarded as honored by the spirits and treated with great respect. There is also some expectation that they will possess unusual powers and abilities that may take years to fully develop. These paranormal powers often eventually lead to the person taking on a new shamanic role as a sacred specialist who can talk to spirits and find lost objects or missing people. These are the "mediums" and "psychics" of the indigenous cultures.

It is important to understand in this context that most traditional native sources are clear that native people do *not* want to become Heyoka or Thunder medicine people. Profound life changes and new social obligations, after all, come with the role. Most difficult of all, these obligations often involve a calling to challenge the accepted social order. I mention this to reiterate my earlier point that locating Elizabeth's experiences in a broader comparative perspective does not normalize them or deny her confessed feelings of being "weird." It only makes these feelings and social experiences more understandable. It normalizes her, but not too much.

I also mention this because I have often heard people or read commentators wanting to claim that the paranormal is normal. No, it is not. Sorry. The whole point of a paranormal event or experience is to *not* be normal. It wants to catch our attention. It wants to be noticed and heard. And to do this it must stand out. It must appear as strange and out of the ordinary. Paranormal processes may, of course, end up having a "natural" explanation (whatever that means). I have even translated the paranormal as the "super natural." But I have also insisted on the "super" part. Again, that is the whole point. That is why these things happen in the first place. To normalize supernormal events, to remove the super-, is to fundamentally misunderstand them. It is also to erase and deny them yet again. So please don't do that.

To return to our indigenous American comparisons, it is not too difficult to see all sorts of other correspondences here with Elizabeth's experiences and her subsequent life, or, for that matter, those of any number of other individuals. Consider the enigmatic and tragic figure of Ted Owens, also affectionately known as the PK Man (the Psycho-Kinetic Man), who after a series of brain traumas and a dramatic UFO encounter in central Texas claimed to be able to direct lightning bolts (and hurricanes) at will.[66]

We do not need to land on any final verdict with respect to any of these remarkable lives and stories to recognize this: Elizabeth Krohn's experience of the lightning strike and its psychical aftermath may have taken on all sorts of clear and profound Jewish shapings (from the invisibility of God in the paradisiacal Garden to the synagogue locale of the strike to, as we shall see soon enough, the kabbalistic motifs of auras, reincarnation, and the spiritual pair), but it also exploded beyond any Jewish framework, really beyond any particular religious complex. Indeed, its original thunderous roar and its later more distant rumbles in her lifelong experiences have resonated almost perfectly with a more global lightning lore.

Once again, everything depends on the framework that we are thinking and imagining in, not just the facts themselves. Those facts mean little, or nothing at all, until we place them in a particular framework. And the bigger the framework, the more they mean.

SYNESTHESIA AND THE SENSING OF DIFFERENT REALITIES

There are other possible frameworks to consider with some of Elizabeth's phenomena. She herself has invoked the set of fantastic phenomena captured under the umbrella of synesthesia, a neurological gift that appears to run in her family and may have been awakened in her by the electric shock of the lightning strike. Thanks to the work of neuroscientists like Richard E. Cytowic and David M. Eagleman, we know quite a bit about synesthesia, even if we are very far from understanding it in any full way. Very briefly, synesthesia is the fairly common condition of "joint sensation" (*syn-esthesia*) within which sensory streams that are separated in other individuals are joined and combined in the synesthete. So a voice or a shape might be tasted; or a day of the week, a letter, or a number might be seen or sensed as a color; or a number might take on a three-dimensional form.[67]

There are many ways that the literature on synesthesia can help us understand and affirm Elizabeth's experiences. One of the most elementary and common kinds of synesthesia, after all, is that in which "subjects see colored outlines or auras around people and objects."[68] There is, in other words, a very strong scientific basis for affirming the reality of seeing auras. *The seeing of auras, it turns out, is a real thing.*

There is good evidence, moreover, to suggest that in some cases the colors of such auras are emotionally mediated; that is, the different colors are translations of emotional fields the percipient is picking up. Hence Elizabeth senses that her relative in the car next to her is close to death and sees a black aura around him. Most synesthetes do not have a reliable code for the colors. This is the case for Elizabeth. But some do. Marnie Loomis, for example, explains her own conscious translation code: "Instead of seeing a person as mad, sad, or sick, ... I see a person who is red, green, or black."[69] We might guess that there is a similar code at work in Elizabeth's perception of auras; she simply cannot read it.

Yet.

The literature on synesthesia can also help us with one other mystery of mystical literature—the key role that sexual arousal and orgasm appear to play in visionary experiences and altered states of consciousness. Synesthetes report a whole range of synesthetic experiences in and around orgasm. In their book, *Wednesday Is Indigo Blue: Discovering the Brain of Synesthesia* (2011), Cytowic and Eagleman quote a number of these: "brilliant flashes of colored lights"; "two dimensional, brightly colored shapes moving against a black background," like a black opal. One woman explained that "my favorite orgasms are brown, two-dimensional squares, which I know doesn't sound very exciting, but they are extremely pleasurable."[70] Another man reports intense libidinal arousal associated with specific tastes and food: "There are times when I am eating when I just want to push the table over and screw whoever is nearby."[71] The historian of religions would recognize in this last (somewhat humorous) moment an ancient symbolic connection reported and explored in numerous literatures: that between eating and sex (recall Adam and Eve, whose "eating of the fruit" made them realize they were naked, that is, made them realize their genitals).

It would be very easy to misinterpret all of this. Cytowic and Eagleman caution us against any easy conclusions here. They thus open their book with a philosophical bomb, that is, the basic idea that synesthesia is not just about sensing things differently. *It is about living in a different reality.* Put most simply, it is not simply a matter of synesthetes confusing an objective reality that the rest of us see, hear, feel, and taste correctly, as if we had everything right and they are mixing and messing it up. Not at all. They actually experience a different reality. *Reality itself changes as human beings neurologically engage it differently.* Reality, in short, is not "out there" in some kind of easy universal and objective way. Rather, reality is a combination or fusion of what is "out there" and what is "in here."

Sound familiar by now?

Think I am making this up? Think again. If you need a scientist to tell you a truth, here are two of them saying the same thing:

This fact brings us back to a central point—namely, that reality is much more subjective than most people suppose. Far from being objectively fixed "out there" in the physical world and passively received by the brain, reality is actively constructed by individual brains that uniquely filter what hits the outside senses.[72]

In short, we cocreate our realities. We do not experience a single objective reality "out there." This, of course, is very similar to my central point in the present book, namely, that this is how near-death experiences work as well—as super science-fiction movies that we cocreate individually and collectively, that live and shine in the in-between.

I suspect that synesthesia has played a major role in the history of religions, and especially in the hypercolorful literature of mystical vision and ecstatic states. My colleague Jonathan Garb, for example, tells me that in the context of Kabbalah or Jewish mysticism, the different sapphire-like dimensions of the Godhead (called *sefirot* in Hebrew, *sefirah* in the plural) are each assigned a color and a day and month. In other words, the mystical system looks synesthetic in the way it associates time and color. Jonathan told me that one famous Jewish mystic, Rabbi Moshe Cordovero, even encouraged his readers to match the color of their clothes to the appropriate *sefirah* or divine dimension of that particular day or month. This, of course, is highly reminiscent of Elizabeth's practice of assigning colors to the days of the week and wearing appropriate clothes on each. I would be very surprised if Cordovero was not a synesthete, like Elizabeth.

In a very similar vein, my colleague Brian Ogren explained that Elizabeth's son Jeremy's ability to "count letters" is very similar to how *gematria* or Jewish numerology works. The latter is a complex system in which each Hebrew letter is assigned a number, and so each Hebrew word adds up to a particular total number, which itself has meaning and can be associated with other words and meanings.

One cannot also but help wonder if the extraordinary colors and sensory "Wow!" of the Garden are not also somehow a function or expression of a synesthetic reality. This, too, would give such an experience a sense of being "more real" than our ordinary reality. Maybe it is. Maybe more sensory modes are activated and combined in such a fuller encounter with the real. Maybe our present sensory modes "split up" and separate what is in fact a single coherent electromagnetic world. Maybe the mutant synesthete actually has a *better* picture of the real than the rest of us Muggles.

FROM THE THEOLOGY OF ELECTRICITY TO THE PHYSICS OF CONSCIOUSNESS

Allow me to end this chapter on both a historical and a contemporary note. As we have seen above, and true to my theory of religion as a kind of practiced science fiction, Elizabeth often resonated deeply with different science fiction movies and books that we talked about over the two years that we worked toward this book. One of these, again, was Mircea Eliade's *Youth Without Youth*. I have written about this deep resonance elsewhere (including just above), but it is also worth exploring in a different direction here, as this new direction speaks to the deep connection between "energy" and "consciousness" so apparent in the near-death literature and so dramatically displayed in Elizabeth's lightning strike.[73]

The novel, recall, is about an aging Romanian intellectual named Dominic Matei who is about to commit suicide on the night of Easter when he is struck by lightning in a rainstorm behind a church while holding an umbrella. The strike initiates a whole series of profound paranormal transformations in Dominic while he recovers in a hospital. He can hear people's thoughts. He has dreams of the near future. He experiences the guiding presence of a spiritual double or guardian angel and becomes convinced of the reality of reincarnation. In short, he becomes Elizabeth Krohn.

What I did not tell you earlier is that toward the very end of this nonfiction fiction, Eliade reflects on Dominic's electrical transformation through various literary devices, specifically through the voices of various fictional figures. Dominic, for example, speaks about the "theology and demonology of electricity" and, again, about the "eschatology of electricity." Theology, demonology, and eschatology are all technical expressions from the comparative study of religion.

Theology is the discipline that seeks to intellectually determine or describe the nature of God. Demonology is a branch of theology that attempts to classify demons and their various appearances and habits. And eschatology is a branch of theology interested in understanding "last things" or ultimate ends or purposes, as in the end of the world or the death of an individual. With these phrases, then, Dominic (really

Eliade) is suggesting that there may be an electrical dimension to people's experiences of God and of demons; and that there might be a final
purpose or goal of electricity that is fundamentally religious or spiritual
in nature.

Dominic explains that he first heard the latter expression, the "eschatology of electricity," from the mouth of a young scholar he met at a
conference in 1964. It is always impossible to identify literary sources
with absolute certainty, but I am willing to bet that this is a clear allu-
sion to Ernst Benz (1907–1982), a German historian of religions whom
Eliade could have easily met about then and whose *Theologie der Elec-
trizität* (1970) or *The Theology of Electricity* was published just six years
before Eliade finished *Youth Without Youth* in Paris, in 1976. The timing
is perfect.

Benz's book is a little gold mine for those who wish to think beyond
the schizophrenia of our present "religion" and "science" wars. Indeed,
Benz calls our present cultural situation "a classical case of schizophrenia." It is so labeled because the divisions we draw with such words are
finally false and very destructive. Actually, they are pathological—crazy-
making. Why? Because "the experience of one and the same ultimate
reality that we are faced with as human beings determines our religious
as well as our scientific consciousness." In other words, religion and science are engaging the same reality, one through symbol and experience,
the other through mathematical modeling and experiment.

Or at least *they should be*. And they certainly once did. Indeed, what
Benz attempts to show is that when both electricity and magnetism were
first discovered in the seventeenth and eighteenth centuries, they ush-
ered in an entirely new way—an energetic way—of thinking about the
relationship of the soul and the body, of mind and matter, of "God" and
the natural world, and of various "electrical species," that is, apparitions,
angels, and so on. In effect, "electricity and magnetism became a new
symbol for God."[74]

This is not the place to get into a detailed description of Benz's history of the spiritual and occult dimensions of electricity and magnetism. We might simply recall here, as a single telling example, Mary Shelley's *Frankenstein* (1818), which equates lightning and electricity with a resurrecting but dangerous occult life force that can animate a corpse. Nor is this the place to discuss the astonishing healing career of Anton Mesmer (1734–1815), who worked with an invisible "animal magnetism" in the human body (he also thought of calling it "electricism") to affect astonishing cures and healings and whose followers did the same for decades before they were effectively shut down by official government commissions in France and the rise of the medical profession.

One simple observation about Benz's "theologies of electricity" will suffice. Before the discovery of these different forms of electromagnetic energy (we now know that electricity and magnetism are manifestations of the same physics), Western writers tended to think in terms that separated the supernatural and the natural. There was "spirit" or "God," and then there was "matter" or "creation." The natural and the supernatural were related (through the act of creation), but they were definitely separate and finally not the same. What the new languages of electricity and magnetism did was provide a third mode that could mediate these earlier natural and supernatural domains. Words like "energy" or human "magnetism" still named fundamentally mysterious processes or powers in the eighteenth and early nineteenth centuries—they signaled a both-and or in-between state. They were at once natural and supernatural. They could thus function symbolically.

And that was only the beginning. Indeed, eventually, with Einstein, we would learn that matter *is* energy, an energy whose nature became more and more mysterious as the decades ticked by (for example, the speed of light and its function in relativity theory). The same unifying trend would continue, and in the heart of physics itself. Consider the large quantum mystical literature, that is, that modern literature that draws explicit parallels or correspondences between the apparent philosophical implications of quantum physics and the paradoxical and unitive expressions of mystical literature. We saw a bit of this above with the work of Elliot Wolfson on the quantum nature of dreams. Mircea Eliade was also enthusiastically reading this literature before he died, in 1986.

Still, forays into this literature, however careful, are tricky at best and are often labeled dilettantish by physicists and philosophers of science, or worse. But such easy labels forget one simple historical fact: it was the founding quantum physicists themselves who encouraged this kind of thinking and who wrote books about the implications of quantum physics for the lay public. Many of them were also explicitly interested in mystical thought. In picking up this literature here, I am following those founding quantum physicists and not the contemporary naysayers.

In any case, one does not need to be a physicist to recognize what is at stake here, which is everything. Everything physical, after all, is composed of quantum particles and follows the "laws" of quantum mechanics, which are weird and wonderful beyond measure (literally, it turns out). One of the strangest features of quantum reality is this "beyond measure," that is, the already noted fact that, at least in some standard interpretations, quanta or particles cannot be said to exist in any definite or localized way until they are observed or measured. Before such an observation, a quantum particle can only be described mathematically and statistically as a probability, as a "quantum wave function." Put differently, a quantum particle is perfectly real, even perfectly mathematical, but there is nothing material or even "actual" about it. It possesses a potential existence, not an actual one. Numerous physicists have marveled at the apparent fact that this strange feature of quantum physics brings consciousness back into the heart of physics, since the wave function appears to require a conscious intervention to collapse and take on material or "particular" properties, that is, as a particle. It is as if material reality requires some kind of observation to appear at all.

It is tempting to imagine this weirdness as a function of our ignorance. "We just don't know where the particle is, but it's somewhere, goddamn it." But this does not appear to be the case: in this interpretation of the physics, this indeterminable feature of quantum reality—which, please note, means *the entire universe* on a quantum level—is in fact the way things really are down there, "where" there are actually no "things" at all. Moreover, and weirder still, not only does it look like this is the way reality works "down there." There is increasing evidence, in new fields like quantum biology and quantum computing, that these same quantum effects scale up to our world "up here." Historically, physicists and philosophers of science have protected themselves from quantum weirdness (and their obvious mystical and paranormal implications) by arguing that such effects wash out as we move from the subatomic realm to the molecular and biological levels, where the Newtonian physics of hard stable objects bouncing around in absolute space and time reigns. But it is now looking more and more like this is not always the case.

The possible implications of such thoughts for our thinking about energy and consciousness are immense, since we now have a form of energy (a quantum particle or wave function) that seems to involve consciousness in its most basic behavior. Few writers have carried these implications further than the political scientist Alex Wendt. In deep conversation with his brother, who is a physicist, Wendt has written a book on quantum physics and the social sciences in an impressive attempt to show how quantum effects likely "scale up" into the social world and help determine human behavior, human freedom, and human consciousness itself. Indeed, Wendt has argued that human beings are actual "walking wave functions," that is, that *consciousness itself is a quantum phenomenon.* He has also argued that we will misunderstand the nature of consciousness as long as we think of it in "Newtonian" terms, that is, in the ways that Newtonian physics understands hard physical objects interacting in three-dimensional space.[75]

Wendt wishes to push against the notion that he is simply being metaphorical when he writes of consciousness as a quantum wave function. He is not. He wishes to make a claim about the physics of consciousness and its fundamental relationship to all of reality. He thinks that quantum effects are manifested constantly within consciousness, that this in actual fact is what consciousness *is*. Which is to say: *who we are*. This, of course, would mean that consciousness is a kind of conscious energy or wave function, *literally*.

The entire distinction between "energy" and "consciousness" begins to dissolve here. As does the whole ancient problem of the relationship between "mind" and "matter." In this model, at least, the former "mind" follows quantum rules; the latter "matter" Newtonian rules. But both are natural features of the same physical world; they simply do what they do at different levels of that world.

And although Wendt does not go there (these are my sins, not his), one could also now make some sense of all of the "lights," "energies," and "illuminations" of mystical literature. These would no longer be simple metaphors. These would be actual descriptions of consciousness itself manifesting in especially intense quantum ways. Similar readings would now be possible for what we now call paranormal phenomena, which— if we just think about it for a few seconds—look more than a little like quantum effects scaled up into our experiential world.

I do not mean to hopelessly confuse things here, or open a Pandora's box (although I just did). I simply mean to observe that the early modern "theologies of electricity" that so fascinated Benz and Eliade continue to this very day in new and increasingly sophisticated forms. Bizarre phrases like the "physics of consciousness" or "conscious energy" are not at all impossible, it turns out. Neither are the knowing energies, conscious lightforms, and living auras of Elizabeth Krohn.

13

"I SEE TIME IN LAYERS"

How to Think about Precognition and Elizabeth's Dreams

Now he has departed from this strange world a little ahead of me. That means nothing. People like us, who believe in physics, know that the distinction between the past, present, and future is only a stubbornly persistent illusion.

—ALBERT EINSTEIN ON THE DEATH OF
HIS FRIEND MICHELE BESSO (1955)

The dreaming brain is simply feeling its future.

—ERIC WARGO, *TIME LOOPS*

Elizabeth's problem with watches may be more than simply electronic. It may also be symbolic. Many of her exceptional experiences, after all, clearly violate our ordinary experience of time, that is, the way we think of time on a watch face as faithfully ticking or spinning away in a regular, orderly fashion and from whose regular, straight-arrow direction we can never escape. By "dreaming the future," that is, entering an altered state of consciousness and cognizing events that have not yet happened (at least from our perspective in the present), Elizabeth in effect "breaks" our ordinary linear experience of time. She leaps forward into the future, or the future reaches back to her, or some part of her steps out of time altogether and scans the entire temporal landscape, as if she were in a balloon floating above ordinary history. Whatever is happening, time is no longer functioning like it usually does. It is "broken." And so her watch breaks to signal this. *Ordinary time stops.*

This again is a very old theme, and again it can be connected to technology, low or high. The lore around death is filled with various sorts of technologies "stopping" at the moment of death. In Europe, before the widespread use of clocks, candles would go out at the moment of death. This was very low-tech, for sure, and maybe it was sometimes just a breeze, but still—the symbolism is there, particularly since gradually melting candles also measured a kind of time. After the advent of clocks, things got a bit more dramatic: mechanical clocks would stop at the moment of death. The message here appears to be at least double. The stopped clock marks the precise time of death, but the stopping of the marking of time also honors the person's entrance into "no time," that is, into eternity. For this was how eternity was often imagined: not as endless time, but as a state outside of time altogether.

Another double message may well be at work in Elizabeth's case, since she did not begin dreaming the future and so transcending ordinary time until "after" the lightning strike and the altered temporal stream of the afterlife. It is as if her two-week experience "there" within a few minutes "here" somehow rendered her capable of experiencing temporal bending in her dreams, as if the "gravity" of that original near-death experience somehow warped the fabric of space-time in and around her sleeping brain so that information from the near future could flow backward and be cognized in the present. This is all speculation on my part. I am not exactly arguing this. But I am certainly leaning, really falling back, in this direction.

It also seems important in this context to note that the modern sense of time as completely homogenous, straight, inviolable, and empty of meaning is a very rare one in the history of human civilization and virtually unknown in the history of religions. Indeed, our modern "empty" sense of a strictly linear time may well be entirely unique. For most human cultures, time is not straight or inviolable, and in very special moments or in-breakings it can be pregnant with meaning. Time can also, as it were, flow backward, as has been assumed and commonly experienced for millennia now in countless divination practices (rituals designed to intuit or see the future), oracles, omens, and prophetic states all over the world.

Indeed, although intellectuals have yet to come to terms with the fact, there are few human practices more universal, more globally distributed, and more widely accepted (including and especially among the elites of these cultures) than those ritual technologies dedicated to divination and dream. It is tempting to brush this off as nothing more than "superstition," but such easy rationalizations cannot explain the global distribution or the historical commonality of the divination practices. It is almost certainly the case that such practices are so universal because different human cultures have found them extremely practical and helpful, that is, *because they work.*

To take one iconic example, the Greek philosophers and intellectuals who laid the foundations for Western thought, civilization, and modern empirical science did not seriously doubt the efficacy of prophecy, divination, and precognition. They recognized that human beings routinely know things that go far beyond any sensory datum or rational deduction. And they did not just accept this. They thought and wrote about it a great deal. As the classicist Peter Struck has recently demonstrated in rich detail, these foundational thinkers theorized this "surplus of knowledge," this "foresight in dreams," this "extra-sensory knowledge" in nuanced and very careful ways: as a part of human nature, as a function of the natural world, as something that happens spontaneously in dream or coincidence, as something that can be induced by the proper ritual technology (*techne*), as a special gift of the gods in a particular prodigy or trance specialist and, perhaps most famously, as a privileged way to "know yourself," as the two-word saying cut into the temple wall at Apollo's temple at Delphi had it (and still has it).[76]

Precognition or divination, then, was not some "woo-woo" to dismiss and make fun of in the ancient Greek world. Nor was it tangential to serious thinking and an adequate understanding of the natural world. It lay at the very root of human being and human knowledge. It lay at the root of us.

A PROVISO AND A PROPOSAL

There are more modern versions of the sense that time is not homogenous, that it can change its speed, nature, or even direction. These, of course, are generally devoid of any reference to the afterlife, eternity, or sensing the future, but they are nevertheless quite striking and well worth discussing here.

Before I begin to engage them, however, allow me to issue a very important proviso. It is this. The following discussion of time in contemporary neuroscience and physics should in no way be construed as an authoritative discussion of these sciences. If I were to claim such a professional mantle, you should be immediately suspicious. (Alternately, if a neuroscientist or a physicist claims to speak on the historical or philosophical nuances of religious experience, you should be immediately suspicious. I certainly am.)

I do not claim to speak for or about neuroscience or physics as sciences. My goals are much more humble but also, be forewarned, much more radical. My aim is to suggest that neuroscience and physics, with or without the permission of a particular scientist, can provide new intellectual frameworks and striking new images that allow us to "see" the historical data (that is, the reported anomalous experiences) as real and important aspects of the actual world in which we live. Put a bit differently, as I explained in my first pages, I am not after proof in what follows. I am after new plausibility structures. I am not after the facts. I am after a better framework to help us see and understand what is right in front of us but that we cannot yet see because we do not possess a sufficiently nuanced framework in which to fit them and so make some sense of them. We cannot admit that "burning rocks are falling from the sky," because we still lack a worldview in which that is thinkable, possible.

I also have a proposal. This is where it gets much more radical. I want to propose that scientists take anomalous experiences as signs or signals of where these sciences should go with their research agendas and theorizing about space, time, matter, energy, and mind. I want to suggest that the human being is the most sophisticated form of technology of any kind on the planet, *far* more sophisticated than any of the clunky machines this same human being has yet conceived and constructed, like the computer, the international space station, or the Large Hadron Collider underneath central Europe. Along these same lines, I want to suggest that human beings like Elizabeth can actually *experience* (and have long experienced) some of the realities that the formal scientific theories are just beginning to encode in their formal mathematical models, and that, if we are really serious about understanding the cosmos and consciousness, we should look first and foremost to these experiences and to these individuals. The sciences study and mathematically map the "outside" of reality. Mystical and paranormal events are experiences of the "inside" of reality. It is the same reality, though, and we will never really understand reality until we embrace both sides of the coin: the outside and the inside.

With such a proposal, please note, I am *not* suggesting that the mystical experiences are the same thing as the scientific experiments. They are not. Nor am I proposing that the mystical experiences somehow "prove" a particular scientific idea or proposal. Nor am I proposing that a particular scientific hypothesis "proves" a particular mystical worldview. I am suggesting that both the experiences and the experiments are engaging or expressing the same fundamental reality, and that we would do well to ponder both in respectful and constructive conversation.

THE GLASS-BLOCK UNIVERSE AND SELF-PRECOGNITION: THE WORK OF ERIC WARGO

I claim no originality with the suggestion that time might be a brain-created illusion and not an objective feature of the external cosmos. As the opening epigraph to this chapter makes clear, Albert Einstein thought the same, as do many physicists with whom I have interacted over the years. It is by no means an uncommon conviction among such professionals. Einstein famously described time as "a stubbornly persistent illusion." What is so interesting about this overused quote is that it is almost never quoted in full. The context is also usually removed: the death of the physicist's lifelong friend, Michele Besso. Einstein, it turns out, was not just speaking about time; he was also speaking about death.

Einstein also insisted on the "frameworks, not facts" principle that I introduced earlier and am pursuing again in this chapter. Here is how he put the situation: "Whether you can observe a thing or not depends on the theory which you use. It is the theory which decides what can be observed."[77] In short, if you lack a plausible model of something, you cannot see it, you cannot even recognize it, even if it is staring you right in the face, as it were (as psychical experiences have been doing for millennia).

One such theory that might well determine what we can see and recognize is something called the "block universe." The block universe is built on Einstein's theory of relativity. It is most often associated with Einstein's teacher, the Jewish German mathematician Hermann Minkowski, who demonstrated that space and time cannot be considered independently of one another, and that his most famous student's special theory of relativity could be figured geometrically as a four-dimensional object, sometimes referred to as "Minkowski space-time." The basic notion here is that space and time are woven together into a single field or medium. You have probably seen the artistic representations of the rubber-like "sheet" warped or stretched by large objects like planets and stars sitting "in" it. That's Minkowski space-time.

The same model possesses profound implications for how we think about time. In a block universe, the past, present, and future exist all at once, woven into a four-dimensional block of space-time. Some models have us "moving through" this block, like a spotlight moves across a dark room, to create the illusion of moving time. Other models have us "spread out" in time and space, like some kind of weird, four-dimensional worm or temporal snake. MIT professor Brad Skow, one proponent of the block universe model, described the theory this way: "If you could look down on the universe, you would see things spread out in time as you would see the universe spread out in space. You could see that things are one way at earlier times and different at later times, but you wouldn't say the universe as a whole is changing."[78]

I am especially intrigued by such a description, because it sounds eerily like what individuals sometimes report in a near-death experience or extreme religious experience, which is often exactly about "looking down on the universe" from some esoteric perspective outside of time and space.[79] Actually, it sounds *exactly* like that. Traditionally, we call such perspectives "transcendent." For most intellectuals, such transcendent experiences are not supposed to exist or be possible at all. Still, they are commonly reported and, if we are willing to imagine ourselves living inside a block universe, they are clearly not impossible. But neither, please note, would they be supernatural or outside of nature in such a universe; they would be entirely natural, or better "super natural" to our present historical linear perspectives. Perhaps this is why these experiences of the transcendence of time happen—forgive the expression—all the time.

Certainly such a block universe and its model of time jive exceptionally well with Elizabeth's simple metaphor for her precognitive dreams: a kind of slicing through an infinitely layered cake. The layers are all already there. One simply moves around in the layer cake with the knife. Indeed, when the string theory physicist Brian Greene describes the block universe and relativity theory, he actually uses the metaphor of a giant loaf of bread through which different actors at different points of space-time in the universe cut a "now" or "world-line" at different angles, depending on their movement and place in the space-time continuum.[80] The similarities in the two images are striking, to say the least. But how did a Houston mother and wife with no physics training or advanced mathematics arrive at the same conviction as a Columbia University theoretical physicist, mathematician, and string theorist?

Simple. She *experienced* it.

For a contemporary example of how the block universe can help us think about remarkable experiences like those of Elizabeth and so "make the impossible possible," consider the elegant blog of Eric Wargo, "The Nightshirt: Sightings, Portents, Forebodings, Suspicions," and his subsequent book *Time Loops*.[81] The subtitle of the blog signals the author's main interest: precognition or, put in the more technical language of quantum physics, *retrocausation,* that is, the notion that on a subatomic or quantum level causality might well move backward (retro-) in time, that is, from the future to the present or past. This quantum bizarreness in turn sometimes creates a phenomenon that Wargo calls "time loops."

Allow me to intervene here for a moment and explain both retro-causation and the time loop with a concrete example. I once wrote about an academic colleague of mine who wishes to remain anonymous.[82] After I gave a lecture on the paranormal at her university, she told me a most remarkable story about how she once sent her young son to visit a zoo with their nanny. After they left, at 10:06 A.M., she felt an impact in her body and "saw" in a kind of flash-picture her young son screaming in the car seat as the car filled up with a strange white smoke. She just knew that something terrible had happened.

Except that it had not. She called her nanny, learned that they were safe, and asked the nanny to drive back immediately on local slow roads. They got back safely. The next morning, the son wanted to go back to the zoo. The mother took no chances. She drove herself this time. On the way there, the mother and son were in a high-speed accident and crashed. The airbags released and filled the car with the white powder that coats airbags and helps them release quickly. After the car crashed, the mother looked back and saw, in the present now, the exact same scene that she had witnessed the morning before, like a "video rerun." A screaming son in a car seat and "white smoke." The man who had caused the accident came to her aid and called her husband. The call came in at around 10:08 A.M. Her earlier vision even had the time right, but twenty-four hours off.

There are two really interesting features of this story that concern us here. First, it dramatically demonstrates that what we call "clairvoyance" (seeing something at a distant point of space in the present) might easily be confused with an experience of "precognition" (that is, knowing about something before it happens). Note that this mother mistook the two phenomena and, by so doing, literally drove right into the accident: by trying to prevent the precognized event on day one, she ended up participating in the causal chain that produced it on day two. It seems difficult to avoid the conclusion that she was caught in what Wargo calls a time loop, with the events of the first day causing the events of the second day that in turn caused the events of the first day that in turn caused the events of the second day, and, well, you get the picture.

Loopy, right?

The second thing that is fascinating here is that, logically speaking, it is not possible to know which self or brain of the mother caused this particular vision. I mean, do we think that the mother on day one somehow "saw" what the mother was seeing on day two? Or do we think that the mother on day two "sent back" a signal to the mother on day one, perhaps as a kind of warning or hesitation that would prevent an even worse accident on day two? The former option would be a classical case of precognition. The latter option would be a near-perfect example of retrocausation. Logically speaking (since we are caught here in a logical loop), these two options are identical. We cannot choose between them with any degree of certainty. All we can do is make the honest but mind-bending observation that a very clear information flow occurred between the two mothers, on day one and on day two. In *which direction* that information flowed we cannot say. Hence the time loop.

Which brings me back to Eric Wargo. His central claim in "The Nightshirt" blog is that many paranormal events are in fact camouflaged or misrecognized forms of precognition, and that these work through retrocausal flows from the immediate or distant future back into the present. For Wargo, these retrocausal flows are entirely normal and are happening all the time, even though we seldom recognize them as such, for example in our nightly dreams, where they are disguised by all of the mental processes Freud mapped more than 100 years ago (free association, puns, displacement, condensation, reversal, symbolization, and so on). Wargo speculates that these retrocausal flows are the secret of evolution (that is, they are what make a biological organism so surprisingly "lucky" in a world otherwise ruled by chance and randomness) and occur in living organisms on some kind of deep quantum biological level. Wargo brings a stunning array of training to imagining this impossible possibility, from anthropology and neuroscience to Zen Buddhism and the history of science fiction. The implications of all of this for how we understand ourselves, history, psychology, much of religion, and— please note—the act and powers of interpretation (which, for Wargo, actually end up determining or guiding the past) are so profound that it is difficult to know where to begin, or end.

But let me try.

Wargo adopts Minkowski space-time as one of the secrets of understanding precognition, as the framework that makes visible the otherwise invisible retrocausal facts. He prefers to call this the glass-block universe. The universe here is a single object likened to a see-through glass block, which implies "that things in the past are still here, and that things that haven't happened yet are here already." Or again: "The considerable evidence of precognition (and more generally, retrocausation) points to the reality of something like the glass block, the already-ness of the future and the persistence of the past." The point here is not that we have conclusive proof of such a model of the universe. We do not. The point is that, in such a glass-block universe, we would not doubt precognition as logically impossible. Quite the opposite, we would expect it as entirely logical and entirely natural.

Significantly—and here comes the radical proposal again—Wargo does not just think the glass-block universe is an abstract theory for scientists to think about. He thinks we can actually *experience* the glass-block universe, and indeed, that many people already have reported on their realizations of the same, always of course in the cultural code of their place and time. Some of his favorite examples here are the masters of Chinese and Japanese Buddhism, who have known "a direct enlightenment experience of the glass block." Hence paradoxical Buddhist one-liners like this one: "Streams and rivers run into the ocean and yet there is no flowing." And then Wargo goes further and gets a bit personal: "I too have had these brief altered perceptions that 'nothing is really happening' even when things are visibly in flux in front of my eyes. I think there's real truth to what those guys were experiencing back on their misty Chinese mountainsides (and are still experiencing)."

So what does this have to do with Elizabeth's precog dreams and how we might think of them today? Well, quite a bit, actually. I can see at least three obvious takeaways for us in Wargo's writing on precognition and retrocausation: (1) the apparent evolutionary function of psychical capacities (hence all my mythical references to the mutant); (2) the "semiotic" (meaning making) or creative nature of paranormal events, that is, the way they seem to goad or push us toward our own creation of meaning (hence my refrain that "we are changing the afterlife"); and, perhaps most originally, (3) the nature of precognition as a cognition not of the event itself, which would make it clairvoyant, but of one's own brain cognizing itself in the future learning of this event through an ordinary physical channel, like a newspaper or online news report. Allow me to treat each of these in turn.

1. Evolution. First, there are the apparent evolutionary functions of psychical capacities like precognition. Something like precognition, be it conscious or unconscious, would carry immense survival benefits, of course. Just think about how useful it would be in avoiding danger or death on the battlefield, on an ancient hunt, or on a modern highway. I mean, really, what could be more useful in all of these real-life situations than the ability to "see" or intuit even just a few seconds into the future? Often, this would be literally lifesaving.

As a perfect cinematic example, I encourage the reader to watch the sci-fi film *Next* (2007), based on a short story by Philip K. Dick. The protagonist of the film is a Las Vegas magician and gambler named Cris Johnson, played by Nicolas Cage, who can see a few minutes into the future. Johnson makes a living by gambling, but he has to be careful not to be too successful lest he get recognized and caught. He gets noticed anyway, by the intelligence services of the U.S. government, which need his extraordinary ability to prevent a terrorist threat. They come after him, he thinks, to arrest him. He runs. The next scene, a chase through a casino lobby in which Johnson easily slips through dozens of secret agents like some invisible ninja (since he knows which direction each will look and when), is a powerful example of how just a few seconds of reliable precognition would make one basically invincible, and practically invisible, in these situations. Johnson will later learn that there is one way to magnify his powers in super ways: loving sex.

This is a Hollywood exaggeration, but it is an exaggeration of something that appears to be quite real on a much more humble level. There is in fact laboratory evidence pointing to a few-second version of precognitive ability in the work of researchers like Daryl Bem and Dean Radin, both of whom have also demonstrated a connection between these forms of "ESP" or "presentiment" and erotic stimulation.[83] This, of course, also makes good evolutionary sense, since erotic arousal is a classic evolutionary reward toward reproduction and survival. If precognition serves an evolutionary function, one would expect to find something like this. And, indeed, one does.

Wargo goes one step further with the laboratory research by engaging Benjamin Libet's famous research on volition or human agency. What Libet appears to have shown is that the decision to perform a manual act (say, the moving of a finger) actually occurs about one-fifth of a second *after* the finger moves. The conventional claim here is that our conscious sense of having free will is illusory, and that this false sense of agency is only an after-the-fact interpretation of something our bodies were in fact doing on their own and had already "decided" without us.[84]

Wargo flips this standard deterministic reading to suggest that, actually, what Libet's results might well show is that our true acting, deciding selves exist one-fifth of a second or so in the future and reach back to the body to manipulate and guide it, as if the body were some kind of Golem or meat puppet. In this thought experiment, *we actually live in the near-future,* where we already know the outcome of our actions and so can act in uncannily successful and "lucky" ways. In yet another provocative flash, Wargo suggests that this might explain the subtle but real altered sense of things one gets in moments of intuition, literary creativity, and athletic flow. Being "in the zone" is, in effect, acting from the near-future *and sensing this.*

In yet another moment of insight, still in this evolutionary current, Wargo links the survival advantage of acting from the slight future to a theme treated in these pages: the key role that trauma so often plays in paranormal events. Trauma, Wargo points out, is another word for survival: "Although psychical phenomena and ESP have always been linked to 'trauma,' this notion masks the fact that they really seem to key in on signals of survival: Implicitly, if you're traumatized, then you've survived. If psi, as precognition, is a biological function, it has to have emerged and prevailed as an adaptive trait, orienting the organism toward its own future survival/reproduction or that of its kin."[85]

Recall the earlier story of my correspondent and the ways that the strange event in the trenches allowed a particular genetic line to survive and pass on:

Then he heard a voice, a Greek voice, that he was sure was his father's voice. "Demetri, Demetri, get out of there."

My uncle shuffled down the communications trench to his platoon, which was filled with Greek immigrant boys, and asked them, "Have any of you guys been calling for me?"

"No, sergeant Moskhopoulos," they all said.

All this time, my uncle had been telling us this story with his eyes down, looking at his cards. Now he looked at us all and said, "When I started to go back a shell blew up the whole place where I'd been. After the war, when I went back to the family in Greece. I found out that day was the day my father died."

2. Meaning. Second, there are all the ways that paranormal events work through the communication and production of meaning. I know this sounds terribly abstract (what is more abstract than "meaning"?), but think of meaning as information or communication that is manifesting *between* two domains, much as we thought of the imagination as translation above. Please also note that meaning is not just involved in human speech, reading, and writing. It is also integral to how genes work. DNA carries what biologists have chosen to call "code." This code, composed of different combinations of just four "letters" (again, their chosen term), in turn instructs the cells to act in particular ways to build this or that feature of an organism. Genetics works through information and translation, then. It is also, of course, all about reproduction and survival. It is evolutionary. Which implies, of course, that evolution itself works through the transmission of "meaning."

   But there is also the sense in which human beings do not just receive meaningful information but also *create* it. We call this meaning-making "interpretation." I know that most people think of interpretation as finding something that is already there, but I trust that the reader realizes by now that this is not how this second kind of meaning actually works. As George Bernard Shaw is supposed to have put it, "Life isn't about finding yourself. Life is about creating yourself." That seems simple, even cute, but, again, the implications are vast, and they bear directly on paranormal events like precognition for Wargo, who argues that a future interpretation or meaning-making act actually causes or helps create the events in the past that are going to be interpreted as such! He turns everything upside down. We do not interpret past events that are already determined.

Meaning arrives from the future and guides the present and past events that will find their ends in the future interpretation or meaning.

Wargo commonly invokes science fiction concepts to explain this mind-boggling thought. Indeed, he turns to the same movie that so moved Elizabeth: *Arrival.* Wargo reads the movie as an uplifting film that gets it just right, that functions as "a brief and inspiring peek into a world where we realize that we are prophetic beings but just don't know it."[86]

When Wargo writes that we are prophetic beings without knowing it, he does not mean to say that we are called by some god to proclaim this or that local revelation. He means something much more universal, and much more significant. He means to say that we really can "see" or "feel" the future a few seconds, days, sometimes even years out, and that these acts of vision, intuition, and interpretation are all about helping us to adapt, survive, and create the future, which is in turn reaching back to us to create us. It is not, then, that we choose an arbitrary interpretation of a past event (or scripture), or that anything goes. Not at all. It is more that our future interpretations help determine what happens in the past. Time flows both ways. It's a circle, not a line. It's a loop.

Remember Elliot Wolfson?

For Wargo, then, the deepest message of *Arrival* is that "meaning always is something that *arrives from the future. We make* our lives meaningful, and renew those meanings in our actions; and our best and most creative insights seem to come from reaching into the Not Yet in obscure and subtle ways." Or, if you prefer, our best and most creative insights seem to come when the Not Yet reaches back to us in obscure and subtle ways. Again, it's a loop, not a line.

Perhaps not accidentally, Wargo sees the genre of film or the movie as the best metaphor for this meaning-making message: "It seems no accident that (as my wife pointed out when we saw *Arrival*) the heptapods' glass screen is the same dimensions as a movie screen, and the whole experience of the film is staged to express the idea that we are basically spectators of something."[87] There is the sci-fi movie metaphor again, in a sci-fi movie no less. It just goes round and round.

3. The Brain Precognizes Its Own Future. Thirdly and finally, there is Wargo's central claim that when a person precognizes a future event, what is really happening is that the brain is precognizing its own future cognition of learning of that event through some ordinary channel, say, a conversation or a piece of media. Here at least, clairvoyance (traditionally understood to be a kind of "leaving" the body or "traveling" to some other place and time to witness some event) is really precognition within the brain *of that brain's own future state.* Clairvoyance is precognition in disguise.

Wargo's writing on this subject orbits around one of the classics of parapsychological literature, J. W. Dunne's *An Experiment with Time* (1927). Dunne was an important early aviator inventor with a distinguished military career in World War I. Significantly, he was also an avid reader of Jules Verne, that is, of early science fiction. Dunne first honed his theory of time through his own precognitive dreams of historical events, including the eruption of Mont Pelée on the Caribbean island of Martinique. He eventually realized that these precognitive dreams were not of the event itself but of himself reading newspaper accounts of those events. He also had numerous dream precognitions about events that would play out in his own life (that is, in his own brain) in the near future or the next day, including one involving a stopped pocket watch (there is the stopped watch again) and another involving a crazed horse that escaped a fence.

Dunne was a trained engineer and had a skeptical mind. He did not just believe these things. He tested them. To test whether his precognitions were false memories, he began to scrupulously record his dreams (like Elizabeth). He concluded that these were genuine dream precognitions, even if they were often slightly distorted, like all dreams. "No, there was nothing unusual in any of these dreams as dreams. They were merely *displaced in time*."[88]

He called his theory of time Serialism. Wargo is worth quoting in full here as he explains the basic idea (I hope you are sitting down):

Dunne's dreams seemed to him evidence for what Einstein and other physicists and mathematicians were just beginning to assert: that since the present moment depends entirely on where you stand in relation to objects—what might be in the past for one observer may still be in the future for another observer, and vice versa—then the future must in some sense already exist.

Einstein's theory of relativity suggested time was a dimension like space; to help visualize this, his teacher, Hermann Minkowski, pictured "spacetime" as a four-dimensional block. Let's make it a *glass* block, so we can see what is happening inside it. Our lives, and the "life" of any single object or particle in the universe, is really a line—a "world line"—snaking spaghetti-like through that glass block. The solid three-dimensional "you" that you experience at any moment is really just a slice or cross section of a four-dimensional clump of spaghetti-like particles that started some decades ago as a zygote and gradually expanded in size by incorporating many more spaghetti-strand particles, and then, after several decades of coherence (as a literal "flying spaghetti monster") will dissipate into a multitude of little spaghetti particles going their separate ways after your death. (They will re-coalesce in different combinations with other spaghetti-strand particles to make other objects and other spaghetti beings, again and again and again, until the end of the universe.[89]) What we perceive at any given moment as the present state of affairs is just a narrow slice or cross-section of that block as our spaghetti-clump-bound-consciousness traverses our world-line from beginning to end.[90]

Working with this vision (minus the flying spaghetti monster), Dunne arrived at a classic mystical model of the Human as Two. Here is Wargo again, summarizing Dunne for us:

Precognitive dreams, Dunne argued, show that at night, as well as other times when the brain is in a relaxed state, our consciousness can wriggle free of the present moment and scan ahead (as well as behind) on our personal world-line, like a flashlight at night illuminating a spot on the path ahead. This ability to be both rooted mentally in our body, with its rich sensory "now," and the possibility of, as novelist Kurt Vonnegut would later put it, "coming unstuck in time," suggested to Dunne that human consciousness was dual: We possess an "individual mind" that adheres to the brain at any given time point; but we also are part of a larger, "Universal Mind," that transcends the now and the body. The Universal Mind is ultimately shared—a consciousness-in-common—that is equivalent to what has always been called "God." Universal Mind is immortal. The body-bound individual mind is, in some sense, a "child of God and Man."[91]

Dunne, then, arrived at a belief in God as a Universal Mind—a very high bar. But the data of his precognitive dreams, as Wargo points out with a graceful honesty, do not actually require such a belief, nor do they support it. These precognitive dreams, after all, were all examples of a body and brain precognizing its own future state, for example, while reading an account of a precognized event in a newspaper (note the paranormal role of reading again).

Wargo, then, wants to think about precognition as self-precognition, as Dunne did, but he is not a theist, as Dunne was. His bar is lower, in the sense that his model does not rely on any supernatural event, any transcendent Mind, or any soul leaving the body. For Wargo, those traditional religious understandings are understandable metaphors or visionary displays that are attempting to translate what is happening, but they are not what is actually happening. What is happening is that a human body-brain—"spread out" in time in the glass-block universe like some four-dimensional space-time worm (the three dimensions of space and the fourth dimension of time)—is communicating with itself, probably through quantum processes, that are moving from the future of that glass block universe back to the present or past. The space-time worm is simply communicating with itself through its own world-line, since it is literally and physically "spread out" along this same line.

Got that? Did you think that thinking about something like dreaming the future would be easy, that it would not violate your normal way of thinking and imagining? How could it be otherwise?

Let me try to explain the model a bit more. I think I can, since this is where Wargo allows me to see much more clearly what I earlier intuited but could not quite explain in any clear way. Early in my conversations with Elizabeth, I began to suspect that what she was often picking up in her dreams was not the plane crashes themselves, *but the future media events reporting the plane crashes.* After all, what she dreamt about the US Airways and TransAsia cases corresponded *perfectly* to the images that appeared in the media the next day.

She saw in her dreams, moreover, the exact same image that *she herself* would see on the television and internet the next day: the people standing on the wing of the US Airways plane floating in the Hudson River and the dramatic sidewise crash of the TransAsia Airways flight over the bay and highway. The same was true of her remembered precognition of the San Francisco earthquake of 1989. She did not see some random image of destruction and death. She saw a policeman looking into an immense crack in the concrete, more or less exactly as it would appear in the newspapers. These images are simply too specific to be coincidental.

The same model, note again, works beautifully for the Brazilian soccer team dream. The actual crash happened a few hours before Elizabeth dreamed of it in the middle of the night. Her instincts here were two: (a) that the dream was precognitive, but then (b) to discount it as such, since she learned the next day that the accident actually happened before the dream. Both of these instincts can be immediately affirmed in Wargo's model, however. Her dream was indeed precognitive, exactly as it felt to her, but not in the literal sense that she was thinking. She was precognizing her own future reading about the event, not the event itself.

Eric Wargo has convinced me. I think that this in fact *is* the case, and we are always, each of us, unconsciously sending our psychic tentacles into the near future to scope out the environment and help us negotiate what is about to be. We are remembering the future and, in the process, creating it within a constant series of time loops. Or maybe this is still all too time-bound. Maybe we are actually living, right now, in the near future, reaching back every second of every day to work our bodies like a biological puppet.

I know that is mind bending. Of course it is. We are used to thinking in straight, one-directional lines from the past to the present. We need to start thinking in circles from the future to the present and back to the future.

BACK TO THE PROPOSAL

Let me return to my proposal. Whether we are thinking in terms of an abstract formal description of the block universe of a philosopher of science or a physicist, as we have it in the work of Minkowski, Skow, and Greene, or an emergent theory of precognition as we have it in a gifted writer like Eric Wargo, we arrive at the same striking suggestion, namely, that *the future already exists.*

If this is true, it would, of course, render Elizabeth's precognitive dreams entirely plausible. They would no longer be impossible. They would be possible. We would not yet have a precise "how," of course, but at least we would have a framework that could render these experienced facts thinkable. We could accept what happened instead of invoking an endless series of denials and distraction devices.

The implications here—at once spiritual and scientific—are *vast*. Can human beings actually experience, directly and personally, features of reality mapped out by the advanced mathematics of modern physics but not normally accessible to our senses and brains? A figure like Einstein could *imagine* the structure of space-time as a four-dimensional, malleable "sheet," and he could establish this mathematically in a way that predicted the actual behavior of the cosmos, say, the light from a distant star "bending" around the sun as the latter warped the space-time field around itself. But Einstein never claimed to actually *experience* the universe as such, that is, to know it directly as such. He was a physicist, not a mystic. He was advancing an abstract theory or formal model, not a technique to experience the truth of the same.

But this is precisely what Wargo is claiming for both his Buddhist masters in China and for his own meditation experiences. He also proposes the glass-block universe as our best model to explain the universal phenomena of precognition, which he considers utterly normal and common. Elizabeth's precognitive dreams imply the present of the future as well, and her image of slicing through a layer cake is highly reminiscent of the block universe of the theoretical physicists.

Is this really possible? Can Einstein's thought experiments become actual human experiences? Einstein marveled at how human reason and its mathematics could rationally or intellectually comprehend the universe. Turns out it may be even weirder than that. Turns out that there may be depths to the human being that go far beyond even the mathematics and that may be able to *know* the universe as it really is before and beyond any scientific theory or mathematical formula. "I just knew." Turns out that Einstein's thought experiment or Brian Greene's cosmic loaf of bread might morph into an actual mystical experience of the same. Here to be enlightened is to know and experience the glass-block universe, where everything is always and already so, and where time flows inside the utter stillness of eternity.

14

"THEY WERE ALL PAIRED UP"

The Evolution of the Double Soul
and Its Angelic Destiny

We are told that when each person dies, the guardian spirit (daimon)
who was allotted to him in life proceeds to lead him to a certain
place, whence those who have been gathered there must, after having
been judged, proceed to the underworld with the guide who has been
appointed to lead them thither from there.

—PLATO'S *PHAEDO*

The transmigration of souls is no fable. I would it were, but
men and women are only half human.

—RALPH WALDO EMERSON

This last chapter is about last things. As I noted earlier, in the study of
religion, we call this branch of religious thinking "eschatology," from the
Greek adjective *eschaton* for "last" or "final." The word and notion carry
more than simply a place in a list or group, though. "Last" or "final" here

also mean the "end" of a thing, as both its final destiny and its ultimate purpose or meaning. So when scholars refer to a religion's eschatology, they are really speaking about the ultimate end, purpose, and meaning of human life in a particular religious tradition. They are referring to who or what we might yet become.

Most developed religious systems have multiple visions of such ends, be it the end of an individual human life or the end of the entire universe. "Heaven," "paradise," and "resurrection" constitute such eschatological visions (although there are countless versions of heaven, paradise, and resurrection in Jewish, Christian, and Islamic history), as does the coming "Messiah" or "Messianic age" (again, countless versions), "hell" (again, countless versions), "purgatory" (you get the picture by now), "judgment," "reincarnation," "enlightenment," "liberation," the "end of the world," and so on.

Elizabeth's near-death experience and the messages that emerged from those two weeks on the alien planet constitute their own eschatology. Much of this "end" or "purpose," however, needs to be drawn out or interpreted. Her visions do not constitute a systematic system in their own right. The meanings are largely implied or implicit. Such thinking is expressed mostly through images and story, not through any systematic thought, although Elizabeth freely and insightfully thinks out of her experiences and visions when asked a particular question. So much that I have to say in this chapter is my own interpretation or drawing out of what I think the images and stories of her visions imply, always, of course, in conversation with Elizabeth. I want to be clear about that (actually, I have tried very hard to be clear about everything).

BE AN ANGEL

I have grown more and more intrigued by the many spiritual pairs, doubles, twins, and doppelgängers of the history of religions (including the literature on telepathy between identical twins[92]). I was especially interested, then, when Elizabeth began talking about how everyone in the afterlife is paired up, and how the other half of the pair acts as a kind of guide both in this life and in the next. But I was also especially interested because I had been reading Charles Stang's *Our Divine Double* on the same theme in the ancient world of the Greek philosophers, the early Christians, and some ancient religious communities.[93] The shared details were remarkable and simply impossible to ignore.

The teaching of the divine double in Stang's analysis of the ancient world is complex and nuanced, but the basic idea is that the human self or ego ("you" and "me") is, in effect, a distant function or reflection of another form of human being that is transcendent, divine, and immortal. Different metaphors are used to get this idea across. The human being is said to be a "reflection" or "image" of this heavenly divine self, for example. Or the whole human system is likened to a giant tree growing upside down, with its roots in the heavens and its branches and leaves growing "down" into this world. Social and familial metaphors are also used. In the ancient sources, this other heavenly self is sometimes called our "angelic twin," spiritual "guide," or "companion."

Like all religious expressions and experiences, there are many ways to read such claims. One would be to understand this comparative pattern of the Other Self or Divine Double as so many local traces of individuals who have been given access to some other dimension or aspect of the human who never really descends completely into this world. To borrow Elizabeth's visionary language, this spiritual double is another dimension or aspect of us that remains "in the Garden." In the ancient sources, as in Elizabeth's visions again, such an angelic guide helps shepherd the little human self through a particular life cycle and then helps determine the next life cycle, that is, the next rebirth or reincarnation.

Stang is very careful here. It is not that we are "really" this Other Self and that our personal sense of self here and now is not real or unimportant. It is rather that we are *both* this named ego or individual person *and* this other Angel Self. In mythical language, each one of us is actually two of us. We are each a spiritual pair. The Human as Two.

It is probably relevant here that in the Bible God himself seems to have his own divine double, which is imagined in various forms, including under the mysterious figure of the "angel of the Lord."[94] I understand, of course, that the common understanding is that angels are not God, but this is not at all clear in numerous biblical texts, in the scholarship on those texts, or in people's contemporary experiences of angels, which continue apace right down to the present. Much too briefly, we could say that angels are intermediary or both-and figures at once human and divine. They thus express God's, and our own, twoness in particularly clear and dramatic ways. If I may express myself in my own poetic code, the angel sits somewhere in between the Human as Two and God as Two, linking and uniting all four, which are not really four but One.

Significantly, Jewish thinkers have often commonly linked both dream and prophecy to the presence of an angel. Two angelic species, for example, functioned in the Jewish philosopher Maimonides (1135–1204) as a way of speaking of the imagination and the intellect: "When man sleeps, his soul speaks to the angel, and the angel to the cherub. Thereby they have stated plainly to him who understands and cognizes intellectually that the imaginative faculty is likewise called an *angel* and that the intellect is called a *cherub*."[95]

As the above quote makes clear, often this "link between prophetic vision and the angelic presence" could become extremely nuanced. For example, among the Rhineland German Jews called "pietists" of the early modern period, the angel was sometimes understood to be a form of God that appears within a person's subjective experience but also "exists in a universe parallel to an individual's mind" as a kind of doubling, as a kind of mirrored reflection, much as we saw above with Stang's work on the Divine Double. In the words of Elliot Wolfson, "God's volition is communicated through an angelic presence that corresponds to a person's inner thought and its corresponding celestial angel (*sar mazzal*), which assumes the image of that person upon descending to the world."[96] This, of course, is uncannily close to Elizabeth's teachings on the angelic guide or mentor who accompanies us into the world and into the next.

Other scholars have noted similar forms of human-divine twoness throughout the history of religions. Andrei Orlov has very recently written an entire book on the "heavenly double" motif in ancient Jewish literature through figures like Enoch, Moses, and Jacob. He begins with the ancient seer Mani (from whose visions emerged the ancient religion of Manichaeism and whom Stang also treats). Mani's heavenly counterpart or spiritual partner first appeared to him at the age of twelve and continued to appear throughout the prophet's life. At the moment of his death, Mani was beholding this heavenly counterpart with "eyes of light." Orlov goes on to describe how such seers would acquire new "luminous bodies" on their celestial journeys and how, in the Jewish sources, these transformations and journeys were often mediated or guided by angelic presences, who would help the seer unite with his or her heavenly double or identity.[97]

Again, the comparative resonances are extremely precise. Although there is no way to establish this with certainty, I personally think that systems like those of the German Jewish pietists and Mani are based on out-of-body experiences and encounters with luminous beings similar to those of Elizabeth and the modern near-death experiencers. Or put differently, I think contemporary near-death experiencers are our own mystics and seers.

April DeConick, whose work on the "gnostic New Age" we looked at earlier, has also written about the Gospel of Thomas, a brief enigmatic text that many scholars think is as old, or older, than the four gospels that made it into the New Testament. Significantly, Thomas was known as the "twin" of Jesus. In this same context, DeConick writes about the guardian angel or twin as a Jewish version of a more ancient trope—that of the *daimon* or *genius* (both of which meant something like "guiding or inspiring spirit") of the Greeks and Romans.[98]

We could go on and on here, and through numerous cultures. Really, the motif of the heavenly double, companion, or twin is *everywhere* in the ancient world, and it continues to appear again and again in the Jewish mystical traditions of Kabbalah, in Iranian Islamic mysticism, and in various modern paranormal notions like the German doppelgänger or occult double. In the contemporary world, angelic visits and apparitions are even embraced by conservative Christian communities that would reject almost every other form of the paranormal. The angel is thus a mediating figure again, linking or connecting that which we otherwise want to separate.[99] The angel just never goes away, perhaps because, well, we never go away. We just keep coming back—as Two, it turns out.

As I listened to Elizabeth talk about the spiritual pairing that is so central to her near-death experience and subsequent convictions, I realized that what Elizabeth had "seen" in the Garden was too close to these historical sources to dismiss as coincidental or accidental, much less as some simple hallucination of her psyche or pure projection of her local culture. I realized, in short, that whatever set of experiences the ancient traditions were based on had been repeated in Houston, in the fall of 1988, in a Jewish woman mourning the loss of her beloved grandfather. I realized, to put it bluntly, that the theme of the spiritual pair is not a simple function of ancient culture and belief, and that it gives witness to something that is not simply historical. It is something that we can and do experience right here and right now. Charles Stang was correct to title his book *Our Divine Double* and not *Their Divine Double*. It is ours, too. It is us.

Both of us.

This is not some recent casual conclusion of mine. It lies at the core of all that I think and write. I have in fact captured and crystallized this same notion in multiple books since 2007. I call it the Human as Two. There are many aspects to this simple four-word poem that could be explained at this point. I will resist most of these, as I have done that elsewhere, and multiple times. But allow me to treat just a few of the historical precedents and spiritual implications of the Human as Two, as I think these, together, get at the very heart and final "end" of Elizabeth's fantastic experience and subsequent convictions. I begin with the "soul."

HOW MANY SOULS ARE YOU?

At the end of the day (and this book), what Elizabeth's visions and experiences are about is the soul: its double nature, its fantastic abilities to know things outside or before the ordinary senses, and its multiple futures both in the other world (via biological death) and in this one (via reincarnation). "Soul," to be sure, is an old-fashioned word, and one that has been on the defensive for some time. Indeed, most of modern science seems hell-bent on convincing us that there is no such thing.

And yet . . . and yet the soul returns, with a literal explosion in Elizabeth's case. What I find so very interesting about these modern cases is that, when the soul appears in the modern world, it often looks very much like it did in the past, that is, it often brings in its wake entire theological structures and specific convictions that find clear precedents in the history of religions, even when the subject has no training or knowledge of this history. This makes sense only if we can move out of the naive assumption or belief that human beings are completely defined by their present place in the temporal stream; that, to employ the technical speak of the humanities, we are entirely "historical" and "conditioned" agents. The historian's temptation here is to assume that this is so because a person like Elizabeth read this book or heard that teaching. In other words, the assumption is that we live in a purely materialist world in which ideas can only be passed on through material events, like reading books with our eyes and hearing things with our ears. Often, of course, this is the case. Sometimes it is not. The means of transmission are not always clear, and they seem to extend far beyond any simple "she read this" or "she saw that." History is just weirder than that. So are people.

April DeConick again has the balance exactly right with respect to the history of gnostic spirituality, whose heavenly ascents, divinization of the soul, and claims to direct salvific knowledge bear more than a passing resemblance to Elizabeth's "I just knew" experiences, as we have already seen. DeConick spends many pages explaining how gnostic ideas have been transmitted by specific texts throughout Western history, including in what she calls the "Trojan horses" of the Gospel of John and Paul's letters of the New Testament, which glow with radical gnostic ideas once read outside their usual policed orthodox interpretations. As we have already seen, DeConick also turns to science fiction and film as especially potent sites of gnostic ideas and their transmission. But then toward the very end of her book, DeConick turns to another transmitter of gnostic convictions and writes of

> another factor that most modern people are uncomfortable trying to explain, because it is irrational, but it has happened and still happens and will happen over and over again: rapture. The spontaneous religious experience. The sudden overwhelming revelation. The ecstatic encounter with transcendence, with ultimate reality, with the God Beyond All Gods.

And the result of such spontaneous ecstatic encounters? "The ecstatic experience of an all-encompassing transcendent reality, a source of being that is goodness and love, prompted many Gnostics to seek religious truth beyond their ancestral and regional religions."[100] To speak anachronistically, the gnostics were the original spiritual seekers, the ancient

New Agers or "spiritual but not religious" who sought God beyond any religion or culture.

We can debate whether or not Elizabeth should be described as such a gnostic. I think there are good reasons to affirm and qualify such a distinction. But that is not my point here. My point is that the ultimate sources of Elizabeth's experiences do not lie solely or exclusively in anything she read or heard in her own family and personal history. They lie in her ecstatic visions, transtemporal nightmares, and those key moments in which she "just knew."

And none of these ecstatic moments are simple or singular. In each, a kind of doubling takes place. There is an Other speaking to Elizabeth or showing her things. In her own experience, she is not the one generating the precognitive nightmare or projecting the visionary 3-D display. An Other is doing all of this. If we want to express this obvious fact more simply, we might say that there are many different forms of consciousness implied in Elizabeth's story. The soul here appears to possess many dimensions or, if you prefer, "levels" (although that doesn't sound quite right—it sounds too much like a department store in a mall).

In any case, I count at least four. There is Elizabeth Krohn whom I talk to in this world and know as a friend. That's one. There is the subtle body that floated just off the ground in the synagogue and sat on the bench in the heavenly garden for two weeks. That's two. There is the spiritual double or angelic guide in the Garden who appeared to be other or "not Elizabeth" but with whom, we learn, the soul must eventually merge. That's three. Finally, there is the glow on the other side of the mountains, the unseeable and unspeakable realm of the near-death vision that nevertheless functions as the final destiny and, we assume, ultimate nature of the soul. That's four.

Similarly, the Jewish kabbalistic tradition often identifies five different dimensions or levels of soul. There is the "body-soul" or animating principle of the human form (*nefesh*). There is "spirit" (*ruah*), the

Hebrew term commonly used in the Torah for the "spirit" of God, as well. There is the "true soul" (*neshama*). There is the "life force" (*haya*), which is usually taken to mean something like the divine life force and is understood to be that level of soul that achieves divine "attachment" or "cleaving" to God (*devekut*). And, finally, there is the "soul of the soul" or literally the "complete unity" (*yehida*), which is sometimes identified with the Godhead itself. As Moshe Cordovero put the matter most simply: "Man is a part of divinity above."[101] These are different systems, but it is not difficult to place Elizabeth's own story in them. One suspects—I do anyway—a common experiential background.

I recognize, of course, that many readers generally assume that there is only one soul, one person, one form of consciousness. But this is clearly not the case even in our ordinary experience. Consider dreaming. When you dream, who is it exactly that dreams? Okay, but then who is it that is telling you all those crazy stories each night? You again? So some aspect of you is telling some other aspect of you stories in your sleep? Tell me, which one is you? Both of them, of course. See what I mean?

And that's just dreaming. This doubling of human consciousness is even more extreme in reincarnation systems. Just which person are you if you are reincarnating through many lives as different persons? Something similar is true in ecstatic religious experiences, where the soul commonly doubles, triples, quadruples, sometimes even "becomes God." It looks very much like we split up like subatomic particles in some grand physics experiment, spinning off here, flashing off there, before we realize that we are a part of, well, *everything*.

TRAUMA AND REVELATION

But alas, such a splitting and uniting often require a great deal of violence. One of the most basic aspects of the human experience of soul is that, generally speaking, this realm of soul is not apparent or even accessible to the person unless the "container" of the body-ego is somehow broken, compromised, punctured, or temporarily taken offline. This is why so many of us have no experience of being Two, of being a public persona and a secret soul. We have not been sufficiently broken, pierced, or cracked open. Perhaps this is also why so many eschatologies, so many visions of the "end of the world," are so violent and destructive: to make something new, one must first destroy that which is old. An eschatology in this symbolic reading is a vision of human suffering writ large onto the cosmos, a vision that sees the breaking as a breaking open.[102]

People can be broken open, or just broken, in all sorts of ways. Such "little ends to the world" can happen, for example, in aesthetic, erotic, and psychedelic states. But probably the most common situations are those that we might gather under the general umbrella of trauma. Physical and/or emotional trauma, of course, normally does tremendous damage to the person. I do not wish to romanticize or idealize anything here. Many people struck by lightning are not changed in a flash. They are instantly killed. But it would simply be dishonest not to observe that in rare cases trauma can also open up an individual to other levels and dimensions of human being.

This is obviously the case in the near-death experience, which is nothing if not a traumatic event. By definition ("near-death"), are we not in the realm of physical trauma? Whatever psychospiritual mechanisms kick in to allow a near-death experience also appear to be functioning in many traumatic events. Among these mechanisms is what the psychiatric community calls "dissociation." To dissociate is to split into two (or more) personalities, usually in order to endure some unbearable situation. The person "splits" into two (yet another mode of the Human as Two) so that she or he can survive a particularly terrible situation, be it a car accident, an illness, extreme anxiety, political torture, a beating, a rape, or too many other horrible things that human beings routinely suffer. This, of course, is how the psychiatric community would generally read a near-death experience: as a massive hallucinatory dissociation. That explains something, but not much.

When I explained this "traumatic secret" to Elizabeth, it made immediate sense, and she quickly incorporated the idea into her own self-understanding. But I did not bring the subject up. She did. It is important to realize that Elizabeth basically *started* our conversations with the story of the childhood abuser. This was no tangential side story. This was the beginning of her story. Here is a snippet from our conversation about the same, where one can actually see Elizabeth take up my reading in a kind of "Aha!" moment. Recall that Elizabeth had been sexually abused by a male babysitter for six years, from the age of six to twelve, and that she had not told her parents about these horrors until much later. Listen:

> J: *Was [the early childhood sexual abuse] connected to the NDE in some way? Did you feel somehow that you had some kind of need to tell your parents after the NDE?*
>
> E: *Yeah, I did. It was within a year after the NDE that I felt like I had to tell them. And they honestly had no clue and felt really guilty about it. Because I had tried to drop hints when I was little, like, "I don't want him to babysit," "I hate him," "He's mean to Debbie," and so on.*
>
> J: *Yeah, the way a six-year-old would talk. As soon as you said something about your childhood and how good it was, my immediate unspoken guess was that there was something else, like this. And I think it's significant. I don't think we need to talk a lot about it now. Whitley [Strieber] is the same way.*
>
> E: *What do you mean?*
>
> J: *Well, he describes how he had some incredible trauma as a little boy on a military base in San Antonio. Apparently, his dad volunteered him for some kind of experiment on the base. Whatever they did*

to him was so bad that his immune system collapsed. He had to be hospitalized for weeks.

E: What did they do to him?

J: We don't know. He has no memory of it. But he thinks that his later visitor experiences were made possible by this early trauma. He does not think that they are the same, or that the early trauma "caused" the later abduction events. He thinks that what trauma does in some cases is "crack open" the psyche, as it were, so that it can "let in" these other kinds of experiences.

E: I can tell you that when I was being raped, I went somewhere. I didn't stick around and hover. I left. I would go walk on beaches. That was my thing. As a six-year-old, I would go to the beach.

J: You disassociated.

E: I totally was not there.

J: Yeah.

E: I couldn't be there.

J: Right.

E: So I think that when I had the NDE I was already accustomed to leaving. I knew how.

J: Right. See, that's the point. That's the observation that Whitley has made.

E: I never even thought about that until you brought it up.

Elizabeth went on to explain to me that she had always felt "different." She felt different "because of what he was doing to me." So when she had the near-death experience, her reaction was, and still is on one level: "Yep, there I go again just being weird. Of course this weird thing happened to me, because I'm weird." That is the "one big reason I never talked about it in public. That's why I kept it secret."

If I might translate here, one major reason that Elizabeth did not talk about the near-death experience in public was because she intuitively linked its strangeness with the weirdness of her earlier sexual trauma. She could not speak about the sexual trauma, so she could not speak about the near-death experience. They were linked. So here again we have a sexual secret become a spiritual secret. We also have a horrible trauma become revelation, a breaking become a breaking open.

THE EVOLUTION OF THE SOUL

Elizabeth speaks of the long cosmic process by which the human soul becomes its own double, becomes an angel, in two different vocabularies that have become historically linked in Western culture in the last century and a half. She speaks of "spiritual evolution" and of "reincarnation." Here we are in a situation not unlike the one above when we tried to relate the physics of the light encountered in mystical and near-death experiences and the various electromagnetic effects of paranormal events. There we addressed the rather shocking phrase: the "physics of consciousness." Here we address an equally shocking expression: the "evolution of the soul." Obviously, we are in the double structure of the paranormal again, that third language somewhere between and just beyond the languages of science and religion.

Do such ways of speaking make any sense at all? What does an expression like "spiritual evolution" have to do with the chromosomes and DNA of contemporary genetics? Is such a way of speaking and thinking simply a series of misplaced metaphors, a kind of fuzzy spiritual speak that is best ignored and left behind? Or are there genuine insights to be had here? These are big questions, obviously, and we are not going to answer them in any adequate way here. But we can at least raise them and honestly describe some of their complexities.

Again, I will lay my cards on the table. For my own part, I think that these ways of speaking and seeing are nothing more, and nothing less, than modern modes of acknowledging the profound connections that really do exist between those two realms of the human experience that are otherwise (falsely) separated in our thinking and speech—the spiritual and the sexual, the mystical and the erotic, the paranormal and procreation, mystical forms of consciousness and evolutionary biology. I understand that none of these expressions are precise, and that they are jarring when placed next to one another, as I have just intentionally done. That is my point.

These same jarring connections are particularly obvious in the manner that Elizabeth invokes the horrendous account of being raped as a young girl for six years. It was in these traumatic conditions, she tells us, that she learned "to leave," a psychospiritual skill that she again drew on when she was struck by lightning and had her all-loving near-death experience. She even speaks of the earlier dissociative skills as "saving" her in the lightning strike. They were, in a word, adaptive. So, clearly, there *is* a connection there between sexual trauma and spiritual tran-scendence, at least in Elizabeth's mind. I have found the same connec-tion between early sexual trauma and later adult mystical prodigies in other contexts, really in almost every literature in which I have looked.

As we have already noted above, these sex-to-spirit connections are again apparent in one of the major reasons that Elizabeth chose to come back from the afterlife: to have a daughter, which of course requires a sexual act and an entire invisible universe of genetic processes. There are profound sexual and genetic implications again in Elizabeth's obser-vations about what she once called in my presence her "weird, crazy family," an affectionate and not inaccurate descriptor of the four genera-tions of people whose lives have been consistently inspired and awed by a whole spectrum of uncanny events.

What *do* we do with the implicit genetic components of Elizabeth's family lore and the remarkable spiritual gifts that run through her gen-erations? The haunted necklace, the office plant gifted by the beloved grandfather that died on the day he died, the son who became an

Orthodox rabbi in the Chabad movement, the mother who believes in reincarnation and was radiated by a comforting light from the sky on a cruise ship, and the female ghost both mother and son saw in their home. There is no getting around it: this family has spiritual mojo.

There are similar genetic or evolutionary implications embedded in reincarnation systems, of course, although we seldom think of it in quite that way. Both reincarnation and evolution take a *lot* of sex to happen. Sex *is* the biological mechanism of rebirth. No sex, no reincarnation, no enlightenment, no release, no spiritual advance. But it's way sexier still. Just think about it. In a world defined by reincarnating souls, in some profound sense beyond any of our present temporary selves, everyone is always becoming everyone else, and so everyone is having sex with everyone else all the time everywhere. It's one big cosmic orgy.

I always think of a funny song when I read the reincarnation stories, be they traditional or contemporary. I think of a little ditty called "I'm My Own Grandpa," originally performed by Lonzo and Oscar in 1947. The song is sung by a young man who marries an older widow with a daughter, who then marries the young man's father, which makes the man's father also his son-in-law (since his stepdaughter just married him). The two families then begin to have children, which confuses all of the family relations further, until the singer eventually, somehow, becomes his own grandpa. I doubt a first-time listener can follow the familial complexity of the humor (I certainly didn't, and still cannot), and *that,* I am sure, is the point. But here is something I do understand: the same can happen in a reincarnation story, and in a much more clear fashion. A dead grandfather can really become a future grandson or granddaughter. It's *that* twisty.

If one wants to be rescued here from the sexual, gender, and familial rabbit hole you just fell into, I suppose one could think of all of these reincarnation stories as one long metaphysical meditation on human identity, a meditation with a single moral lesson: We are not who we think we are. Each of us, spread out over countless lives, is everyone else.

Just think about that.

COMPARING REINCARNATIONS

As you think about it, it is important to also understand that the meaning and experience of something like "reincarnation" shifts dramatically from culture to culture and time period to time period. Numerous cultures assume some kind of reincarnation process, and most of the models differ profoundly—the nature of the preexistence of the soul before it takes on a body; what spiritual or moral mechanisms determine the future birth; how long a temporal "gap" the soul waits between births; the nature of the intermediate world one encounters at death; whether this process is something to embrace or escape from; whether one can reincarnate as an animal, an insect, or a simpler life form still; and finally, what the point of it all might be. To put the matter bluntly, *reincarnation is not one thing*. Models of what it is and how it works are extremely diverse, and they are still morphing, still changing right in front of our eyes up to this very day.[103]

Such morphing models, then, are in no way restricted to the famous and ancient karma theories of the Asian religions, as is often assumed. Moreover, even the different Hindu and Buddhist traditions differ profoundly on key points, like the nature and permanence of the soul or self that reincarnates and the presumed goal or purpose of all of this living and dying. These beliefs and convictions also differ profoundly *within* the Hindu and Buddhist traditions themselves, which are not one thing either. To complicate things further, reincarnation belief systems are also apparent in ancient Greece, in early Christianity, in some of the mystical branches of Judaism, in numerous indigenous traditions of the Americas and Africa, and in an immense swath of twenty-first century individuals often collected under the rubric of the "spiritual but not reli-gious." And that, no doubt, is just the beginning. Really, reincarnation beliefs (and experiences) can be found pretty much anywhere we choose to look.

Seen in this broader historical and comparative perspective, Eliza-beth's insistence on the reality and centrality of reincarnation is not par-ticularly surprising. Actually, it makes very good historical and cultural sense, even in her own religious environment. Reincarnation is not at all foreign to the history of Judaism and is quite common in those mysti-cal schools within the Jewish traditions often gathered under the general umbrella of Kabbalah. Known as *gilgul* in Hebrew, reincarnation or trans-migration is a central teaching in some of these esoteric schools. It can be found as early as the ninth century and is widely discussed in the tra-dition, from the kabbalistic masters of the Italian Renaissance to modern mystical traditions like the Chabad-Lubavitch movement inspired by the remarkable "Rebbe," Rabbi Menachem M. Schneerson (1902–1994).[104]

There is nothing necessarily "non-Jewish" about reincarnation, then, although it is indeed an esoteric or undiscussed teaching within many mainline strands of Judaism today. I do not want to suggest that it is somehow common or required in Judaism. That is simply false. But nei-ther should we think that it is entirely foreign or out of place. If we want to stick to a historical and local framework (although I have no idea what a "local historical" framework might mean when reincarnating souls in many systems can effortlessly hop families, societies, continents, and even species), Elizabeth's own understanding of reincarnation could easily be traced back to Jewish kabbalistic and mystical roots.

Having said that, the present shape of reincarnation in her thought and experience probably owes as much to modern esoteric, Theosoph-ical, human potential, and New Age strands as it does to any medieval or modern kabbalistic ones, particularly in its embrace of "evolution-ary" language, which did not really appear until after Darwin, in the second half of the nineteenth century.[105] Having said that, it is even more important to keep in mind that nineteenth-century Theosophy (the real granddaddy, or grandmother, of the later New Age) was itself influenced by Jewish Kabbalah, and that the Hebrew term for "reincarnation" (*gilgul*) actually means "revolution," as in a "turning round," a meaning which, of course, is also embedded in the English "evolution," a "rolling out," and in the Sanskrit *samsara* (the "cycle of birth and death"). What we appear to have here is a kind of esoteric history of evolution before evolution, if you will.[106]

It is also crucial to understand that the modern revival and global renaissance of Kabbalah is in deep conversation with the same modern esoteric and New Age currents (including counterculture, trance techniques, and Asian religions), and that this revival of Kabbalah is taking place on a scale that is far greater than in any previous historical era, including the alleged "golden ages" of Kabbalah in the thirteenth and sixteenth centuries.[107] At no point in Jewish history has the Kabbalah enjoyed such widespread enthusiasm and attention. We may not yet have an adequate theory about why, but there is no getting around the fact that the New Age is often shaped by the Jewish tradition, and much of modern Jewish mysticism is shaped by the New Age. The two should not be facilely separated, then, but neither should they be equated or conflated. They are different, and they are connected.[108]

TAKING IT ALL IN: FROM NEAR-DEATH TO REINCARNATION

What to make of all of this, here at the end, not of the world or of a life, but of this little book? What follows are my thoughts—obviously speculative, but also entirely sincere.

One of the most basic questions that any eschatology must answer is what happens to us after we die. Respectfully setting aside the materialist answer for just a moment (that is, "Nothing happens"), there are two basic, seemingly competing models at work in the modern mystical literature: a one-life model and a multiple-life model. On one level, the question seems easy enough to phrase: "Do we live once, or do we live many times?" On another level, it is not at all so clear.

In the spring of 2016, I visited the Department of Perceptual Studies at the University of Virginia in Charlottesville. It was a visit long overdue. I have known and interacted with many of the faculty there for some time. Bruce Greyson is a psychiatrist, now retired from the university, who is the doyen of near-death studies in the United States. Bruce showed me an entire wall of files of near-death cases that he has been studying for decades now—about a thousand in all, give or take a hundred. One is marked "Elizabeth Krohn."

Jim Tucker is on the present faculty. He is a child psychiatrist who also specializes in studying CORT or Cases of the Reincarnation Type. These involve young children, usually between the ages of two and five (at the onset of language but just before full socialization), who claim to remember previous lives. The details can be eerily precise, and many can be corroborated with coroner reports and historical research. This research project, now in its seventh decade, was begun by the psychiatrist Ian Stevenson (1918–2007), also formerly of the University of Virginia. Jim showed me two walls of file cabinets of such cases—about 2,700 in all. And they are still collecting them.

The file cabinets on the near-death experiences and the file cabinets on the cases of the reincarnation type are not twenty feet apart. I mention this not to dwell inappropriately on office spaces but to make a very important point: the modern near-death experience and the phenomenon of past-life memories are clearly related *historically* (the same individuals have studied and written about them), *institutionally* (the University of Virginia has played an outsized role here, since both Bruce Greyson and Jim Tucker have been on the faculty and even Raymond

Moody, the coiner of the modern near-death experience, received his PhD in philosophy from the same university—what is in the water there?), and *conceptually* (since both forms of human experience suggest the postmortem survival of some aspect of the human person).

And once again, Elizabeth's experience fits in extremely well here: the file on her own near-death experience is just a few feet from the files of the reincarnation memories. One cannot help but sense that it is all somehow related. There are even files on precognitive dreams of plane crashes in the same archives.[109]

But all of this begs the questions: What *is* the relationship between the near-death experience and reported memories of a previous life among small children? How do we relate these two sets (or file cabinets) of human experience? Or, if you prefer, how do we keep them apart?

At the end of the day, these two literatures confront us with serious questions that individuals and cultures have struggled with for millennia. We are not likely to solve them in these last few pages. There appears to be a basic contradiction here, after all. In one set of stories (the near-death literature) we have what looks like a one-life model—we live once, we die once, we encounter some being or presence, and then we go "into the Light" or some other afterlife state or place. In the other set of stories (the past-life memory literature), we have an unabashed multiple-life model—at least some of us (an important qualification) live many times, die many times, and pass through some intermediate state from death to birth, hopefully toward some sort of enlightenment, release, or other unspecified end or goal. We usually associate the former with the monotheistic traditions (Judaism, Christianity, and Islam) and the latter with the Asian traditions (Hinduism, Buddhism, and Daoism). Elizabeth's story reminds us that this division is too easy and not always accurate.

What are we to make of this apparent dilemma or seeming contradiction? It seems to me that, again, we basically have three options here, each of which lines up with one of the models of the imagination explained above: the hallucinatory, the literalist, and the translational.

First, we can adopt a reductive explanation and argue that *all* of these experiences are fundamentally shaped (and so entirely bound) by culture. There is no real contradiction here, since there is no afterlife. The differences are all traceable to the differences of culture. This lines up perfectly with what we called the hallucinatory model of the imagination outlined above.

Certainly there is much to recommend such a view to us even within a Western historical frame, as Carol Zaleski's artful comparisons of near-death experiences in medieval Europe and modern America suggest. Medieval souls, for example, often reported seeing such Catholic realities as purgatory, saints, the Virgin Mary, and the punishments of hell, whereas modern ones tend to see more abstract white lights and loved ones and seldom emphasize postmortem punishment or intermediate states (like purgatory). But even here we must be careful, as Zaleski also points out, for there is also much that is similar between the medieval and the modern, including the life review and the powerful and positive aftereffects of the visions.[110] Zaleski's comparative balancing of similarity and difference within the Western narratives is admirable, but it does not yet resolve for us the cross-cultural problem, since she does not treat the reincarnation memory cases, which can be found in Asian as well as Western and numerous indigenous cultures around the world.

Second, we can adopt some literalist position and argue that one or the other of the models of the afterlife is the correct one, and that the others are false, heretical, diabolical, in error, and so forth. Many a monotheist (not all) will want to argue that the "true" afterlife is the single-life model defined by judgment and reward, whereas the Hindu, Buddhist, or Daoist will want to argue that the "true" afterlife is the multiple-life model defined by some form of karma or other similar moral mechanism. Even here we must be careful, though, as we can also find monotheistic traditions, like Sikhism or mystical forms of Judaism, that will combine reincarnation and judgment in different ways, and much of ancient Greek religious culture (presumably "Western") assumed reincarnation. In reality, there is no easy "West"/"East" or one-life/multiple-life division here. Nevertheless, the point remains solid enough: any such religious traditions will usually argue that its own model is the correct one, and that everyone else has it more or less wrong. This religious sensibility lines up well with the literalist model of the imagination outlined above.

Third, we can incorporate elements of both of these positions but reject their final conclusions. We can posit that reported experiences of the afterlife are often just that—experiences of a real afterlife—but that their specific content or visionary displays are clearly products of the cultural religious imagination. The religions are all in some sense correct, and they are all in some sense incorrect. None of them should be taken literally. The science fiction movie can always be written and directed in different ways. This, of course, lines up with the translational model of the imagination outlined above, as well as with my general thesis here that "we are changing the afterlife."

There is a further payoff here with this third model, since, once we adopt it, we might also begin to wonder whether there are certain "stages" or "levels" of the death process. We might wonder whether the further one gets into the death process, the less translation is necessary and the more the movie is absorbed back into the projecting Light.

An important figure like Robert Monroe, who helped bring into the English language the expression "out-of-body experience," otherwise known as the OBE (which bears close descriptive and historical connections to the near-death literature), is suggestive here. Having experimented with hundreds of out-of-body experiences during his own lifetime, Monroe believed that there were in fact stages in our spiritual journeys after death, and that in the early stages an individual could well dwell in a world shaped by whatever his or her religious beliefs happened to be. He called these "belief system territories." There were many *further* realms beyond these, whose complexities involved numerous teachings, such as a distinction between the "I Here" (the individual in this lifetime) and a cosmic continuum of personalities involving thousands of lifetimes that he called the "I Theres," as well as the existence of various intermediate realms and beings.[111]

We need not dwell on Monroe's system here. I am not asking you to sign your name to its details. That is not my point. My point is that we could well imagine a model of the afterlife that features something like his "belief system territories" early on in the death process, but that also displays features or realms that are less and less cultural and more and more universal the further one journeys "in" (or "out"). Culture and religion might eventually fall away and a person, any person, could experience the same afterlife realities as any other person (whatever a "person" or personal identity might mean in such a far-death state and its continuum of consciousness).

If we were to adopt such a stage theory, as a thought experiment if nothing else, this third option could rather easily coordinate the two afterlife models—that of one life and multiple lives. Such a model, after all, begins by observing that the modal Western near-death experience does not seem to be a full death experience. It is rather a *near*-death experience. The researchers are fairly consistent in their consensus that the person does not actually die in these events. He or she, after all, *always* comes back. Otherwise, we would have no story of a near-death experience. The past-life memories, on the other hand, clearly represent or at least claim to represent, a death that was complete and carried all the way through. There can be no rebirth without an actual death.

The easiest way to synthesize both the one-life and the multiple-life models, then, is to adopt an "Asian" model of reincarnation as the more complete one and assume that the "Western" near-death experiences are just that—*near*-death experiences, which, if carried through, would have led, in some cases at least (for there is no way to know if all souls reincarnate), to a next-life scenario, perhaps more or less similar to what we find reported or remembered in Asia but no longer bound to those particular cultural framings and assumptions (around karma, caste, purity and dietary codes, and so on). Those cultural framings, after all, are also culturally determined and local, and so relative. They are not absolute or universal.

This third option, please note, cuts both ways. It gives us something very powerful (a way of coordinating the afterlife experiments of different cultures), but it also takes away a great deal, including the primacy of the one-life model and the typical interpretations of the many-lives models that the Asian religions profess. If we choose to take up this thought experiment, we should not underestimate that gift *or* those costs.

There is another way to say this. We might want to insist on making sharp distinctions between ancient scriptures and modern identities in our social or religious lives (as if the past is somehow more holy or authoritative than the present, and as if the "they" of the past were not actually the "we" of the present), but whatever or whoever is writing the scripts and projecting the movies of extreme religious experiences like those of Elizabeth Krohn obviously cares little for such quibbles. It simply does what it does, and one of the things it does is combine and recombine ideas, traditions, and persons from the store of memory and culture (wherever that is). Again, *we* might want to draw distinctions, but *it* wants to link, compare, and (con)fuse. We might want to be stable and individual religious egos and pretend that we are all separate from one another, but it knows that all such egos are temporary and finally illusory, and that every little ego flows seamlessly into another from life to life, like one whirlpool or current flowing into another within a single giant ocean.

BEYOND THE MOUNTAINS

Again, I am speculating here. Please remember that. Please do not mis-read me as claiming that I somehow know this, or that I think that this must be the case. I am not saying that. Still, it is true, perfectly true, that I think these things, and that I find them plausible given the total wit-ness of the history of religions (as opposed to just this or that religion, community, or individual). I also honestly think that much of this spec-ulation on my part is already carried in Elizabeth's visionary experience in the afterlife.

Consider the visionary fact that everything she experienced was "in the Garden," which may have been on another planet but which also looked, smelled, and sounded just like the natural world of this earth, only more so. It was a deeply ecological vision of the afterlife. But it also encoded its own transcendence. The Garden was not the ultimate destination of the visionary landscape, after all. The other side of the mountains in the distance carried this particular symbolic function. The mountain path was the path that moved away from both near-death and a return to this life and toward some kind of ultimate truth or final tran-scendent state that was never actually given in the experience.

This all makes good sense in both a comparative or global and a local or Jewish context. Comparatively speaking, mountains have long functioned as a place of revelation and epiphany, as the place closest to the sky and so to the gods who dwell there (this, of course, presumes a naive version of transcendence as the third dimension in relationship to a flat, two-dimensional plane, that is, as "up"). So too in the Jewish tradition, God is most directly encountered in a burning bush by Moses on a mountain, Mount Sinai. If the Garden, then, carries a sacralization of the earth and the natural world, the mountains signal transcendence and a movement beyond the human toward God and, well, we do not know because we are not told.

It is in this way that Elizabeth's near-death experience can well be seen as an intuition of a kind of stage-theory of the afterlife. The dead see the movies of their own cultural myths and personal inclinations first "in the Garden" (or in whatever setting they choose to see) before they move on to some transcendent state beyond all of this "on the other side of the mountain." It is entirely possible that the latter transcendent or ultimate stage is universal, the same for us all, whereas the former near-death stage is always local and relative, unique to each of us.

◆ ◆ ◆

My central contention throughout these pages has been that we are changing the afterlife. In light of the above, I probably need to qualify this outrageous claim. I need to say that the afterlife we are changing is likely the near-afterlife, the imaginations that we die into and often return from. To speak in the mythical terms of Elizabeth's visionary landscape, I suspect that we can and do change the Garden, but not the glowing Presence on the other side of the mountains.

To switch metaphors and return to one of the central ideas of this second half of this book, the immediate afterlife as a supermovie, we might guess that it is somewhere "in the mountains" that the same pro-jecting movie turns back on its own Light and returns to the projector projecting it. The colorful scenes, characters, and special effects all "enter the Light." Maybe that turning around to the projector at the back of the room is more than a metaphor. Maybe it is closer to the truth than we think. Hence the famous tunnel image and the loving Light shining at its end. Maybe such souls are zooming "back" into the Projector, from which they were originally projected.

Elizabeth's visionary narrative thus encodes in mythical form both the movies of our religions and the Light behind them projecting it all. Hence the (Jewish) Garden and the (transcendent) Light beyond the mountains. As such, Elizabeth's visionary narrative encodes in ecologi-cal or geographic form what I have called the Human as Two.

And the Human as One. Please also note Elizabeth's convictions that, at some point, when the reincarnating soul is mature and awake enough, it realizes that its angelic companion *is also itself* (and this is a fine and accurate gloss on what the kabbalistic tradition calls the *yehida* or the fifth and highest level of the soul as "complete unity"[112]). It becomes one with its own divine double. At that point it then takes on a new cosmic purpose. It becomes a twin, companion, counterpart, double, or angel to *another* soul toward the same unifying end or eschatological purpose. Elizabeth does not say it, perhaps because she has not thought quite like this, but what this entire vision seems to suggest is that we are all one (remember *Arrival?*), that we become one another (or one another's double) again and again throughout countless lives, and that each of us is, has been, and will be everyone else's double before we finally become ourselves and enter the Light from which we all originally emanated or shone.

A FINAL TALE: THE FOUR RABBIS IN PARADISE

Probably the most famous instance of the garden motif in Jewish lore occurs in the second and third chapters of Genesis, the famous Adam and Eve story. But there are other gardens in the Jewish tradition. For example, the Song of Songs describes a "locked garden" (4:12), an image and even title that later kabbalistic traditions take up to name an esoteric space or realm that is not fully accessible to us here, much as Elizabeth describes her own experience of the Garden: "Many things about my visit to the Garden I now struggle to describe. They are simply not imaginable or thinkable. We simply cannot perceive the Garden 'where' and 'when' we are now. And so the words to describe them do not yet exist here. Maybe they never will. Perhaps they are not supposed to exist here."

I should add that the same Song of Songs tradition is infused with a deep mystical eroticism, of which both the Jewish and the Christian mystical traditions were keenly aware and engaged in a variety of symbolic and physiological ways. To take just one of numerous examples, a common metaphor for spiritual enlightenment in the Jewish mystical tradition is *hitorerut,* which literally means "awakening" or "arousal," which takes us straight back to the profound links between mystical awakening, reproduction, and an erotic evolutionary impulse.[113] We also find the garden in early Jewish commentaries on the Bible. Here we often encounter the term *pardes,* which is normally translated "paradise" but literally means "orchard" or "garden." The word is Persian in origin (yet another little sign of how misguided it is to separate cultures and religions or to imagine them as unconnected or incomparable).

As such a Persian "paradise" suggests, the garden or orchard was an ancient Middle Eastern trope that was likely in place for centuries, if not millennia, before the arrival of monotheism and Judaism on the scene. Kings built gardens. Gardens were the place of royalty, wealth, power, pleasure, and privilege. Perhaps these allusions to the power and privilege of kings are reasons gardens were also considered dangerous in Jewish lore. Consider the Garden of Eden—things didn't exactly work out very well there for the lovely couple.

Another garden story that emphasizes danger is the Jewish story of the four rabbis who went to *pardes.* The story is ancient, dating back at least to the first century, and probably before that. It is considered an *aggadah,* which we might translate as "instructive legend" or "sacred story." Another form of religion as "true fiction" or "fictional truth." There are many versions of the story, but all involve four rabbis who went to paradise. The first looked and died. The second looked and went mad. The third "destroyed the plants" (a metaphor, in some readings, for becoming a heretic or losing the correct faith[114]). Only the fourth entered and left paradise "in peace."

I do not want to get into the specifics of the ancient, medieval, and modern interpretations of this story. These historical complexities are not my concern here. I want to do something else. I want to advance my own interpretation. I want to suggest that it does not seem too much of a stretch to engage this story as a commentary on ancient and modern near-death experiences, that is, on the garden of paradise and its potential dangers and gifts.

I hope you, oh reader, have not looked and died, or looked and gone mad. But I certainly have not sought to leave you "in peace" either, that is, unmoved or content in your particular movie we call a self or a religion. And I am not the least bit concerned if you have become a "heretic," not because I am not concerned about you, but because I do not believe in heretics. To label someone a "heretic," after all, one must assume a single correct faith from which this person has somehow strayed, an exclusive, universal way of imagining and entering paradise. I have no such single correct faith for one simple reason: because there is none.

Perhaps you understand that now. Perhaps you do not. Either way, if this little book has moved you in any way, I hope that it has shocked you into the realization that, although paradise and an afterlife there almost certainly are, there is no such single or correct way to get there, no one vision or experience of that paradise and afterlife, no singular movie or imagination into which we die for a time. These are countless forms of paradise and the afterlife, just as there are countless forms of human beings and cultural imaginations. And all of these, individually and collectively, are changing paradise itself each day, little by little, death by death, near-death by near-death, book by book. As fantastic and unbelievable as it might sound, we are all, together, really and truly changing the afterlife.

POSTSCRIPT

"You Were There Too":
How Elizabeth Finally Dreamed This Book

Elizabeth did not just get struck by lightning, talk to God, and come back to dream the future. She also came back to dream this book.

The evening after we completed the manuscript, Elizabeth went to bed and dreamed another dream that was not a dream. She awoke, tapped out another email on her iPhone, and sent it to me at 1:01 A.M. on April 25, 2017. It reads thus:

HI JEFF.

Holy shit. I had a dream just now that I was talking to a man named Corny (??? Must be a nickname) Last name was not Kripal. I think it started with a "W" or a "U." You were there too. This man is no longer living, but was a close relative of yours. I think he died on December 10, but I don't know what year. He told me he died the same date as my grandmother (Dec 10th), but that my grand-mother died the same year as his wife … 14 or 15 years before him I think. We were standing in front of a movie theater at the corner of Lincoln and 5th, but I don't know what city. Looked like a small town. Theater name started with an "M."

Did you also have this dream? It was very vivid to me. There were lots more details, but I want to know if you were part of the conversation also.

ELIZABETH

Sent from my iPhone

When I got up and found the email waiting for me, I did some simple searching for obituaries on the internet, since I knew the general facts but not the specific dates of the deaths of my maternal grandparents. I also knew that the address of the theater of my hometown was very close to what Elizabeth had in the dream, but I wanted to see how close. All of these details were easily found online within a few minutes (in the absence of trust, the stratagem of fraud or conscious deceit can easily be invoked here). Here is what I wrote back, at 6:07 A.M.:

ELIZABETH,

Holy shit is right. Here are the *exact* details, all of which you hit.

My maternal grandfather's name was/is Cornelius. People called him "Cornie." A nickname.

His last name was/is Wiedel.

He died on December 10, 2010.

Here he is: https://www.findagrave.com/cgi-bin/fg.cgi?page=gr&GRid=62910410

His wife, Wilma, died in 1997, two months short of 14 years before him. Here she is:

https://www.findagrave.com/cgi-bin/fg.cgi?page=gr&GRid=115822137

The movie theater in my hometown of Hebron is called "Majestic," and it is on Lincoln Ave. and 5th Street.

Here it is: http://hebronmajestic.com/

I do not recall any dream, Elizabeth, alas.

very, very impressed (as usual),

Jeff

Other details would emerge as we spoke on the phone that morning ("the dream follows the mouth"). Although I had no personal aware-ness or memory of visiting Elizabeth in her dream, she was completely convinced that I was "totally out of the body" and had done exactly this. She is not the first to claim this, by the way. Other friends, colleagues, and readers have reported similar anomalies around the reading of my books, including a close colleague who works in ancient Neoplatonism and claims that I visited him in my "shining light body" (*augoeides*) in a dream to help him solve a particular problem with which he was strug-gling for an academic essay.[115] Still, I have no memory of any of this. In my own understanding, I am a dullard. I am a Muggle stumbling through a banal world just to the side of the fantastic world in which people like Elizabeth live and see.

On the phone now, Elizabeth told me that Grandpa spoke of not being able to find his glasses as he approached death, how his vision became very clear right before he died, and that now he very much wanted "to see a movie." That, I assumed, was why we were standing in front of my hometown movie theater, where my family has watched countless movies over four or five generations.

As I have tried to explain above, I think that significant dreams like this one are often a mixture of "empirical" and "symbolic" material, which the dreams mix in imperceptible ways so that it is difficult for the untrained eye to distinguish between them. Since I know all of the empirical references of this dream as well as its lived context on the night it was dreamed (the night after our book submission), I believe that I also know precisely where these lines between the empirical and the symbolic can be drawn and how this particular dream is a near-perfect case of such a mixing.

The empirical details are obvious and very impressive for anyone who trusts Elizabeth's integrity: the date of Grandpa's death and the street address of the theater are precise, and the beginning letter of the name of the theater is obviously partial but equally precise. On the phone, Elizabeth also told me that she knew the theater was red because of the "M," since the dream was synesthetic and her synesthesia codes the letter "M" as red. Which leaves begging the question: Why does the actual theater "cooperate with" her synesthesia coding? The actual building is red brick. Or is this synesthetic link what drew her to this building in the dream in the first place? Other details are displayed in the dream in the approximate ways that are very familiar to students of paranormal cognition: one is given an option (fourteen or fifteen years, a "W" or a "U"), and one of the options is the correct one. It is also striking how the dream works in an associative way, linking the years and dates of death to loved ones in a kind of free associative but nevertheless accurate manner.

The rest of the dream is different. I do not believe, for example, that the alleged deathbed scene of the lost glasses or the dream scene itself with Grandpa wanting to see a movie are reflections of any historical reality. I believe rather that they are symbolic. That is, I do not think that it matters whether Grandpa lost his glasses or not at the end of his life. (I have asked my mom and aunt, and the matter remains inconclusive.) Nor do I think it is necessary that we assume that Elizabeth was actually talking to Grandpa in the afterlife (recall that she herself did not think that she was speaking to her own grandfather in the Garden, even though she was hearing his voice). I think that these two scenes are expressing truths of which they otherwise cannot speak in literal ways and that need our own interpretations to draw them out and make them clear.

More specifically, I think that these two scenes speak directly to this book (which, please remember, we had just submitted a few hours before the dream) and my central thesis that the near-death landscape is a kind of superreal virtual movie that we are all creating through our cultures and religious beliefs over the generations. When Grandpa appeared in the dream and told Elizabeth and me that he "wanted to see a movie," what he was saying was, in effect, "I want to have a positive afterlife experience." The lost glasses scene communicates something like, "But I could not understand any of this while I was alive. My sight became clear only when I approached death and died."

Any skilled dream interpreter will ask why it was my grandfather who appeared in the dream and not someone else.[116] I will be intimate and vulnerable here, as is necessary for any adequate dream interpretation. If you are going to understand such a dream, you'd better be honest to the point of discomfort, or no real understanding will follow.

So here goes.

Grandpa was the unquestioned elder and patriarch of our family on my mother's side. He held and continues to hold immense family meaning and cultural weight, a weight to which even his nickname alludes. "Cornie" was affectionate and related to his birth name, of course, but it also obviously alludes to the staple of Nebraska agriculture—corn. He was a very successful farmer. A very big part of his legacy in our family has to do with the farms he left his four children and their families. He was—also, I think, significantly—the last family member to pass as of the date of Elizabeth's dream.

Grandpa's central presence in the dream is no accident then, and suggests, to me anyway, that the dream was quite genuine and not made up by Elizabeth in any fraudulent or deceitful way. I could have well spoken to Elizabeth about Grandpa, although I do not have any clear or certain memory of this. Elizabeth has met my parents (while they were visiting us in Houston) but none of my other family, so it is possible that she would have picked up some family details from Mom, but certainly not something like the street address of the town theater. In any case, no other deceased figure could have more powerfully signaled "the family" on my mother's side and in my own rural home culture.

What I think that Elizabeth was reading was my own mind and, more specifically, my own mind's feelings about this book. For example, I take Grandpa's description of "not being able to see" as ironically comforting, since it represents quite accurately the general attitude of most people to the basic ideas of this book. They cannot "see" what we are trying to tell them here about the afterlife, namely: that we do not really die; that consciousness is not finally a function of the mortal brain and body; that we ourselves are projecting, like a movie, the visionary landscapes reported in near-death experiences; that we "come back"; and that none of our specific religious identities should be taken as absolute or final. Grandpa's unseeing is a very apt stand-in for the general culture of our families and the broader society in which we happen to live. As a scholar of comparative religion, I constantly feel that "no one sees me," that is, that no one really understands what I am saying. I feel very much alone.

This, then, is how I would translate in my own words what Elizabeth's dream is "saying" to us, and particularly to me: "We cannot see what you are trying to tell us, Elizabeth and Jeff, not at least before we die. But we will all see very clearly and soon enough. And, oh by the way, you are on the right track with that movie analogy. We want to see a (better) movie now. That is why the book you just submitted is so important."

Please note that none of this speaks to how my or Elizabeth's family members, living or dead, actually feel or think about any of this. I am not speaking for any of my family members, much less am I claiming anything about how my deceased Grandpa feels or thinks. I am speaking only about and for myself. In the end, I think Elizabeth was reading my mind, not theirs. And she was reading it in an uncannily accurate and insightful way.

AND THEN IT GETS WEIRDER

But how did Elizabeth get all of those historical details exactly right? These were no metaphors or dream symbols. Nor did they speak to any anxieties on my or her part. These were precisely correct.

I had a hunch about this right away, drawn mostly from my reading of my colleague Eric Wargo, whom I discussed earlier and whose recent work on precognition sets a new standard as it reorients us around an established but largely forgotten model of the brain precognizing its own future state.[117] Having corresponded with Eric previously, I suspected that Elizabeth got all of those details right because she had "read" or heard them all from my email and phone response to her dream in the future and so "just knew" these same details in the past (that is, the present of the dream). In short, I think she got them from her reading and speaking to me the next day, very much like her precognitive perceptions of the near-future plane crashes that she would see in the media the next day. I do not think she was really talking to Grandpa. I think she was talking to me in the future. So she received the details in her dream from my email about the same dream in the future—another perfect time loop.

As we have seen, Eric Wargo has written extensively of these time loops and the manner in which information does indeed appear to flow from the future back into the present, that is, its own past. I sent Eric Elizabeth's dream email and my response to it and asked him if my time-loop reading of it would be his as well.

It was.

Actually, I had recently sent him the entire book manuscript well before this exchange about Elizabeth's psychic dream. He wrote back the next day. His email is reproduced below. The only details I probably need to provide the reader for context involve the "X" of which he writes.

In the summer of 2006, just after watching the third X-Men film, *X-Men: The Last Stand,* I entered a kind of manic creative fury in the theater (there is the science fiction movie motif again). I walked out of the theater and noticed something glimmering in the sun in the parking lot. I picked up what I thought was a gold Christian cross, lying just under my minivan door, as if it had been placed right there and right then for me. It was not a cross. It was an "X." I have since written quite a bit about this magical moment and its symbolic transformation from a Christian cross into a mutant X. The important point here is that this X was found in a parking lot, and that it fundamentally changed the shape and direction of my life and writing career.

With that explained, here is Eric's email. You should probably sit down and, if you already are, take a deep breath.

Jeff, I'm about ⅓ of the way through the book. Maybe what I'm about to suggest is roughly where you are going with it, or maybe not, but…Has it occurred to you that you yourself had a major hand in shaping Elizabeth's experiences, even as far back as her lightning strike?

I'm reading her story and it's almost as if she is a fictional character you would have created if you were a fiction writer (and everyone tells you [that] you should write fiction). Think about it: Given whatever is going on in her brain, she is much more responsive than most of us to what happens in her future. This includes not just the occasional air crash dream—those vivid experiences are likely the tip of a largely unconscious iceberg.

What if she is literally in some sense your creation, her experiences during and since the lightning strike framed and shaped through a three-decade premonition of her collaboration with you, the world expert on zapping and mutation? It seems clear from what I've read so far that this collaboration with you has been "super" important in her life, helping transform her curse into a superpower. I really, literally think that as far back as 1988 her story was being shaped by this framing you would ultimately provide, well in her future at that point.

This struck me all of a sudden when I read your passage about lending her Eliade's novel [*Youth Without Youth*]. I haven't read that (I need to), but one of the recurring themes in what I'm writing are the time loops between friends, between colleagues, between spouses, between doctors and patients, that center on books and book-lending, sharings and convergences that are pre-cognized and therefore that much more powerful because of it (I think there's a possible model of religious conversion in this notion of coming to a book or idea we've dimly precognized). These moments get called "synchronicity" (or Koestler's "library angel") but that term obfuscates more than it reveals. I think you and Elizabeth are an outrageously clear example of this.

And another thing—you call yourself a Muggle—but don't you think your whole paranormal oeuvre since encountering an X in a parking lot (a little bit like being struck by lightning) has been precognitive of Elizabeth's "case"? I mean, the whole thing is uncanny—I think you say she was struck in a parking lot just a couple blocks from your work (?). This collaboration is a precognized convergence from both sides.

And it's super powerful.

Eric

What Eric is describing here is not quite as outrageous as it might at first sound. It actually fits into a much larger and hauntingly consistent pattern. I opened my recent memoir-manifesto, *Secret Body*, which describes how readers of my books routinely write to me and report various bizarre occurrences around the reading of my books, as if these books were tapped into something, as if these pages express some superpower, as if the words themselves can invoke or conjure that which they are about.

I am beginning to believe that. Still, Eric's musings above are the most extreme example of this that I have ever heard, much less considered. I cannot also help but observe that his thoughts are not at all foreign to Elizabeth's own self-understanding. She has her own way of speaking of this same self-fashioning from the future, this same time loop. As we were writing the book, she once wondered out loud whether the point or purpose of the lightning strike and NDE was this book. She wondered whether that was all "for" this. She is also convinced that the two of us were destined to write this book, that it was written before it was written, as it were.

We can flip this thought, reverse its direction in time, and ask the same question in a different way. Or in both ways. Perhaps, as Elizabeth intuits, the lightning strike occurred so that she could cowrite this book. But perhaps this book has also occurred so that she could be struck by lightning. Certainly the past event resulted in the present book, as we normally assume. But perhaps the present book also somehow produced the past set of events, as only a figure like Eric Wargo can presently imagine. Perhaps time flows both ways at once, as a kind of snake biting its own tail, in a constant return, in a loop of mind and matter that none of us quite understands yet but in which all of us are caught all the time.

What does it feel like to finish a lightning bolt that cracked forward in time to become a book? What does it feel like to finish a book that reached back in time to become a lightning bolt?

APPENDIX

THE EMAILS

Come and see what is written of Daniel, "The mystery was
revealed to Daniel in a night vision" (Daniel 2:19), and it is
written "Daniel saw a dream and a vision of his mind in bed;
afterward he wrote down the dream."

—THE ZOHAR IN ELLIOT WOLFSON'S
A Dream Interpreted Within a Dream

As I have lectured on Elizabeth's experiences over the last two years, audiences are often taken aback by the apparent empirical nature of the time-stamped emails. They are used to hearing stories about religious experiences, but they have generally never heard a story or vision that interacts so clearly with the physical and historical world. In the question-and-answer sessions that follow the lectures, I am often asked the same two questions about the emails. How many precognitive dreams did not come true? And could Elizabeth have faked the date and time stamps? Both questions really boil down to the same question: Do these emails constitute scientific evidence for precognition?

I once thought I would write an extensive appendix on these matters, but such an appendix quickly "got into the weeds" of the nature of scientific evidence, the differing methods of the humanities and sciences, and, in particular, the complexities of digital forensics, about which I know next to nothing. It also quickly became obvious that we had neither the time nor the financial resources to do real justice to the latter forensic research, which can be exceptionally expensive.

Not that we avoided the question. We spoke to three computer professionals, including a computer security expert with experience in government, academic, and industrial settings. These conversations and an initial series of forensic tests (for the knowing, a DKIM) that the latter professional ran on Elizabeth's home computer (at her invitation) convinced me of the following tentative conclusions:

1. The digital forensics performed could not prove that the time stamps are fraudulent.

2. The digital forensics performed could not prove that the time stamps are genuine.

In short, we could neither disprove nor prove the authenticity of the emails. It was a draw. Much of this nonconclusion was a function of the unfortunate historical fact that as Elizabeth has used and retired various devices and computers over the years (specifically, an old iPad, two very old BlackBerry phones, three old iPhones, two different laptops, and now a desktop computer), she has forwarded the precognitive emails to herself in order, she thought, to preserve them. But as she did this, the Yahoo server appears to have lopped off the metadata of the forwarded emails. For most of the emails, then, we simply lacked a sufficient digital train to authenticate them. At least one precognitive dream email (of the Tokyo earthquake) could be authenticated in a very weak way, but again, we lacked the full metadata to be sure.

This does not mean that I think that the emails are fraudulent. I am convinced that they are genuine for reasons that I will explain below. But what this *does* mean is that nothing involving the emails can or should be read as scientific evidence for precognition. We simply lack such evidence. The email data as it stands at the moment is extremely suggestive for those who are already open to the possibility that precognition is a real thing, but they do not constitute scientific proof of precognition, and the data certainly will not convince the committed skeptic. I want to be very clear about that.

In the end (and we are at the end), these are very technical conversations, and this is not a technical book (nor is it a book about precognition or the emails). Allow me, though, to make a few general observations about these particular matters for those who might be interested in such questions. What follows is what I wish I had time to say to my audiences but never do.

ON THE NATURE OF SCIENTIFIC EVIDENCE

Allow me to begin on a personal note. I have had probably a few hundred thousand dreams in my life, but *only one* that I remember as precognitive, and only then after the fact. That is, I recognized it as precognitive only after the events that it encoded in symbolic form played out the following day. In light of Eric Wargo's work, I strongly suspect that my later interpretation of the dream as precognitive of the day's forthcoming events was what retrocaused the dream from the future to the previous night. It was an extremely important dream. Indeed, this particular dream (interpretation) helped me to respond to these events in a way that would prove crucial for my family's well-being and my own professional survival. The symbolic dream actually encoded the answer to a series of events and an urgent moral question that would not arise until later that day and the next. My realization that it was all encoded in the dream allowed me to respond correctly and precisely to the situation.

But here is my point. If I set this single, life-changing dream and its message in the context of all of my other dreams, it would be statistically meaningless. It would *disappear.* Statistical approaches effectively "erase" such remarkable moments, which is, I believe, precisely why they are used by professional debunkers. In other words, I think that statistical approaches to paranormal phenomena are privileged in order to deny the phenomena in question, which is inherently anomalous and so, generally speaking, statistically insignificant. I am *extremely* skeptical of this statistical approach when it comes to assessing the presence and importance of anomalous or rogue spiritual phenomena, then, since the method erases that which we are trying to understand.

Let me push this further. I think that sometimes an extremely rare event, or an absolutely unique one with no corroboration or confirmation in a broad set of experiments, can be deeply significant from a religious, historical, or philosophical perspective. Indeed, a singular anomaly—that is, something that happened, and will happen, only once—can be *the most meaningful event of a person's or community's life.* I understand perfectly well that this is not how science works, but it is exactly how religion, history, and life often work. It is the anomalous that so often changes history and determines the shape and direction of a life or even an entire civilization.

When assessing a question like "How many of the dream precognitions did not come true?" we have to be very aware of these historical matters and what method we are using to determine their significance and meaning. I do not personally think that the statistical approach is the best method here. Moreover, I think the question about "how many" is understandable but is finally both distorting and unanswerable.

It is distorting for the reasons articulated just above.

It is unanswerable because we do not have all of the dream emails to work with and arrive at an accurate statistical answer, and this for two perfectly reasonable reasons. First, many of Elizabeth's precognitive dreams are of a deeply personal nature or involve family members. She is understandably reluctant to share these with anyone. I fully understand that moral decision, since I just hid most of the details of my own pre-cognitive dream to protect a number of living individuals. So already we are missing a good number of them, including, no doubt, many of the "hits." Second, Elizabeth has had more dreams than she can remember over the last three decades, and many, if not most, of these would have occurred before she landed on her email verification method in 2008. The 1989 San Francisco quake dream falls here, for example, but so do no doubt dozens of others. So we are missing all of those as well.

FRAUD OR TRICKSTER?

One email that did pass the forensic test and did preserve the metadata was the 2009 Captain Sully landing in the Hudson River. This is a very good example of just how complicated things can get, and how quickly.

Recall that we have a third-party witness of this dream description and its afternoon occurrence in Jerusalem. Matt Krohn listened to the dream seconds after it happened and watched Elizabeth type out the email to herself. He also reported that she was immediately talking about "people standing on the wings." The email was sent, with Matt as a witness, at 2:57 in the afternoon in Jerusalem, or at 7:57 A.M. in the morning in New York City. The plane went down at 3:31 P.M. New York time, which would have been at 10:31 P.M. in Jerusalem, that is, roughly seven hours after the dream. So we seem to have a very clear example of precognition here.

Still, we lack any hard scientific evidence. Despite Matt's unequivocal confirmation of when the email was composed, the date stamp on it in the metadata shows that it went through the Yahoo server twenty-six minutes *after* the actual crash in the Hudson. This would have been enough time for the floating plane image to appear on the internet and on television, but barely. To be specific, the metadata shows that it went through the Yahoo server at 12:57 Pacific Standard Time or at 3:57 P.M. Eastern Standard Time (New York time). Eric Wargo has done some initial research on the internet history of the Sully river landing. He observes that the first image actually appeared on a Twitter feed at 3:36 P.M., just five minutes after the landing. The first news stories began to appear about fifteen minutes after that.[118] So the times are all extremely close, and almost anything is possible here. But one can certainly not rule out from the digital evidence that Elizabeth composed the email after the crash. That is one possible reading.

In the end, what we have with this single email is an apparent conflict of evidence. We have Matt's eyewitness account and Elizabeth's own sworn story, which agree with one another in every detail. But then we also have the computer metacode, which does not agree. This contradiction can be resolved in two ways. First, one could simply posit fraud on the part of Elizabeth and Matt. This would resolve the contradiction. Perhaps the technologies would have allowed Elizabeth to change the time stamps on her emails by changing the clocks on her different computers. But then why would she have taken such care to preserve such fraudulent emails and have forwarded them to herself for years? That makes little sense. Still, it is possible that she is some kind of pathological liar, a perpetrator of a long-meditated fraud. Recall that fraud is one of the four options with which I began the book. There it is, if you choose to take it.

Second, we could posit that the email sat in her computer for about seven hours before it "decided" to send it to the Yahoo server, oddly enough, immediately after the crash began appearing on the internet. Most readers have probably experienced this frustrating phenomenon, particularly when they are traveling (which she was) and dealing with various kinds of Wi-Fi signals and computer systems: the email just will not go out until one gets a better signal. It has certainly happened to me, many times. This is Elizabeth's theory of the time delay. She finds the whole thing eminently frustrating.

I do not find the first fraud explanation plausible, and for two reasons.

First, it seriously violates my own two-year sense of the honesty and integrity of these two individuals, whom I know quite well. Such a moral charge simply does not "ring true." I recognize that this cannot satisfy the skeptic, who will say that this is no proof. I recognize that, but again, I am making no such scientific claims.

There is a very profound point to make here. In the humanities, we sometimes call this a "hermeneutic of trust." A "hermeneutic" is an interpretive stance or method that—and this is the key—will shape or even largely determine how a phenomenon appears, or does not appear. We saw this earlier with Elliot Wolfson and his nuanced notions of how an interpretation of a dream might determine the meaning of the dream, much as an observation in a quantum physics experiment appears to determine the nature of a particle or wave. "Interpretation," then, is much too weak a translation here. A hermeneutic is more like a "conjuring," an "enactment," or a "cocreation," that is, a state of consciousness that evokes whatever it is attempting to understand. A hermeneutic of trust, then, is an interpretive state of consciousness that trusts the report or individual *with the understanding that this trust will reveal information and insights, even conjure phenomena that a more suspicious or doubting approach would not and could not produce.*

This is not naiveté. This is a very serious claim about how we arrive at knowledge in the humanities, and in particular in the humanistic study of paranormal phenomena. The same claim also resonates deeply with something called the "sheep-goat" effect in parapsychology, namely, the well-known phenomenon that a trusting experimenter (the "sheep" in this case) will tend to find positive results with respect to the presence of psi, whereas the doubting or suspicious experimenter (the "goat" in this case) will tend to find negative results. Put more simply and less technically, I am convinced that my own attitude toward Elizabeth matters a great deal. The simple truth is that Elizabeth would not have shared what she shared with me were it not for this trust and this collaboration. Nor would have I learned what I learned. And, of course, there would have been no book. Everything in fact hinged on that trust and what it revealed and made possible.

And this, of course, is the very opposite of the scientific method, which would seek objectivity and emotional distance from the subject being studied, and, as a result, could have never produced this book. That is not a criticism of the scientific method. It is simply an observation about how the sciences and the humanities work in very different ways.

The second reason I reject the fraud charge is that I think of Elizabeth's precognitive experiences in the larger context of the historical record, which is chock-full of hundreds, indeed thousands, of other cases and incidences like hers (including my own precognitive dream). Elizabeth's dreams fit seamlessly into a much larger pattern. It is for these larger historical reasons that I am convinced that precognitive phenomena are real and intimate, if largely invisible expressions of the natural world in which we all live.

I recognize that for the skeptic such "extraordinary claims require extraordinary evidence," but I have never understood that claim, mostly because it is obvious to me that "extraordinary" is entirely relative to one's worldview and philosophical assumptions. Such things are certainly not extraordinary in the world I inhabit and the assumptions I think out of. I live in a "glass-block universe" in which the past, present, and future all exist right *now* (again, just watch Brian Greene's *The Elegant Universe* or read Eric Wargo's *Time Loops*).

Moreover, I know that divination is one of the oldest and most common human practices and experiences on the planet. For these two reasons, there is nothing especially extraordinary or even surprising about precognition for me. Such phenomena are all quite natural and to be expected in such a (perfectly scientific) cosmology and (massively documented) history of religions. Hence the burden of proof for me is on the skeptic, not on those who honestly report precognition with the consistency and detail that Elizabeth does. Still, I recognize this is a reasonable difference and is ultimately a function of differing worldviews and philosophical assumptions.

There is possibly something much stranger afoot here, though. If one chooses to believe Elizabeth and Matt about the Jerusalem plane crash dream, the late time stamp of this particular email may well be the most valuable part of the entire email story. After all, it almost looks like the computer was waiting for the internet to report the crash before it would send the email and so prevent us from having any clear and hard evidence of precognition. This is called the "trickster effect" in parapsychology. The trickster is a mythical name for the often observed phenomenon that psi or paranormal events appear to have their "own minds" and seem nearly omnipotent at avoiding clear detection.[119]

I recognize, of course, that this will be much too much for those who will opt for the fraud answer. So be it. That is their choice. That is the world they choose to live in.

IN THE FUTURE...

Finally, I should add that this book is not a finish line but a snapshot of an ongoing conversation and living experiment. The security expert recommended that Elizabeth switch email accounts to Google, since Google has a very reliable date- and time-stamped system that would give us strong and reliable evidence for any future precognitive dreams.

As of November 6, 2017, Elizabeth has agreed to send me any emails about her precognitive dreams through a new Gmail account. And the security expert has offered to look at new data. So we are moving forward now with those instructions and that promise.

I frankly worry a bit about this as well, though. I happen to think that we are scared to death, terrified, of our own human potentials and our own paranormal powers. We all share in the Superman, but we want to pretend that we are only Clark Kent—you know, put on a pair of glasses and go write boring stuff for the *Daily Planet*. Apparently, that's the reality in which we want to live. The ruse works. Accordingly, paranormal effects happen precisely when we are not looking, or better, when we are not taking responsibility for them. In a word, they work best when they work *unconsciously*.

The séance worked in the nineteenth century, for example, because it involved a dark room and many people sitting around a large table. Since it was never clear who was responsible for what psychical effects (tables floated, apparitions appeared, minds were read), the individuals around the table could "let loose." In parapsychological speak, they became "disinhibited." They could manifest psi effects while at the same deny their own responsibility for these effects. They could act like Superman but still pretend to be Clark Kent. This is why the séance ritual worked. This is also, of course, what made fraud possible under the cover of darkness and under the table (literally). There is the trickster again.

Put bluntly, it is my own position that scientific focus on paranormal effects has an inhibiting effect on them. It makes them go away. But then this was one of the reasons Elizabeth wanted to write this book anyway: to make the terrifying vision-dreams go away. I am not sure this book will do that, but I am pretty sure an ironclad scientific test will. In any case, we are open to whatever comes. We are game. Let us see what happens in the future, or perhaps better, what has already happened in the future.

ORIGINS AND GRATITUDE

Elizabeth would like to thank the following people, without whom this book could not have been written:

I would like to thank my husband, Matt Krohn, for his love, patience, and belief in my ability to write this book. His editing skills are only surpassed by his husbanding skills. Matt amazes me every day with his power to provide just what I need, just when I need it. I will forever be grateful to him for his physical and emotional support as I slowly got my story down on paper at last. He is a calming and loving presence and is the best friend a person could have. I am a lucky wife indeed.

My children also were so very supportive of this project, and I could not have written my story without all of them being on board and encouraging me to finally tell the details of what happened on September 2, 1988, and in the years since. After all, so much of it is about them.

First, I owe a huge thank you to Jeremy Balkin for heroically running back out into the storm to save his little brother. Jeremy was a four-year-old hero in 1988 and has grown into such a fine man. He has been supportive of me and has nudged me to share the details of what happened that day as I wrote this book. He is a terrific dad, and it gives me tremendous pleasure to watch him in his role as a parent. My pride in Jeremy is enormous and well deserved.

I also owe many thanks to Andy and Shana Balkin for their unwavering support of my emotional ups and downs as I wrote this book. They are exemplary parents, and their children are especially fortunate to have them both as role models. I thank Andy especially for holding my hand when I was struck by lightning, and for being by my side ever since. He is a principled and caring man any mom would be proud to call her son, and I am especially proud to be his mom.

A tremendous thank you also goes to Mallory and Harrison Botwin for supporting me throughout this journey. I am very fortunate that they are a major part of my life. Special thanks to Mallory for giving me the honor of being her mom. I am grateful every day that I came back for the opportunity to raise such a spunky girl into such a sparkling woman. That opportunity has always been such a gift. Every time I look at her it makes me know I did something right. She makes me proud every day.

No one on earth has ever been gifted better, more loving, cuter, smarter, or sweeter grandchildren than I. Maxwell, Efrayim, Yehuda Moshe, Evelyn, Leo, and Lillie have brought so much sunshine and pleasure into my life, each in his or her own unique way. Their gorgeous glowing faces and big hugs helped support me throughout this project. In addition to my children, I love each and every one of these special grandchildren more than there are stars in the sky.

I would also like to thank my loving and supportive parents, Marianne and Larry Greenfield, for being exactly the parents I have always needed them to be. From the day I was born, they have seemed to know intuitively exactly how to respond to me in any given situation. Their support has always been unwavering, especially as I worked on this book. They are both such amazingly wonderful people who I am so proud and lucky to call Mom and Dad.

Finally, and perhaps most importantly, I will be forever grateful for the serendipitous occurrences that brought me together with Jeff Kripal in October of 2015. I am indebted to Jeff for his endless patience and for helping me to get my thirty-year-old story written in as dignified a manner as possible. I thank him for becoming not only my coauthor and my teacher, but also a close and trusted friend. My gratitude to Jeff is boundless.

Jeff would like to thank the following people:

First and foremost, I would like to thank Elizabeth for trusting me and for revealing so much of her soul in these pages. I was always deeply moved by her integrity and fierce honesty. We laughed a lot, it should be noted.

I would especially like to thank Anyang Anyang, Cyrus Wirls, and Stuart Nelson of the Institute for Spirituality and Health in the Texas Medical Center, all of whom played important roles in arranging the original event at which Elizabeth and I first met and spoke. My PhD student Timothy Grieve-Carlson also helped considerably with researching databases on plane crashes and earthquakes that might have corresponded to Elizabeth's nightmares. All of this work did not finally make it into the book but may well form the basis of a future website on the same.

I would also like to thank all of my colleagues in the professional study of religion and my friends and coconspirators here in Houston, all of whom helped me in different ways think through these questions in various professional and private formats. In November of 2016, I invited Elizabeth and Matt to a special symposium called "Bodies of Light and Super Saints" at the Esalen Institute in Big Sur, California, in order to get the feedback of close colleagues in the humanities and sciences who study such events. We spoke about the book project to the Houston IONS (Institute of Noetic Science) group in January and co-taught a course on the book manuscript at the Houston Jung Center in the spring of 2017.

I have also lectured on this material at Duke University, to their Paranormal Working Group; Stanford University, to the departments of anthropology and religious studies; the University of California, Berkeley, for two courses on the philosophy and neuroscience of consciousness;

the northeast regional meeting of the American Academy of Religion, as their plenary address; the 60th anniversary celebration of the Parapsychological Association; and a conference on Judaism and the Chabad movement in New York City. Michael Murphy of Esalen; Lydia Dugan of Houston; Sean Fitzpatrick of the Houston Jung Center; Priscilla Wald, Joseph Donahue, and David Morgan of Duke University; Tanya Luhrmann of Stanford University; David Presti and Robert Sharf of the University of California, Berkeley; Diana Walsh Pasulka of the University of North Carolina, Wilmington; Annalisa Ventola of the Parapsychological Association; and Philip Wexler of the Institute of Jewish Spirituality and Society were my hosts for these specific events. Other key conversation partners, mostly via correspondence, were Cherylee Black (about her own negative NDE and other related phenomena); Jonathan Garb, David Halperin, Brian Ogren, and Elliot Wolfson (on the Jewish materials); and Lee Irwin (on the Native American traditions).

Finally, my reading of and correspondence with Eric Wargo were particularly important and especially formative with the precognitive materials. I just think Eric is brilliant. His "tesseract" model of the brain and his glass-block universe could revolutionize not only the study of precognitive prodigies like Elizabeth, but neuroscience, physics, evolutionary biology, psychology, history, the humanities, and the social sciences in the process. I am not exaggerating. But that must wait for another time and another book, both, I hope, shimmering already somewhere down the glass-block universe.

ENDNOTES

1   For the statistics and basic data of lightning strikes in this paragraph, I am relying on https://mosaicscience.com/story/what-its-be-struck-lightning.

2   For a perfect textual example, see John Keel's description of debunker Phil Klass, who stood up in such an audience and addressed, in a loud voice, Keel's honest observation that he saw so many UFOs in West Virginia during the Mothman episode that he lost count: "That man is a terrible liar!" And then "he stalked out of the hall." John A. Keel, *Flying Saucer to the Center of Your Mind,* ed. Andrew B. Colvin (Seattle: Metadisc Books, 2013), 69. This is childish.

3   John W. Price, *Revealing Heaven: The Christian Case for Near-Death Experiences* (New York: HarperOne, 2013).

4   Additional information about Holland and this particular sermon can be found at https://en.wikipedia.org/wiki/Henry_Scott_Holland.

5   *Sabbath Rest and Renewal: A Service for Reclaiming Shabbat* (1995). This document was reedited in 2004 by a subcommittee of the Ritual and Music Committee at the synagogue.

6   The healer's name and city have both been changed to protect her privacy.

7   The snapshot I saw in my nightmare can be viewed at https://archives .sfexaminer.com/sanfrancisco/1989-loma-prieta-temblor-shook-up-need -for-earthquake-solutions/Content?oid=2909383.

8   The exact snapshot we saw on the news, and that I had seen in my nightmare, can be viewed at www.cbsnews.com/news/trauma-lingers-for-flight -1549-survivors/.

9   To see the awful snapshot that I saw in my nightmare and that later appeared in the news, go to: http://pulseradio.fm/2015/02/05/taiwan-pilot-hailed-a -hero-for-pulling-plane-clear-of-buildings/.

10 Dannion Brinkley, with Paul Perry, *Saved by the Light: The True Story of a Man Who Died Twice and the Profound Revelations He Received* (New York: Villard Books, 1994).

11 See www.lightningsafety.noaa.gov/odds.shtml.

12 For a learned discussion of this phrase, see Elliot Wolfson, *A Dream Interpreted Within a Dream: Oneiropoiesis and the Prism of Imagination* (New York: Zone Books, 2011), 143–50. I will be engaging this book extensively below.

13 Ibid., 171.

14 I am especially grateful to, in alphabetical order, Jonathan Garb, Brian Ogren, Ohad Rosenberg, Philip Wexler, and Elliot Wolfson. I also learned a great deal from Esther J. Hamori, *Women's Divination in Biblical Litera-ture: Prophecy, Necromancy, and Other Arts of Knowledge* (New Haven, CT: Yale University Press, 2015), a remarkable piece of work that came to my attention too late to incorporate into this book but that I have engaged in a scholarly essay: "The Gnostic Garden," *Gnosis: Journal of Gnostic Studies* 3, no. 2 (Fall 2018).

15 Whitley Strieber and Jeffrey J. Kripal, *The Super Natural: Why the Unex-plained Is Real* (New York: Penguin Tarcher, 2017).

16 For a history of Esalen and the larger California and countercultural scenes from which it emerged and influenced, see my *Esalen: America and the Reli-gion of No Religion* (Chicago: University of Chicago Press, 2007).

17 Jeffrey J. Kripal, *Mutants and Mystics: Science Fiction, Superhero Comics and the Paranormal* (Chicago: University of Chicago Press, 2011).

18 Martin Riesebrodt, *The Promise of Salvation: A Theory of Religion*, trans. Steven Rendall (Chicago: University of Chicago Press, 2010), 74–75.

19 Raymond Moody, with Paul Perry, *Paranormal: My Life in Pursuit of the Afterlife* (New York: HarperOne, 2012), 70. Please note the key line: "that I think was Jesus." Here is a clear sign that the man was interpreting the vision.

20 I am relying here on Andreas Sommer, "Crossing the Boundaries of Mind and Body: Psychical Research and the Origins of Modern Psychology,"

doctoral thesis, Science and Technology Studies, University of London, 2013, 22. The original text is Francis Bacon, "Of the Proficience and Advancement of Learning, Divine and Human" (1605).

21 Nancy Evans Bush, "Distressing Western Near-Death Experiences: Finding a Way through the Abyss," in Janice Miner Holden, Bruce Greyson, and Debbie James, eds., *The Handbook of Near-Death Experiences: Thirty Years of Investigation* (Santa Barbara: ABC-CLIO, 2009), 81.

22 There are voices that have tried to speak out on this particular issue, including Cherylee Black, who experienced such a negative NDE, who has been active in the NDE research community, and who has corresponded with me about the matter for years now. My comments here on the subject are very much inspired by those conversations.

23 Ibid. Contrary to what many people want to believe, there actually is no necessary relationship between mystical experiences and moral behavior. "Bad" people can and do have profoundly positive mystical experiences, including positive near-death experiences, and "good" people can and do have negative ones. And vice versa. I have addressed this difficult pattern at length in many other contexts. See Jeffrey J. Kripal, *Secret Body: Erotic and Esoteric Currents in the History of Religions* (Chicago: University of Chicago Press, 2017), especially the index under "gnomon 4."

24 There is, of course, commonly a correlation between belief and the content of a near-death or visionary experience. Christians do not generally see Krishna, Buddhists do not generally see Jesus, and so on. Even here, though, there are exceptions.

25 Moody, *Paranormal,* 110–11.

26 Wolfson, *A Dream,* 16, 20–21. For a discussion of "paranormal phenomena" and "extrasensory perception," see ibid., 76, 122. For a discussion of the paranormal (here as the interpretation of the formation of birds in the sky) as a stepped-down version of sagely wisdom and, higher still, of prophecy itself, see ibid., 162.

27 F. W. H. Myers, *Human Personality and Its Survival of Bodily Death*, abridged edition (Newburyport, MA: Hampton Roads Publishing, 2001), 340.

28 Ibid., 8.

29 Ibid., 9, 126.

30 Jeffrey J. Kripal, "Visions of the Impossible," available at www.chronicle
   .com/article/Embrace-the-Unexplained/145557.

31 Personal correspondence from Pericles Georges, July 2, 2014. My thanks to
   Pericles for giving me permission to use this letter.

32 I am indebted to Whitley Strieber for this insight.

33 The sci-fi buff cannot help but recall here the final scenes of the movie *Contact* (1997).

34 Elsewhere I have distinguished between the "empirical imaginal" (e.g., Elizabeth's historically precise precog dream-visions) and the "symbolic imaginal" (e.g., Elizabeth's sensibility that the near-death experience will be
   different for different people). See the discussions around gnomon 12 in
   Kripal, *Secret Body,* for a discussion.

35 Wolfson, *A Dream,* 189.

36 It is instructive to compare this tripartite model of the religious imagination
   to the standard kabbalistic four-part model of how to interpret scripture (a
   similar system, by the way, was in place with the medieval Christian writers with respect to the Christian Bible). Allow me to quote my colleague
   Brian Ogren on this, as the system is quite complex and deserves an expert
   voice: "Classical Judaism from the early middle ages on usually falls back
   on the four-fold method of literal (*Peshat*), allegorical (*remez*), homiletical
   (*derash*) and secret (*sod*) levels of interpretation. The first letter of each of
   these put together forms the acronym of *Pardes,* the Garden or the Orchard,
   which works deeply into Elisabeth's narrative. Within classical Judaism, all
   four levels are accepted as 'true.' Here the [symbolic] veil remains necessary,
   but not as a mere veil. For example, the idea is that there really were historical figures named Adam and Eve. In their very being, and in their (true)
   historical narrative (*Peshat*), they perhaps point to allegory, such as Adam
   as Form and Eve as Matter (*remez*), to stories woven that don't actually exist
   in the biblical text, like Adam's first wife Lilith (this would be *derash*), and
   to a secret level, such as God herself/himself being androgynous (*sod*). *All*
   of these, according to classical Judaism, are true, and the secret level cannot
   exist without the literal, and vice versa. It is a holistic system … a classical
   Kabbalist would find the Bible entirely true, in all of its aspects."

Brian also explained to me that the most interesting thing for him about kabbalistic modes of interpretation is that "it is all literal and not-literal, all at the same time. And true insight theoretically comes from the embrace of the paradox of that coincidence of opposites." Put a bit differently, it is all about "the in-between (which seems to parallel to the state of being that is near-death: death but not death, life but not life, etc.). For the kabbalists, this leads to the danger of going crazy, of heresy, or even of [physical] death" (as we will see in our final pages in this book). This "embrace of the paradox" of the "coincidence of opposites" is *precisely* what I am trying to get at here, if in a different more modern mode. Although I firmly reject the historical or literalist claims of the first level of interpretation (there was no historical Adam and Eve), I want to take the literal/not-literal claim very seriously. Here I wonder about the possible phenomenological origins of such paradoxes; that is, I wonder if they might have something to do with how human beings experience visionary states (like the NDE) whose landscapes are indeed experienced as *literally* real or true but are also clearly "imagined" in some supersense. Put simply, I wonder if this traditional sense of the literalness of scriptural interpretation is visionary in origin and so based on phenomenological (if not historical) fact.

37 I am indebted to Jonathan Garb for this line of thought.

38 Wolfson, *A Dream,* 124. See ibid., 199, for a succinct statement of the logic. See 209 for an application of the same truth/falsehood paradox to the practice of religion itself in a contemporary rabbi of the Chabad-Lubavitch movement.

39 Ibid., 161.

40 Ibid., 112.

41 For a discussion of this pattern, see ibid., 131–32.

42 Ibid., 114, 165.

43 Ibid., 166.

44 Ibid., 51.

45 Ibid., 53.

46 Ibid., 203.

47 Jonathan Garb, *Yearnings of the Soul: Psychological Thought in Modern Kabbalah* (Chicago: University of Chicago Press, 2015), 32.

48 Wolfson, *A Dream,* 151.

49 There are in fact numerous competing interpretations of the bizarreries of quantum mechanics. This one is known as the "Cophenhagen interpretation," so named because it was classically articulated by Niels Bohr in Copenhagen. For a lay explanation, I recommend Robert Nadeau and Menas Kafatos, *The Non-Local Universe: The New Physics and Matters of Mind* (New York: Oxford University Press, 1999).

50 Wolfson, *A Dream,* 103–04.

51 Ibid., 151.

52 Ibid., 108. For Wolfson's fullest explication of what I want to call his "gnosis of the timeswerve," see his "Prologue: Timeswerve/Hermeneutic Reversibility," in Elliot R. Wolfson, *Language, Eros, Being: Kabbalistic Hermeneutics and Poetic Imagination* (New York: Fordham University Press, 2005). This is one central text that has inspired me in my engagement with Elizabeth's notion of time looping back on itself.

53 Cited in Wolfson, *A Dream,* 153.

54 Ibid., 163. In this same context, Wolfson describes interpretation as "theurgical," a technical term from Western esotericism that refers to the ability to ritually act as or influence the divine presence.

55 Hilary Evans, *Sliders: The Enigma of Streetlight Interference* (San Antonio: Anomalist Books, 2010).

56 William Thomas Walsh, *Our Lady of Fátima* (Garden City, NY: Image Book, 1954), 167–68.

57 Diana Walsh Pasulka, *Heaven Can Wait: Purgatory in Catholic Devotional and Popular Culture* (New York: Oxford University Press). Not accidentally, Pasulka is now working with UFO contactees.

58 See, for example, Cynthia Nelson, "The Virgin of Zeitoun," *Worldview* 16, no. 9 (September 1973): 5–11.

59 Without getting into a long discussion of Bible verses that invoke lightning, here are a few sample ones that give the general flavor of threat and punishment: Exodus 9:23–24, 2 Kings 1:10–12, Psalms 144:6, Luke 9:54, Revelation 20:9.

60 Ernst Benz, *The Theology of Electricity: On the Encounter and Explanation of Theology and Science in the 17th and 18th Centuries,* trans. Wolfgang

Taraba, ed. and with an introduction by Dennis Stillings (Eugene, OR: Pickwick Publications, 1989), 36.

61 Exodus 13:22, Daniel 10:6, Matthew 28:3.

62 Ezekiel 1–3.

63 Michael Lieb, *Children of Ezekiel: Aliens, UFOs, the Crisis of Race, and the Advent of End Time* (Durham, NC: Duke University Press, 1998), 12–13.

64 For a variety of comparative examples, see Mircea Eliade, *Shamanism: Archaic Techniques of Ecstasy*, trans. Willard R. Trask (Princeton, NJ: Princeton University Press, 1964), 19, 55, 81, 100, 170, 206.

65 I have corresponded with my colleague Lee Irwin, who works with and writes about the indigenous cultures of North America. The following few paragraphs on indigenous cultures are drawn more or less directly from our correspondence, with my own alterations and comments.

66 Jeffrey Mishlove, *The PK-Man: A True Story of Mind Over Matter* (Charlottesville, VA: Hampton Roads, 2000).

67 For the philosopher or historian of ideas, this might throw some real light on the famous ideal "Forms" of ancient Platonism, which connected the Forms to numbers.

68 Richard E. Cytowic, MD, and David M. Eagleman, PhD, *Wednesday Is Indigo Blue: Discovering the Brain of Synesthesia*, afterword by Dmitri Nabokov (Cambridge, MA: The MIT Press, 2009), 151.

69 Ibid., 154.

70 Ibid., 157.

71 Ibid., 159.

72 Ibid., 21.

73 For my fuller treatment of the novel, see my memoir/manifesto, *Secret Body*, particularly chapters 11, 12, and Closing.

74 Benz, *The Theology of Electricity*, 1–2. The same is happening today with what is sometimes called the quantum turn, that is, the turn to quantum physics as a new mediating language or set of metaphors.

75 Alex Wendt, *Quantum Mind and Social Science: Unifying Physical and Social Ontology* (Cambridge, UK: Cambridge University Press, 2015).

76 Peter Struck, *Divination and Human Nature: A Cognitive History of Intuition in Classical Antiquity* (Princeton, NJ: Princeton University Press, 2016).

77 This was related by Werner Heisenberg in Abdus Salam and John C. Taylor, *Unification of Fundamental Forces: The First 1988 Dirac Memorial Lecture* (Cambridge, UK: Cambridge University Press, 1990), 99.

78 Bradford Skow, *Objective Becoming* (New York: Oxford University Press, 2015). For the interview, see www.ibtimes.co.uk/block-universe-theory-time-where-past-present-future-exist-all-once-1485965.

79 I am thinking of the work of the French researcher Jean-Pierre Jourdan, "Juste une dimension de plus," an English translation of which, "Just Another Dimension," can be accessed at www.iands-france.org/FRAMES/frame.html.

80 See www.youtube.com/watch?v=MO_Q_f1WgQI.

81 Eric Wargo, *Time Loops: Precognition, Retrocausation, and the Unconscious* (Charlottesville, VA: Anomalist Books, 2018).

82 See Jeffrey J. Kripal, with Ata Anzali, Andrea R. Jain, and Erin Prophet, *Comparing Religions: Coming to Terms* (Oxford: Wiley-Blackwell, 2014), 366.

83 For a nice review of Bem's work and its controversial reception, see Daniel Engber, "Daryl Bem Proved ESP Is Real: Which Means Science Is Broken," *Slate*, May 17, 2017, at https://slate.com/cover-stories/2017/05/daryl-bem-proved-esp-is-real-showed-science-is-broken.html.

84 It is important to note that not every researcher agrees that the evidence points in this direction. Some argue that Libet confused the brain's "readiness potential" (RP) with the causal decision itself. Others observe that the conventional reading of the Libet experiment has been fantastically exaggerated for ideological reasons, that is, to argue for determinism and against free will. I am adopting the conventional reading simply to observe how Wargo turns it upside down with a simple loop.

85 "What Was Your Original Face on Mars?—Zen and the Prophetic Sublime" at http://thenightshirt.com/?p=4024.

86 "Zen, Signs and the Arrival of Meaning," at http://thenightshirt.com/?p=3961.

87 Ibid.

88   Dunne, *An Experiment with Time* (1952/1927), 50; referenced in Wargo, *Time Loops,* 64.

89   Wargo is being funny, but his flying spaghetti monster image is uncannily similar to the Buddhist notion of *skandha*s, the various "strands" that make up a person, unravel at death, and lead to a "rebirth" as other combinations. For Buddhism, there is no stable self or soul that reincarnates, but life does carry on, or reincarnate—as living strands or "flying spaghetti monsters."

90   Wargo, *Time Loops,* 66.

91   Ibid., 67.

92   Guy Lyon Playfair, *Twin Telepathy* (Stroud, UK: The History Press, 2008).

93   Charles Stang, *Our Divine Double* (Cambridge, MA: Harvard University Press, 2015). There are other relevant themes here that I cannot pursue, including the doppelgänger or double that is so commonly seen in paranormal experiences and visions.

94   The definitive scholarly study of this "God as Two" (my phrase) is Jarl E. Fossum, *The Name of God and the Angel of the Lord: Samaritan and Jewish Concepts of Intermediation and the Origin of Gnosticism* (Baylor, TX: Baylor University Press, 2017/1985).

95   Wolfson, *A Dream,* 120.

96   Ibid., 156–57.

97   Andrei A. Orlov, *The Greatest Mirror: The Heavenly Counterpart Traditions in the Jewish Pseudepigrapha* (2017).

98   April DeConick, *Seek to See Him: Ascent and Vision Mysticism in the Gospel of Thomas* (Leiden: E. J. Brill, 1996), 150–51.

99   This is one of the many demographic patterns tracked and analyzed by Christopher Bader, F. Carson Mencken, and Joseph O. Baker, *Paranormal America: Ghost Encounters, UFO Sightings, Bigfoot Hunts, and Other Curiosities in Religion and Culture* (New York: New York University Press, 2011).

100 April DeConick, *The Gnostic New Age: How a Countercultural Spirituality Revolutionized Religion from Antiquity to Today* (New York: Columbia University Press, 2016), 350.

101 Garb, *Yearnings*, 29.

102 Do I have to add that a literal reading of such an eschatology is extremely dangerous and misguided?

103 For a rich comparative treatment of reincarnation in the history of religions in America, including among the indigenous cultures, I recommend Lee Irwin, *Reincarnation in America: An Esoteric History* (Lanham, MD: Rowman & Littlefield, 2017).

104 The definitive study is Brian Ogren, *Renaissance and Rebirth: Reincarnation in Early Modern Italian Kabbalah* (Leiden: Brill, 2009).

105 Many of these evolutionary spiritualities have been implicated in colonial and troubling notions of "progress," with Western civilization understood to be at the pinnacle of such a "spiritual evolution." I do not have the space to treat such issues here, but they are issues, and we need to struggle with them. For more, see my discussion in *Secret Body*. For page references, see the index under "esotericism, evolutionary."

106 My thanks to Brian Ogren for initiating this line of thought.

107 Jonathan Garb, *The Chosen Will Become Herds: Studies in Twentieth-Century Kabbalah,* trans. Yaffah Berkovits-Murciano (New Haven, CT: Yale University Press, 2009), 2–9.

108 I have been inspired in this line of thought by three Israeli colleagues: Jonathan Garb, particularly his *Yearnings of the Soul, his Shamanic Trance in Modern Kabbalah* (Chicago: University of Chicago Press, 2011), and *The Chosen Will Become Herds;* Ohad Rosenberg, a PhD student at Tel Aviv University working on the Jewish influence on the New Age movement; and Rachel Werczberger and her *Jews in the Age of Authenticity: Jewish Spiritual Renewal in Israel* (Bern: Peter Lang, 2016).

109 See also *Journal of Scientific Exploration* 22, no. 1 (Spring 2008): 47–48.

110 Carol Zaleski, *Otherworld Journeys: Accounts of Near-Death Experience in Medieval and Modern Times* (New York: Oxford University Press, 1987).

111 For a biography and summary of Monroe's teaching, see Ronald Russell, *The Journey of Robert Monroe* (Charlottesville, VA: Hampton Roads, 2007).

112 My thanks to Brian Ogren for this reading.

113 My thanks to Brian Ogren for this comparative note on the Song of Songs and the Hebrew linking of spiritual awakening and sexual arousal.

114 In traditional accounts, the heresy involved the rabbi seeing two powers instead of one in the heights of heaven: God and Metatron (a kind of superangel in many Jewish sources). Here the Human as Two is so elevated that it morphs into God as Two. My thanks to Brian Ogren for this important historical detail.

115 Gregory Shaw, "Theurgy and the Platonist's Luminous Body," in April DeConick and Grant Adamson, eds., *Histories of the Hidden God: Concealment and Revelation in Western Gnostic, Esoteric, and Mystical Traditions* (London: Equinox, 2013). See note 65 of Shaw's essay.

116 I am indebted to my colleague and friend Kelly Bulkeley for this line of thought. Kelly is a world authority on dreams and religion and the author or coauthor of more than twenty books on the same, including, most recently, *Big Dreams: The Science of Dreaming and the Origin of Religion* (New York: Oxford University Press, 2016) and *Lucrecia the Dreamer: The Spanish Inquisition's Trial of a 16th Century Prophet* (Stanford, CA: Stanford University Press, 2018).

117 Eric actually pursues this very case—Elizabeth and me—to explain how meaning "arrives from the future" in his extraordinary book, *Time Loops*. For a more extensive reading of what follows here, then, go there.

118 Eric Wargo, personal email communication, November 11, 2017, 9:43 P.M.

119 For a brief discussion, see J. E. Kennedy, "The Capricious, Actively Evasive, Unsustainable Nature of Psi: A Summary and Hypothesis," *The Journal of Parapsychology* vol. 67 (Spring 2003): 53–74. For the fullest account of this trickster effect from the perspective of the social sciences and, in particular, structural anthropology, see George P. Hansen, *The Trickster and the Paranormal* (Bloomington, IN: Xlibris, 2001).

INDEX

G

Krohn, Elizabeth (story of) *continued*
decision to return to life, 28–32
experience during lightning strike,
17–21
experience is beyond Jewish
frameworks, 220–221
haunted necklace, 51–57
how she knew what she "just knew,"
187–191
insights right after lightning strike,
20–21
lessons of the Garden. *see* Garden
lives of two authors when writing,
139–140
looking back, 119–122
mourning and shopping, 15–16
new age and. *see* new age
precognitive dreams and nature of
time. *see* time
seeing energy fields (auras), 57–60
seeing her capacities as gifts,
140–141
strange things. *see* strange things
struck by lightning, 17–21
structured religious doctrine and, 95
synesthesia of, 60–66
warm glow and the "Garden," 23–28
Krohn, Matt (husband)
believes stories of Elizabeth, 40, 60
Elizabeth's precognitive visions while
with, 39–40, 84–85, 87–90
at Esalen with Elizabeth, 140–143
as eye-witness of dream, 299–303

L

layer cake, time as, 81–83
Libet, Benjamin, 243–244
Life After Life (Moody), 151, 162–165
light
Elizabeth's visions of, 5–6
every being as spark of eternal, 100
God illuminates all as indivisible, 109
in modern religious experiences, 149
movie as display of refracted, 150

neurobiology and, 152–153
as real in NDEs, 155
as single universal in religion,
213–214
tunnel of, 149
lightning paralysis (keraunoparalysis),
Elizabeth, 34
lightning strike
Elizabeth knew before she
reincarnated, 103
Elizabeth's experience during, 17–19
engagement and interpretation of,
126–128
fate and being hit by, 78–79
likelihood of person being hit by,
1, 102
parallels experience of Dannion
Brinkley, 97
physical side effects of, 97–98
receiving knowledge after, 97, 98–99
voltage of, 1
in *Youth Without Youth* (Eliade),
147–148, 225
lightning strikes, lore from other
cultures/times
book of Ezekiel, 216–217
comparing Elizabeth's experiences
to, 214–215
Jewish tradition, 215
monotheistic traditions, 215
Native American religion, 218
shamans sometimes identified by,
217–218
as sign of God's wrath in Bible,
215–216
signaling divinity in Bible, 216–217
literalist model of imagination
overview of, 192–193
religious intolerance begins with,
193
translational model of imagination
and, 195, 197–198
what happens after death, 275–277
Loma Prieta earthquake of 1989, 85–87,
251
looking back, 119–122

love. *see* unconditional love
Luna, Luis Eduardo, 150
Luria, Isaac, 110

M

Magic Eye books, seeing auras in, 58
magnetism
    electromagnetism, 209–210, 212–214
    healing powers of, 227
    leading to new symbol for God, 226
Maimonides, angelic species in, 258
Mani, heavenly counterpart of, 259
material world, conventional materialists
    and, 168–169
McKenna, Terence, 206
meaning, of paranormal events, 245–247
meaning-making, 246–247
mental world, conventional materialists
    and, 168–169
Mesmer, Anton, 227
military, holding back in *Awake*, 181
mind-brain relations, and telepathy,
    170–171
Minkowski, Hermann, 237, 249
Minkowski space-time
    definition of, 237
    as four-dimensional block, 249
    precognition based on, 241
monotheistic traditions
    God as transcendent in, 215
    one-life model in, 275–277
Monroe, Robert, 277–278
Moody, Raymond
    coining term "near-death
      experience," 13
    "near-death experience" studies,
      161–162
    parable of, 162–165
    PhD from University of Virginia,
      275
moral dilemma, of precognitive dreams,
    86–87
mountains. *see* beyond the mountains
Mourner's Kaddish, 15

Muggle, in Harry Potter, 142–143
multiple-life model
    vs. one-life model, 275–277
    in stages of death process, 278–279
Mutants and Mystics (Kripal), 143
Myers, Frederic, 170–171
mysticism, Hasidic Judaism, 114–115

N

Nancy, energy healer, 71–75
Native American religions, lightning lore
    in, 218–219
natural world
    in monotheistic religions, 215
    in Native American religions, 218
nature of time, in precognitive dreams,
    83–85
near-death experience (NDE)
    biological purpose of, 170
    challenges deep religious
      sensibilities, 165
    changing afterlife via literature of, 205
    coinage of term, 13, 161
    corroboration that death is not final,
      69–71
    of Elizabeth, 2
    Elizabeth knew what she "just knew,"
      187–191
    Elizabeth seeks confirmation about,
      68
    empowers us all, 130
    experiencers are mystics and seers,
      259
    imagery of film/television
      describing, 148
    before it was called that, 161–162
    literalist model of imagination in,
      192–193
    looking down on universe in,
      237–238
    in medieval Europe vs. modern
      America, 276
    negative, 163–164
    religious beliefs irrelevant in, 164, 193

near-death experience (NDE) *continued*
   sacred plant cultures of Latin
      America and, 149
   story in Plato, 162
   as story to be heard, read, and
      pondered, 126–128
   trauma and revelation in, 265–268
   University of Virginia studies on,
      274–275
   visions are like 3-D movies that
      morph, 205
   why it feels so real, 152–155
near-future
   we actually live in, 244
   working our bodies from, 252
negative near-death experiences (NDEs),
   163–164
neo-Darwinians, conventional
   materialists are often, 170
neurobiology, why NDE feels so real,
   152–154
neuroscience, conventional materialists
   and, 168–169
new age
   death is not final, 69–71
   finding needed support, 67–69
   flipping the coin, 76–80
   healer in Houston, 71–73
   Kabbalah's revival in, 273
   psychic readings in Seattle, 73–76
   truths of ancient gnostic Christians
      in, 186
Newtonian physics, consciousness as
   quantum wave vs., 229–230
Next, sci-fi film, 242–243
nightmares. *see* precognitive dreams,
   Elizabeth's
The Nightshirt Blog, *Eric Wargo*, 238–241

O

objectivity, literalist model of
   imagination, 192–193
OCD (obsessive-compulsive disorder),
   synesthesia and, 63–65

octopi
   Arrival film with aliens looking like,
      181–184
   from contact to communication
      with, 179–181
   how to talk to, 178–179
Ogren, Brian, 224
one-life model
   vs. multiple-life model, 275–277
   stages of death process, 278–279
organized religion, Elizabeth's discomfort
   with exclusivity of, 109–111
orgasm, synesthetic experiences around,
   222–223
Orlov, Andrei, 259
Our Divine Double (Stang), 257–258, 260
out-of-body experiences (OBEs),
   277–278
Owens, Ted (PK or PsychoKinetic
   Man),220

P

"The Parable of Plato's Cave"
   gnostic forms of knowledge,
      185–186
   movie theaters reproduce cave in,
      184
   views of reality in, 151–152
paradise (*pardes*), 283–284
paranormal events
   are about meaning, 168
   collapses ordinary experience,
      167–168
   connected to energy, 211–212
   dreams of Elizabeth as. *see*
      precognitive dreams, Elizabeth's
   Elizabeth knew what she "just knew,"
      187–191
   everyone can interact with, 79–80
   evolving soul and, 102–104
   lightning in Native American culture
      and, 219–220
   meaning of, 245–247
   as neither black nor white, 165–170

precognitive dreams of Elizabeth, how to
think about *continued*
  brain precognizing its own future,
    247–252
  as direct seeing into future,
    196–197
  Eric Wargo and, 238–242
  evolution and, 242–245
  future already exists, 252–253
  meaning, 245–247
  modern sense of time, 233
  as part of historical record,
    301–302
  picking up on future media reports,
    251
  problem with watches, 231–234
  as prophecy, divination and
    precognition, 233–234
  provisio and proposal, 234–236
  resonates with ancient
    gnostics, 187
  time as a persistent illusion, 236
  work of Eric Wargo, 236–252
prenotion (precognition), and Francis
  Bacon, 162
Price, Reverend, 68–69, 71
procreation, paranormal and, 170–173
projected light (movie theater)
  religion as science fiction and,
    148–152
  tunnel of light as, 155
prophecy
  Greek philosophers on, 233–234
  Homer on some dreams as, 203
  in Jewish mystical tradition,
    200–201
  link between angelic presence and,
    258
  rabbis on dreams as minor forms of,
    201–202
psi-fi, as sci-fi, 144
psychic readings
  Elizabeth's short career in, 73–75
  from healer in Houston, 69–71
psychophysical interpretation,
  electromagnetism, 210

Q

quantum physics
  beyond measure in, 228–229
  dreams and, 205–207
  mystical literature of, 227–228

R

Radin, Dean, 243
"radioactive" saints, 213
reading
  as empowerment, 125–131
  interpretation and revelation in, 205
  as paranormal practice, 138–140
reality
  synesthetes actually experience
    different, 223
  we cocreate, 223
Reform Judaism
  absence of spirituality in, 113–114
  Elizabeth raised in, 95, 107
  as force for political change, 112
  Hasidic Judaism vs., 114–117
  ritual dimension of, 112–113
reincarnation
  comparing reincarnations, 271–273
  Elizabeth's decision to return, 103
  Elizabeth's insistence on reality of,
    271–272
  Elizabeth's mother's belief in, 48
  genetics and evolutionary
    implications of, 270
  goal is liberation from birth and
    death, 104
  memories in small children of,
    274–276
  one-life vs. multiple-life models of,
    275–277
  revelations in Garden, 30–31,
    100–101
  revelations in this book, 5
  spiritual evolution of soul and,
    271–273
  story in Plato, 162

time loops
  precognized book sharing of authors
    and, 291–294
  remembering future and creating, 252
  retrocausation and, 238–240
Time Loops (Wargo), 238
Torah
  Elizabeth's visions/experiences and,
    129–130
  lightning surrounds presence of God
    in, 215
  linkages between dreams and
    prophecy, 200–201
  rabbis on dreams/visions, 201–202
  revelation and interpretation in,
    204–205
  ritual dimension of Judaism and,
    112–113
  word of God in, 111
TransAsia Airways Flight 235, 90–91, 251
translation
  communicating with other species
    via, 179–182
  of emotional fields in colors of auras,
    222
  genetics works through information
    and, 245
  precognitive dreams and, 196–197
  seeing auras as, 210–211
translational model of imagination
  overview of, 195–197
  in study of religion, 199
  what happens after death, 277
translation-distortion, 180–181, 200
trauma
  and revelation, 264–268
  spiritual transcendence and sexual, 269
trickster effect, parapsychology, 303
trust, hermeneutic of, 301–302
Tucker, Jim, 274–276
TWA Flight 800 crash, 38–39

U

UFOs, around altered states of energy,
  212–213

unconditional love
  experience in Garden of, 25–26
  as lesson learned in Garden, 120
  in Moody's book/Elizabeth's story,
    162–163
  reminder to Elizabeth to feel, 32,
    42–43
  stays with Elizabeth forever, 29
unity between humanity, 198
Universal Mind, Dunne's belief in God
  as, 250
University of Virginia studies on,
  274–275
US Airways Flight 1549
  Elizabeth "sees" future media on, 251
  precognitive dream about, 87–90
  preserved metadata for email about,
    299–303

V

veridical hallucinations, NDEs in
  Victorian England, 162
Verne, Jule, 248
Victorian England, near-death
  experiences in, 162
visions
  as biotechnological projections, 148
  dream space in Judaism linked to,
    200–202
  of end or purpose of human life, 226
  engaging and acting on, 174
  as knowledge given, 97
  religions fund art for sake of,
    174–175
  religious beliefs in NDEs and, 164
  of sacred plant cultures of Latin
    America, 149–150
  from voltage or visitations, 99
"Visions of the Impossible" (Kripal),
  171–172
vision-work, story of Elizabeth requires
  shared, 126–128
visitations
  in the Garden, 97
  vision coming from, 99

ABOUT THE AUTHORS

©SHERYL THOMAS

Elizabeth Greenfield Krohn was a wife and mother of two young boys when she was struck by lightning in the parking lot of her Houston synagogue, and her most fundamental understandings of what the world is and how it works were completely transformed. She is now a grandmother living in Houston.

©MICHAEL SPADAFINA FOR MAX VIDEO PRODUCTIONS, INC.

Jeffrey J. Kripal is a well-known professor of religion at Rice University and the codirector of Esalen's Center for Theory and Research. He is the author of many books on religion and unexplained phenomena, including, with Whitley Streiber, *The Super Natural.* He is a key figure in consciousness studies within academia and beyond.

About North Atlantic Books

North Atlantic Books (NAB) is an independent, nonprofit publisher committed to a bold exploration of the relationships between mind, body, spirit, and nature. Founded in 1974, NAB aims to nurture a holistic view of the arts, sciences, humanities, and healing. To make a donation or to learn more about our books, authors, events, and newsletter, please visit www.northatlanticbooks.com.

North Atlantic Books is the publishing arm of the Society for the Study of Native Arts and Sciences, a 501(c)(3) nonprofit educational organization that promotes cross-cultural perspectives linking scientific, social, and artistic fields. To learn how you can support us, please visit our website.